Criminal Procedures

2005 Supplement

2005 Supplement

Criminal Procedures

Cases, Statutes, and Executive Materials

Second Edition

Marc L. Miller
Professor of Law and
Associate Dean for Faculty and Scholarship
Emory University

Ronald F. Wright
Professor of Law
Wake Forest University

111 Eighth Avenue, New York, NY 10011
www.aspenpublishers.com

Permissions
Aspen Publishers
111 Eighth Avenue
New York, NY 10011

Printed in the United States of America

2 3 4 5 6 7 8 9 0

ISBN 0-7355-5145-6

Library of Congress Cataloging-in-Publication Data

Miller, Marc L. (Marc Louis)
    Criminal procedures : cases, statutes, and
      executive materials /
Marc L. Miller, Ronald F. Wright.—2d ed.
      p. cm.
    Includes bibliographical references.
    ISBN 0-7355-2483-1 (casebound)
    ISBN 0-7355-5145-6 (supplement)
    1. Criminal procedure—United States—
Cases. I. Miller, Marc L., 1959–   ;
Wright, Ronald F., 1959– . II. Title.
KF9618.M52   2003
345.73′05—dc21

About Aspen Publishers

Aspen Publishers, headquartered in New York City, is a leading information provider for attorneys, business professionals, and law students. Written by preeminent authorities, our products consist of analytical and practical information covering both U.S. and international topics. We publish in the full range of formats, including updated manuals, books, periodicals, CDs, and online products.

Our proprietary content is complemented by 2,500 legal databases, containing over 11 million documents, available through our Loislaw division. Aspen Publishers also offers a wide range of topical legal and business databases linked to Loislaw's primary material. Our mission is to provide accurate, timely, and authoritative content in easily accessible formats, supported by unmatched customer care.

To order any Aspen Publishers title, go to *www.aspenpublishers.com* or call 1-800-638-8437.

To reinstate your manual update service, call 1-800-638-8437.

For more information on Loislaw products, go to *www.loislaw.com* or call 1-800-364-2512.

For Customer Care issues, e-mail *CustomerCare@aspenpublishers.com*; call 1-800-234-1660; or fax 1-800-901-9075.

Aspen Publishers
a Wolters Kluwer business

Contents

3

Full Searches of People and Places: Basic Concepts   21

4

Searches in Recurring Contexts   39

5

Arrests 43

6

Remedies for Unreasonable Searches and Seizures 49

7

The Impact of Technology 53

8
Interrogations 71

9
Identifications 93

10
Complex Investigations 95

11
Defense Counsel   99

12
Pretrial Release and Detention   125

13
Charging   133

14
Jeopardy and Joinder

15
Discovery and Speedy Trial

16
Pleas and Bargains

17
Decisionmakers at Trial

18
Witnesses and Proof

19
Sentencing

20
Appeals 273

21
Habeas Corpus 281

Preface

One function of a casebook supplement is to keep teachers and students current with recent events. From one vantage point, the change in this area may not seem so profound. In terms of basic doctrine, most aspects of criminal procedure have changed only modestly over the past few years. This is particularly true for a book, such as this one, that emphasizes nationwide trends within state criminal justice systems. Such nationwide changes take much longer to develop than any shifts in a single jurisdiction.

Nevertheless, these are remarkable times in criminal justice, and these remarkable events must become part of a vibrant criminal procedure course. After the events of September 11, 2001, lawyers and judges in criminal courts all over the country continue to generate questions about how criminal procedure might change with the threat of terrorism in the background. The U.S. Supreme Court has proven remarkably active in the area for several years running, and the high state courts have added important insights of their own. These events are altering the law of pretrial detention, habeas corpus, suspicionless stops, and many other topics.

In practical terms, these events all add up to a lengthy supplement for a casebook published not so long ago. Some of the materials in this supplement will appear in the next edition; other materials may eventually disappear from the print format materials and move to the web site. Many decisions from the U.S. Supreme Court (along with some from the state supreme courts) seem on a first reading to make a dramatic shift in law and practice. However, after a year or two for reflection, some of those cases appear to be less important, because they merely restate or apply established concepts. A casebook supplement is a good opportunity to test the staying power of new cases, statutes, and policies.

This supplement is consistent with our larger goal of creating materials to extend the breadth and depth of the core casebook. We have also created Internet Web pages for this casebook to enrich the resources available for students using this casebook. Our goal is not to create an electronic coursebook. Instead, the electronic resources broaden, deepen, and enliven the core text.

The *Criminal Procedures* Web pages include materials allowing students to test and expand their knowledge, such as practice problems, exams, short excerpts of articles on criminal procedure, a virtual library with a few police manuals and prosecutorial policies that would otherwise be difficult to obtain, and links to criminal justice resources on the Web. The address for these pages is http://www.crimpro.com (or simply "crimpro"). We welcome suggestions for materials to post on the Web pages or to publish in this printed supplement.

We hope you find that the casebook, this supplement, and the Web pages—together—offer a complete, coherent, and challenging set of tools for learning about criminal procedure.

Marc Miller
Ron Wright

July 2005

Table of Cases

Chapter 1

The Border of Criminal Procedure: Daily Interactions Between Citizens and Police

A. Police as Community Caretakers

Page 9. Add this material before the notes.

Courts increasingly rely on the "community caretaker" concept in the areas of frequent interaction between police and citizens, including stops and examination of automobiles. Does an energetic community caretaker function provide a stepping-stone for searches that would not otherwise be legal? Does the community caretaker function interfere with a citizen's right to be let alone, perhaps by sleeping in a car?

State v. Michael Lovegren
51 P.3d 471 (Mont. 2002)

NELSON, J.
... ¶ 3 On the night of October 31, 1998, Officer Gary Hofer of the Richland County Sheriff's Department was on routine patrol. At approximately 3:05 A.M., he came upon a vehicle parked on the side of

Highway 16 South in Richland County between Crane and Sidney. The vehicle's motor was running, but its headlights were off. Officer Hofer stopped to investigate.

¶ 4 When Officer Hofer approached the vehicle and looked in the window, he saw Lovegren sitting in the driver's seat. Lovegren appeared to be asleep. Officer Hofer knocked on the window and, when Lovegren did not respond, Officer Hofer opened the door. Lovegren suddenly woke up and stated: "I was drinking." Officer Hofer smelled a strong odor of alcohol and he noticed that Lovegren's eyes were bloodshot, so he had Lovegren perform various field sobriety tests. Lovegren failed both the one-legged stand and the heel-to-toe test. Hence, Officer Hofer transported Lovegren to the station where a breath test was performed. The test results showed that Lovegren's blood alcohol content was 0.115. Officer Hofer read Lovegren his *Miranda* rights and wrote out a citation charging him with driving under the influence of alcohol in violation of §61-8-401, MCA....

¶ 6 On May 12, 1999, Lovegren filed a motion in the District Court asking the court to suppress all of the evidence obtained in the investigative stop on the grounds that Officer Hofer lacked a particularized suspicion of any wrongdoing on Lovegren's part, thus the stop was not justified. On May 26, 1999, the District Court denied Lovegren's motion stating that a particularized suspicion was not required in this situation, as Officer Hofer had a duty to investigate for Lovegren's own safety.

¶ 7 ... Lovegren was subsequently convicted of the charge and the District Court [fined Lovegren $420 and sentenced him to 60 days in jail with all but one day suspended. The court also suspended Lovegren's driver's license for six months. Lovegren appeals.]

¶ 10 ... Lovegren contends that this investigative stop was not justified because Officer Hofer did not have a particularized suspicion that Lovegren had committed, was committing, or was about to commit an offense.

¶ 11 Lovegren also contends that the District Court overstepped its authority by inferring more from the police reports than what they actually said. Lovegren notes that in the police report, Officer Hofer clearly stated that the driver of the vehicle "appeared to be asleep" and that there were no references in the report to any signs of struggle or trauma to indicate the need of further assistance. Thus, Lovegren argues that the District Court erred in concluding that although the report indicates that the driver appeared to be asleep, the officer could not know whether the driver was asleep, ill, unconscious or even dead.

¶ 12 The State argues, on the other hand, that the District Court correctly determined that Officer Hofer did not need a particularized suspicion of criminal activity in this situation. The State maintains that the court correctly applied the "community caretaker doctrine"—even though the court did not identify it as such—in determining that Officer Hofer was justified in stopping to check on Lovegren's welfare and that Officer Hofer would have been derelict in his duties had he not done so....

¶ 16 [Many courts recognize that some of the least intrusive police-citizen encounters do not] involve any form of detention at all and, therefore, [do] not involve a seizure. This category is generally referred to as the "community caretaker" or public safety function....

¶ 18 Because this Court has not squarely addressed the community caretaker doctrine, we take this opportunity to survey the law from other jurisdictions in this area and to set forth our own test for application of this doctrine.

¶ 19 Of the many jurisdictions that have addressed this doctrine, a majority have adopted it in some form. However, the boundaries of this doctrine that control the judgment exercised by the officers in these situations are not consistent across all of the jurisdictions. Indeed, our review of the cases leads us to conclude that some jurisdictions have expanded the doctrine beyond what would likely be acceptable given the enhanced protection of the right of individual privacy and against unreasonable searches and seizures guaranteed under Article II, Sections 10 and 11 of the Montana Constitution....

¶ 20 [T]he majority of the jurisdictions that have adopted the community caretaker doctrine have determined that a peace officer has a duty to investigate situations in which a citizen may be in peril or need some type of assistance from an officer. [The opinion cited cases from Minnesota, Alaska, New Jersey, Vermont, and Washington State.]

¶ 21 [T]he caretaking duties that come under this doctrine are varied and range from assisting a driver slumped over in his car to stopping a man walking alongside a road. [The opinion cited cases from Alaska, Arkansas, Illinois, North Dakota, Virginia, Wyoming, Alabama, and Wisconsin.]

¶ 22 In addition, many jurisdictions have recognized that the scope of any intrusion following the stop must be limited to those actions necessary to carry out the purposes of the stop, unless particularized suspicion or probable cause subsequently arises. See State v. Dube, 655 A.2d 338 (Me. 1995) (initial entry into apartment by police as they accompanied building custodian so he could make emergency repairs was lawful, but squalid conditions of apartment did not create exigent circumstances justifying officers' continued presence in apartment after repairs were completed); Apodaca v. Taxation & Revenue Dept., 884 P.2d 515 (N.M. App. 1994) (police officer's observation of defendant's motorcycle weaving within its lane of traffic supported officer's stop of defendant based on officer's concern for defendant's safety, but the scope of any intrusion following the stop must be limited to those actions necessary to carry out the purposes of the stop unless reasonable suspicion or probable cause arises)....

¶ 24 [W]hen an officer claims that he or she acted under the community caretaker doctrine, many jurisdictions use a two-step approach to analyze the officer's actions. First, if an officer states that he stopped to assist a person who appeared to be in need of assistance, an objective view of the specific and articulable facts must be examined to determine whether they support the officer's statements. And, second, a determination must be made regarding at what moment the officer "seized" the person and thereby implicated Fourth Amendment protections....

¶ 25 With this survey of the foregoing case law in mind, we adopt the following test in relation to the community caretaker doctrine. First, as long as there are objective, specific and articulable facts from which an experienced officer would suspect that a citizen is in need of help or is in peril, then that officer has the right to stop and investigate. Second, if the citizen is in need of aid, then the officer may take appropriate action to render assistance or mitigate the peril. Third, once, however, the officer is assured that the citizen is not in peril or is no longer in need of assistance or that the peril has been mitigated, then any actions beyond that constitute a seizure implicating not only the protections provided by the Fourth Amendment, but more importantly, those greater guarantees afforded under Article II, Sections 10 and 11 of the Montana Constitution as interpreted in this Court's decisions.

¶ 26 Applying this test in the present case, the facts support the conclusion that Officer Hofer had objective, specific and articulable facts suggesting that Lovegren might be in need of assistance. While Lovegren might simply have been asleep, he might just as likely have been ill and unconscious and in need of help. Under these circumstances, Officer Hofer had the right to check on Lovegren's welfare and to open the door of Lovegren's vehicle when Lovegren failed to respond to a knock on the window of his vehicle. As the State points out, it would have been a dereliction of Officer Hofer's duties if, after knocking on the window and obtaining no response, Officer Hofer walked away and continued on his patrol. Thus, under the community caretaker doctrine, when Officer Hofer opened the door to check on Lovegren, Officer Hofer had not yet "seized" Lovegren.

¶ 27 However, when Officer Hofer opened the door, not only did Lovegren awake, but he voluntarily stated that he had been drinking. At that time, Officer Hofer also noticed other signs of intoxication giving him a particularized suspicion to make a further investigatory stop—i.e., the field sobriety tests—which eventually developed into probable cause for an arrest. This escalation of events leading to Lovegren's arrest is proper....

¶ 28 Accordingly, we hold that the District Court did not err when it denied Lovegren's motion to suppress.

Page 10.   Add this material at the end of note 2.

The community caretaker function has been used to justify entry into homes and stops of automobiles. See Laney v. State, 117 S.W.3d 854 (Tex. Crim. App. 2003) (officer enters trailer after midnight to determine where two young boys lived); State v. Tague, 676 N.W.2d 197 (Iowa 2004) (rejecting application of community caretaker to justify car stop to protect driver and other drivers when car briefly crossed line and state claimed driver might be intoxicated or fatigued). See also State v. Cassidy, 843 A.2d 1132 (N.J. 2004) (rejecting emergency aid exception for enforcement of restraining order in domestic violence case). The community caretaker function is also sometimes referred to as the "emergency aid" exception to the standard requirements of the Fourth Amendment and state analogs. See State v. Ryon, 108 P.3d 1032 (N.M. 2005) (officer can hold both community safety and criminal investigation motives and still make warrantless entry of home; distinguishes emergency aid doctrine from community caretaker doctrine).

C. *Control of Gangs and Kids*

Page 23.   Add this material at the end of note 1.

See State v. J.P., 2004 WL 2609242 (Fla., Nov. 18, 2004) (municipal curfew ordinances that forbid minors to be out at night violate minors' constitutionally protected freedom of movement and right to privacy).

D. *Traditional and Community Policing*

Page 31.   Add this material at the end of note 1.

For a rich collection of reviews showing the variety of policing strategies that can flow from the concept of "community policing," consult the Web site of the Vera Institute's Police Assessment Resource Center at http://www.vera.org/section2/section2_1.asp.

Page 32.   Add this material at the end of note 5.

Does Packer's model suggest anything about different ways that victims of alleged crimes might become involved in criminal investigations or adjudications? For two efforts to supplement the Packer models, see Kent Roach, Four Models of the Criminal Process, 89 J. Crim. L. & Criminology 671 (1999) (proposing "punitive" and "non-punitive" models of victim involvement); Douglas Beloof, The Third Model of Criminal Process: The Victim Participation Model, 1999 Utah L. Rev. 289.

Chapter 2

Brief Searches and Stops

A. *Brief Investigative Stops of Suspects*

2. Grounds for Stops: Articulable, Individualized Reasonable Suspicion

Page 55.   Add this material at the end of note 5.

See also State v. Henning, 666 N.W.2d 379 (Minn. 2003) (striking down statute authorizing traffic stop based on "special series" license plate issued to drivers with previous conviction for driving while intoxicated).

Page 55.   Add this material at the end of note 7.

State courts have applied Florida v. J.L. to anonymous tips in many contexts, often distinguishing that case. See State v. Jordan, 817 N.E.2d 864 (Ohio 2004) (during drug investigation, man on porch flees when police arrive while second man shouts to fleeing man; reasonable suspicion to detain second man).

Page 59.   Add this material at the end of note 1.

State v. Moore, 853 A.2d 903 (N.J. 2004) (nature of crime in area may contribute to reasonable suspicion to stop men engaged in suspicious street-side transaction).

3. Pretextual Stops

Page 67.   Add this material at the end of note 5.

See also Jones v. Sterling, 110 P.3d 1271 (Ariz. 2005) (criminal defendants can assert racial profiling as defense to charges and not rely solely on civil rights claims).

4. Criminal Profiles and Race

Page 73.   Add this material at the end of note 3.

See also Harris v. State, 806 A.2d 119 (Del. 2002) (to establish reasonable suspicion for stop on basis of drug courier profile, state and federal constitutions require officer to explain how training makes apparently innocent conduct suspicious).

Page 83.   Add this material at the end of Problem 2-3.

See Sharon Davies, Profiling Terror, 1 Ohio S.J. of Crim. Law 45 (2003) (creates typology of racial profiling and argues that terror investigations are not fundamentally different from other forms of racial profiling).

Page 84.   Add this material at the end of note 2.

A recent analysis of data about traffic stops between 1995 and 2000 concludes that the Maryland State Police "stopped and searched cars with black and Hispanic drivers much more often than cars with white drivers; it is hard to see how they could have produced these results without taking race into account in deciding who to stop and who to search." Although this practice "seems to increase the probability of finding large hauls of drugs," the large hauls are rare, and about "two-thirds of all drivers searched were not carrying any illegal drugs." Most of the drivers who had any drugs in the car were found with trace amounts; among black and Hispanic drivers, "a larger minority of the searches uncovered substantial quantities of illegal drugs." See Samuel R. Gross and Katherine Y. Barnes, Road Work: Racial Profiling and Drug Interdiction on the Highway, 101 Mich. L. Rev. 651 (2002).

A citywide survey of police stops in Los Angeles, conducted under court order, showed that Black and Latino motorists are three times more likely than other drivers to be asked to step out of their vehicles by Los Angeles police during traffic stops, and are about twice as likely as whites to be searched. "Minorities More Likely L.A. Police Search Targets," N.Y. Times, Jan. 6, 2003.

Problem 2-3A. Click It or Tickets for All

The National Highway Traffic Safety Administration offers grants to local law enforcement agencies to fund campaigns that will increase usage of seat belts. One program, known as "Click It or Ticket," aims at the general population, while a separate program grants money for seat belt programs operating in Hispanic neighborhoods. Both programs combine advertising campaigns with driver checkpoints. Officials at checkpoints in Hispanic neighborhoods stop every car and hand out information. Every tenth driver gets a more thorough inspection and could be cited.

The Hispanic public affairs specialist for the NHTSA said Hispanics are targeted because they are not as accustomed to using seat belts as other groups. Critics of the program point out that NHTSA does not have data on the percentage of Hispanics who buckle up. King Downing, the national coordinator for the American Civil Liberties Union's Campaign Against Racial Profiling, puts the question this way: "In the absence of any data, I would ask why are they targeting Latinos?" Federal officials respond that, according to the Centers for Disease Control, traffic accidents are the leading cause of death for Hispanics ages 1 to 34. According to Lorraine Novak, a senior regional program manager for the NHTSA, "It's not profiling, it's targeting a specific population."

As an administrator in the NHTSA, would you continue the grants for these two seat belt enforcement efforts? See "Seat Belt Checks for Hispanics Denounced," N.Y. Times, May 28, 2003.

B. Brief Administrative Stops

Page 92.   Add this material after note 6.

See State v. Mitchell, 592 S.E.2d 543 (N.C. 2004) (approves checkpoints based on standing permission from supervisor to operate under unwritten guidelines).

Page 92.   Add this material after note 7.

The Supreme Court created a specialized version of the checkpoint rules to apply when the roadblock is designed to obtain information about people other than the motorist stopped. In Illinois v. Lidster, 540 U.S. 419 (2004), a police department seeking information about a fatal hit-and-run accident stopped motorists passing by the scene of the accident several days later. Although one of the stopped motorists was discovered to be driving while intoxicated, the Court ruled that the suspicionless stop was reasonable because the checkpoint sought information rather than arrests of intoxicated drivers.

After this decision, is it still fair to characterize suspicionless searches as "exceptional" techniques that will only be approved under "special" circumstances? Or has the law now evolved (or devolved) to the point that suspicionless searches are regulated and approved on the same basis as more traditional searches?

Page 92.   Add this material after note 8.

See also United States v. Flores-Montano, 541 U.S. 149 (2004) (Customs officials do not need individualized suspicion before removing, dismantling, and searching fuel tank of vehicle crossing the border, despite fact that such searches were not routine).

C. Gathering Information Without Searching

2. Abandoned Property

Page 105.   Add this material in note 1 at the end of the first paragraph.

See also Litchfield v. State, 824 N.E.2d 356 (Ind. 2005) (requires reasonable suspicion rather than probable cause for search of trash left for pickup); State v. Sampson, 765 A.2d 629 (Md. 2001) (officer collected trash left at curb by suspected drug dealer for six days; not a search); State v. Goss, 834 A.2d 316 (N.H. 2003) (expectation of privacy in garbage placed by curb is reasonable under state constitution).

D. Brief Searches of Individuals

2. Scope of a *Terry* Search

Page 119.   Add this material in note 1 at the end of the first paragraph.

Murphy v. Commonwealth, 570 S.E.2d 836 (Va. 2002) (baggie felt during pat-down could not be seized on plain feel theory; illegal nature of object was not immediately apparent).

Page 120.   Add this material at the end of note 6.

See State v. Peterson, 110 P.3d 699 (Utah 2005) (officers could not pat down a jacket before giving it to detained person, who did not request jacket before going outdoors).

Page 121.   Replace the Nevada decision with the following material.

Larry Hiibel v. Sixth Judicial District Court of Nevada, Humboldt County
542 U.S. 177 (2004)

KENNEDY, J.

The petitioner was arrested and convicted for refusing to identify himself during a stop allowed by Terry v. Ohio, 392 U.S. 1 (1968). He challenges his conviction under the Fourth and Fifth Amendments to the United States Constitution, applicable to the States through the Fourteenth Amendment.

The sheriff's department in Humboldt County, Nevada, received an afternoon telephone call reporting an assault. The caller reported seeing a man assault a woman in a red and silver GMC truck on Grass Valley Road. Deputy Sheriff Lee Dove was dispatched to investigate. When the officer arrived at the scene, he found the truck parked on the side of the road. A man was standing by the truck, and a young woman was sitting inside it. The officer observed skid marks in the gravel behind the vehicle, leading him to believe it had come to a sudden stop.

The officer approached the man and explained that he was investigating a report of a fight. The man appeared to be intoxicated. The officer asked him if he had "any identification on [him]," which we understand as a request to produce a driver's license or some other form of written identification. The man refused and asked why the officer wanted to see identification. The officer responded that he was conducting an investigation and needed to see some identification. The unidentified man became agitated and insisted he had done nothing wrong. The officer explained that he wanted to find out who the man was and what he was doing there. After continued refusals to comply with the officer's request for identification, the man began to taunt the officer by placing his hands behind his back and telling the officer to arrest him and take him to jail. This routine kept up for several minutes: the officer asked for identification 11 times and was refused each time. After warning the man that he would be arrested if he continued to refuse to comply, the officer placed him under arrest.

We now know that the man arrested on Grass Valley Road is Larry Dudley Hiibel. Hiibel was charged with "willfully resisting, delaying, or obstructing a public officer in discharging or attempting to discharge any legal duty of his office" in violation of Nev. Rev. Stat. (NRS) §199.280. The government reasoned that Hiibel had obstructed the officer in carrying out his duties under §171.123, a Nevada statute that defines the legal rights and duties of a police officer in the context of an investigative stop. Section 171.123 provides in relevant part:

> 1. Any peace officer may detain any person whom the officer encounters under circumstances which reasonably indicate that the person has committed, is committing or is about to commit a crime. ...

> 3. The officer may detain the person pursuant to this section only to ascertain his identity and the suspicious circumstances surrounding his presence abroad. Any person so detained shall identify himself, but may not be compelled to answer any other inquiry of any peace officer.

Hiibel was tried in the Justice Court of Union Township. The court agreed that Hiibel's refusal to identify himself as required by §171.123 "obstructed and delayed Dove as a public officer in attempting to discharge his duty" in violation of §199.280. Hiibel was convicted and fined $250....

NRS §171.123(3) is an enactment sometimes referred to as a "stop and identify" statute. [The opinion cites statutes from twenty states.] Stop and identify statutes often combine elements of traditional vagrancy laws with provisions intended to regulate police behavior in the course of investigatory stops. The statutes vary from State to State, but all permit an officer to ask or require a suspect to disclose his identity. A few States model their statutes on the Uniform Arrest Act, a model code that permits an officer to stop a person reasonably suspected of committing a crime and "demand of him his name, address, business abroad and whither he is going." Warner, The Uniform Arrest Act, 28 Va. L. Rev. 315, 344 (1942). Other statutes are based on the text proposed by the American Law Institute as part of the Institute's Model Penal Code, §250.6, [which] provides that a person who is loitering "under circumstances which justify suspicion that he may be engaged or about to engage in crime commits a violation if he refuses the request of a peace officer that he identify himself and give a reasonably credible account of the lawfulness of his conduct and purposes." In some States, a suspect's refusal to identify himself is a misdemeanor offense or civil violation; in others, it is a factor to be considered in whether the suspect has violated loitering laws. In other States, a suspect may decline to identify himself without penalty.

Stop and identify statutes have their roots in early English vagrancy laws that required suspected vagrants to face arrest unless they gave "a good Account of themselves," 15 Geo. 2, ch. 5, §2 (1744).... In recent decades, the Court has found constitutional infirmity in traditional vagrancy laws. In Papachristou v. Jacksonville, 405 U.S. 156 (1972), the Court held that a traditional vagrancy law was void for vagueness. Its broad scope and imprecise terms denied proper notice to potential offenders and permitted police officers to exercise unfettered discretion in the enforcement of the law.

The Court has recognized similar constitutional limitations on the scope and operation of stop and identify statutes. In Brown v. Texas, 443 U.S. 47 (1979), the Court invalidated a conviction for violating a Texas stop and identify statute on Fourth Amendment grounds. The Court ruled that the initial stop was not based on specific, objective facts establishing reasonable suspicion to believe the suspect was involved in criminal activity. Absent that factual basis for detaining the defendant, the Court held, the risk of "arbitrary and abusive police practices" was too great and the stop was impermissible. Four Terms later, the Court invalidated a modified stop and identify statute on vagueness grounds. See Kolender v. Lawson, 461 U.S. 352 (1983). The California law in *Kolender* required a suspect to give an officer "credible and reliable" identification when asked to identify himself. The Court held that the statute was void because it provided no standard for determining what a suspect must do to comply with it, resulting in "virtually unrestrained power to arrest and charge persons with a violation."

The present case begins where our prior cases left off. Here there is no question that the initial stop was based on reasonable suspicion, satisfying the Fourth Amendment requirements noted in *Brown*. Further, the petitioner has not alleged that the statute is unconstitutionally vague, as in *Kolender*. Here the Nevada statute is narrower and more precise. The statute in *Kolender* had been interpreted to require a suspect to give the officer "credible and reliable" identification. In contrast, the Nevada Supreme Court has interpreted NRS §171.123(3) to require only that a suspect disclose his name. As we understand it, the statute does not require a suspect to give the officer a driver's license or any other document. Provided that the suspect either states his name or communicates it to the officer by other means—a choice, we assume, that the suspect may make—the statute is satisfied and no violation occurs.

Hiibel argues that his conviction cannot stand because the officer's conduct violated his Fourth Amendment rights. We disagree.

Asking questions is an essential part of police investigations. In the ordinary course a police officer is free to ask a person for identification without implicating the Fourth Amendment. Interrogation relating to one's identity or a request for identification by the police does not, by itself, constitute a Fourth Amendment seizure.

[Questions] concerning a suspect's identity are a routine and accepted part of many *Terry* stops. Obtaining a suspect's name in the course of a *Terry* stop serves important government interests. Knowledge of identity may inform an officer that a suspect is wanted for another offense, or has a record of violence or mental disorder. On the other hand, knowing identity may help clear a suspect and allow the police to concentrate their efforts elsewhere. Identity may prove particularly important in cases such as this, where the police are investigating what appears to be a domestic assault. Officers called to investigate domestic disputes need to know whom they are dealing with in order to assess the situation, the threat to their own safety, and possible danger to the potential victim.

Although it is well established that an officer may ask a suspect to identify himself in the course of a *Terry* stop, it has been an open question whether the suspect can be arrested and prosecuted for refusal to answer. Petitioner draws our attention to statements in prior opinions that, according to him, answer the question in his favor. In *Terry*, Justice White stated in a concurring opinion that a person detained in an investigative stop can be questioned but is "not obliged to answer, answers may not be compelled, and refusal to answer furnishes no basis for an arrest." The Court cited this opinion in dicta in Berkemer v. McCarty, 468 U.S. 420, 439 (1984), a decision holding that a routine traffic stop is not a custodial stop requiring the protections of Miranda v. Arizona, 384 U.S. 436 (1966). In the course of explaining why *Terry* stops have not been subject to *Miranda*, the Court suggested reasons why *Terry* stops have a "nonthreatening character," among them the fact that a suspect detained during a *Terry* stop "is not obliged to respond" to questions. According to petitioner, these statements establish a right to refuse to answer questions during a *Terry* stop.

We do not read these statements as controlling. The passages recognize that the Fourth Amendment does not impose obligations on the citizen but instead provides rights against the government. As a result, the Fourth Amendment itself cannot require a suspect to answer questions. This case concerns a different issue, however. Here, the source of the legal obligation arises from Nevada state law, not the

Fourth Amendment. Further, the statutory obligation does not go beyond answering an officer's request to disclose a name....

The principles of *Terry* permit a State to require a suspect to disclose his name in the course of a *Terry* stop. The reasonableness of a seizure under the Fourth Amendment is determined by balancing its intrusion on the individual's Fourth Amendment interests against its promotion of legitimate government interests. The Nevada statute satisfies that standard. The request for identity has an immediate relation to the purpose, rationale, and practical demands of a *Terry* stop. The threat of criminal sanction helps ensure that the request for identity does not become a legal nullity. On the other hand, the Nevada statute does not alter the nature of the stop itself: it does not change its duration or its location. A state law requiring a suspect to disclose his name in the course of a valid *Terry* stop is consistent with Fourth Amendment prohibitions against unreasonable searches and seizures.

Petitioner argues that the Nevada statute circumvents the probable cause requirement, in effect allowing an officer to arrest a person for being suspicious. According to petitioner, this creates a risk of arbitrary police conduct that the Fourth Amendment does not permit.... Petitioner's concerns are met by the requirement that a *Terry* stop must be justified at its inception and "reasonably related in scope to the circumstances which justified" the initial stop. Under these principles, an officer may not arrest a suspect for failure to identify himself if the request for identification is not reasonably related to the circumstances justifying the stop....

It is clear in this case that the request for identification was reasonably related in scope to the circumstances which justified the stop. The officer's request was a commonsense inquiry, not an effort to obtain an arrest for failure to identify after a *Terry* stop yielded insufficient evidence. The stop, the request, and the State's requirement of a response did not contravene the guarantees of the Fourth Amendment.

Petitioner further contends that his conviction violates the Fifth Amendment's prohibition on compelled self-incrimination. The Fifth Amendment states that "no person ... shall be compelled in any criminal case to be a witness against himself." ... The Fifth Amendment prohibits only compelled testimony that is incriminating....

In this case petitioner's refusal to disclose his name was not based on any articulated real and appreciable fear that his name would be used to incriminate him.... As best we can tell, petitioner refused to identify himself only because he thought his name was none of the officer's business. Even today, petitioner does not explain how the disclosure of his name could have been used against him in a criminal case....

The narrow scope of the disclosure requirement is also important. One's identity is, by definition, unique; yet it is, in another sense, a universal characteristic. Answering a request to disclose a name is likely to be so insignificant in the scheme of things as to be incriminating only in unusual circumstances. In every criminal case, it is known and must be known who has been arrested and who is being tried. Even witnesses who plan to invoke the Fifth Amendment privilege answer when their names are called to take the stand. Still, a case may arise where there is a substantial allegation that furnishing identity at the time of a stop would have given the police a link in the chain of evidence needed to convict the individual of a separate offense. In that case, the court can then consider whether the privilege applies, and, if the Fifth Amendment has been violated, what remedy must follow. We need not resolve those questions here....

STEVENS, J., dissenting.

... It is a settled principle that the police have the right to request citizens to answer voluntarily questions concerning unsolved crimes, but they have no right to compel them to answer. The protections of the Fifth Amendment are directed squarely toward those who are the focus of the government's investigative and prosecutorial powers. In a criminal trial, the indicted defendant has an unqualified right to refuse to testify and may not be punished for invoking that right. The unindicted target of a grand jury investigation enjoys the same constitutional protection even if he has been served with a subpoena. So does an arrested suspect during custodial interrogation in a police station. There is no reason why the subject of police interrogation based on mere suspicion, rather than probable cause, should have any lesser protection.

[The Court] concludes that the State can compel the disclosure of one's identity because it is not "incriminating." But our cases have afforded Fifth Amendment protection to statements that are "incriminating" in a much broader sense than the Court suggests. It has long been settled that the Fifth Amendment's protection encompasses compelled statements that lead to the discovery of incriminating evidence even though the statements themselves are not incriminating and are not introduced into evidence. By "incriminating" we have meant disclosures that could be used in a criminal prosecution or could lead to other evidence that might be so used....

Given a proper understanding of the category of "incriminating" communications that fall within the Fifth Amendment privilege, it is clear that the disclosure of petitioner's identity is protected. The Court reasons that we should not assume that the disclosure of petitioner's name would be used to incriminate him or that it would furnish a link in a chain of evidence needed to prosecute him. But why else would an officer ask for it? And why else would the Nevada Legislature require its disclosure only when circumstances "reasonably indicate that the person has committed, is committing or is about to commit a crime"?[7] [The] Nevada Legislature intended to provide its police officers with a useful law enforcement tool, and that the very existence of the statute demonstrates the value of the information it demands....

A name can provide the key to a broad array of information about the person, particularly in the hands of a police officer with access to a range of law enforcement databases. And that information, in turn, can be tremendously useful in a criminal prosecution. It is therefore quite wrong to suggest that a person's identity provides a link in the chain to incriminating evidence "only in unusual circumstances." [Petitioner], in my view, acted well within his rights when he opted to stand mute. Accordingly, I respectfully dissent.

BREYER, J., dissenting.

... In Terry v. Ohio, 392 U.S. 1 (1968), the Court considered whether police, in the absence of probable cause, can stop, question, or frisk an individual at all. The Court ... set forth conditions circumscribing when and how the police might conduct a *Terry* stop. They include what has become known as the "reasonable suspicion"

---

[7] The Court suggests that furnishing identification also allows the investigating officer to assess the threat to himself and others. But to the extent that officer or public safety is immediately at issue, that concern is sufficiently alleviated by the officer's ability to perform a limited patdown search for weapons.

standard. Justice White, in a separate concurring opinion, set forth further conditions. Justice White wrote: "Of course, the person stopped is not obliged to answer, answers may not be compelled, and refusal to answer furnishes no basis for an arrest, although it may alert the officer to the need for continued observation."

[Sixteen years later], the Court wrote that an "officer may ask the *[Terry]* detainee a moderate number of questions to determine his identity and to try to obtain information confirming or dispelling the officer's suspicions. *But the detainee is not obliged to respond.*" Berkemer v. McCarty, 468 U.S. 420, 439 (1984) (emphasis added). See also Illinois v. Wardlow, 528 U.S. 119, 125 (2000) (stating that allowing officers to stop and question a fleeing person "is quite consistent with the individual's right to go about his business or to stay put and remain silent in the face of police questioning").

[The] Court's statement in *Berkemer*, while technically dicta, is the kind of strong dicta that the legal community typically takes as a statement of the law. And that law has remained undisturbed for more than 20 years.... There are sound reasons rooted in Fifth Amendment considerations for adhering to this Fourth Amendment legal condition circumscribing police authority to stop an individual against his will. Administrative considerations also militate against change. Can a State, in addition to requiring a stopped individual to answer "What's your name?" also require an answer to "What's your license number?" or "Where do you live?" Can a police officer, who must know how to make a *Terry* stop, keep track of the constitutional answers? After all, answers to any of these questions may, or may not, incriminate, depending upon the circumstances....

The majority presents no evidence that the rule enunciated by Justice White and then by the *Berkemer* Court, which for nearly a generation has set forth a settled *Terry* stop condition, has significantly interfered with law enforcement. Nor has the majority presented any other convincing justification for change. I would not begin to erode a clear rule with special exceptions. I consequently dissent.

Page 127.   Add this material at the end of note 2.

See also State v. Warren, 78 P.3d 590 (Utah 2003) (officer's subjective lack of concern for safety is a factor to consider in judging reasonableness of frisk; objective safety concerns might be satisfied by order to exit vehicle); State v. Sprague, 824 A.2d 539 (Vt. 2003) (under state constitution, officer conducting routine traffic stop may not automatically order driver to exit vehicle).

Page 127.   Replace note 3 with the following material.

3. Terry *stops and requests for identification.* Before the decision in *Hiibel,* there was surprisingly little precedent (in either state or federal courts) on the question of whether the state could punish a citizen's refusal to answer an officer's questions during an investigatory stop. If a person refuses to answer a police officer's request for identification because she honestly believes that the officer lacks reasonable suspicion to stop her, would a conviction under the Nevada statute be valid? Does an effort to investigate and prevent acts of terrorism—an objective of criminal law enforcement that gained new urgency after September 11, 2001—make this sort of questioning more common and more valuable?

Related questions now being litigated relate to the subjects a police officer may discuss with occupants of a vehicle after making a stop. See People v. Gonzalez, 789 N.E.2d 260 (Ill. 2003) (officer may ask occupants questions unrelated to purpose of traffic stop; court rejects decisions from other jurisdictions that focus on whether questioning prolonged the stop, or whether questioning expanded scope of stop); State v. Diaz, 850 So. 2d 435 (Fla. 2003) (officer may not check license of driver after realizing that basis for stop—expiration date of tag—did not exist).

A similar issue, dealing with the linkage between the reason for the stop and the investigation, arises when canine dogs arrive at the scene of a traffic stop. See State v. Wiegand, 645 N.W.2d 125 (Minn. 2002) (dog sniff of car exterior during traffic stop requires reasonable suspicion to believe car contains drugs, even if stop takes less time than needed to issue citation); People v. Cox, 782 N.E.2d 275 (Ill. 2002) (unreasonable traffic stop when officer called drug canine unit and took fifteen minutes to write ticket for equipment violation).

Chapter 3

Full Searches of People and Places: Basic Concepts

A. Origins of the Fourth Amendment and its Analogs

1. General Search Warrants

Page 134. Add the following material at the end of note 4.

See also David E. Steinberg, The Original Understanding of Unreasonable Searches and Seizures, 56 Fla. L. Rev. 1051 (2004).

B. Probable Cause

1. Defining Probable Cause

Page 145. Add the following material at the end of note 3.

See also Maryland v. Pringle, 540 U.S. 366 (2003) (officer who found $763 in glove compartment and cocaine behind armrest in back seat had probable cause to arrest driver, front seat passenger, and rear passengers when all occupants of car denied knowledge of drugs).

C. Warrants

1. The Warrant Requirement and Exigent Circumstances

Page 169. Add the following material at the end of note 1.

See also State v. Lovig, 675 N.W.2d 557 (Iowa 2004) (in the absence of hot pursuit, police investigating traffic accident cannot enter a home without a warrant to arrest person suspected of drunk driving; dissipation of suspect's blood alcohol content over time did not create exigent circumstance); Brigham City v. Stuart, __ P.3d __, 2005 WL 387966 (Utah, Feb. 18, 2005) (when officer safety is not a concern, potential harm required for exigent circumstances rises; contrasts emergency aid doctrine).

2. Requirements for Obtaining Warrants

Page 177. Add the following material in note 2 at the end of the first paragraph.

The consequences are severe when the warrant fails to describe particularly the items to be seized. In Groh v. Ramirez, 540 U.S. 551 (2004), the Supreme Court held that a search warrant failing to describe the items to be seized from a home could not be cured by the agent's inclusion of a list of the items in an unincorporated warrant application, or by his oral description to the homeowners of the items to be seized.

Page 180. Add the following material at the end of note 1.

What should police officers do when they obtain new information about the person or place named in the warrant before they execute the warrant? Return to the magistrate for an updated finding of probable cause? See State v. Maddox, 98 P.3d 1199 (Wash. 2004) (officers must return to magistrate for updated ruling only if new facts negate probable cause).

3.   Execution of Warrants

Page 183. Add the following material before the notes.

United States v. Lashawn Lowell Banks
540 U.S. 31 (2003)

SOUTER, J.

Officers executing a warrant to search for cocaine in respondent Banks's apartment knocked and announced their authority. The question is whether their 15-to-20-second wait before a forcible entry satisfied the Fourth Amendment and 18 U.S.C. §3109. We hold that it did. ...

With information that Banks was selling cocaine at home, North Las Vegas Police Department officers and Federal Bureau of Investigation agents got a warrant to search his two-bedroom apartment. As soon as they arrived there, about 2 o'clock on a Wednesday afternoon, officers posted in front called out "police search warrant" and rapped hard enough on the door to be heard by officers at the back door. There was no indication whether anyone was home, and after waiting for 15 to 20 seconds with no answer, the officers broke open the front door with a battering ram. Banks was in the shower and testified that he heard nothing until the crash of the door, which brought him out dripping to confront the police. The search produced weapons, crack cocaine, and other evidence of drug dealing.

In response to drug and firearms charges, Banks moved to suppress evidence, arguing that the officers executing the search warrant waited an unreasonably short time before forcing entry, and so violated both the Fourth Amendment and 18 U.S.C. §3109, [which provides: "The officer may break open any outer or inner door or window of a house, or any part of a house, or anything therein, to execute a search warrant, if, after notice of his authority and purpose, he is refused admittance or when necessary to liberate himself or a person aiding him in the execution of the warrant."] The District Court denied the motion, and Banks pleaded guilty, reserving his right to challenge the search on appeal. ...

A divided panel of the Ninth Circuit reversed and ordered suppression of the evidence found. 282 F.3d 699 (9th Cir. 2002). In assessing the reasonableness of the execution of the warrant, the panel majority set out a nonexhaustive list of "factors that an officer reasonably should consider" in deciding when to enter premises identified in a warrant, after knocking and announcing their presence but receiving no express acknowledgment:

> (a) size of the residence; (b) location of the residence; (c) location of the officers in relation to the main living or sleeping areas of the residence; (d) time of day; (e) nature of the suspected offense; (f) evidence demonstrating the suspect's guilt; (g) suspect's prior convictions and, if any, the type of offense for which he was convicted; and (h) any other observations triggering the senses of the officers that reasonably would lead one to believe that immediate entry was necessary.

The majority also defined four categories of intrusion after knock and announcement, saying that the classification "aids in the resolution of the essential question whether the entry made herein was reasonable under the circumstances":

> (1) entries in which exigent circumstances exist and non-forcible entry is possible, permitting entry to be made simultaneously with or shortly after announcement; (2) entries in which exigent circumstances exist and forced entry by destruction of property is required, necessitating more specific inferences of exigency; (3) entries in which no exigent circumstances exist and non-forcible entry is possible, requiring an explicit refusal of admittance or a lapse of a significant amount of time; and (4) entries in which no exigent circumstances exist and forced entry by destruction of property is required, mandating an explicit refusal of admittance or a lapse of an even more substantial amount of time.

The panel majority put the action of the officers here in the last category, on the understanding that they destroyed the door without hearing anything to suggest a refusal to admit even though sound traveled easily through the small apartment. The majority held the 15-to-20-second delay after knocking and announcing to be insufficient to satisfy the constitutional safeguards.

We granted certiorari to consider how to go about applying the standard of reasonableness to the length of time police with a warrant must wait before entering without permission after knocking and announcing their intent in a felony case. We now reverse. ...

There has never been a dispute that these officers were obliged to knock and announce their intentions when executing the search warrant, an obligation they concededly honored. Despite this agreement, we start with a word about standards for requiring or dispensing with a knock and announcement, since the same criteria bear on when the officers could legitimately enter after knocking.

The Fourth Amendment says nothing specific about formalities in exercising a warrant's authorization, speaking to the manner of searching as well as to the legitimacy of searching at all simply in terms of the right to be "secure ... against unreasonable searches and seizures." Although the notion of reasonable execution must therefore be fleshed out, we have done that case by case, largely avoiding categories and protocols for searches. Instead, we have treated reasonableness as a function of the facts of cases so various that no template is likely to produce sounder results than examining the totality of circumstances in a given case; it is too hard to invent categories without giving short shrift to details that turn out to be important in a given instance, and without inflating marginal ones. We have, however, pointed out factual considerations of unusual, albeit not dispositive, significance.

In Wilson v. Arkansas, 514 U.S. 927 (1995), we held that the common law knock-and-announce principle is one focus of the reasonableness enquiry; and we subsequently decided that although the standard generally requires the police to announce their intent to search before entering closed premises, the obligation gives way when officers "have a reasonable suspicion that knocking and announcing their presence, under the particular circumstances, would be dangerous or futile, or ... would inhibit the effective investigation of the crime by, for example, allowing the destruction of evidence," Richards v. Wisconsin, 520 U.S. 385 (1997). When a warrant applicant gives reasonable grounds to expect futility or to suspect that one or another such exigency already exists or will arise instantly upon knocking, a magistrate judge is acting within the Constitution to authorize a "no-knock" entry. And even when executing a warrant silent about that, if circumstances support a reasonable suspicion of exigency when the officers arrive at the door, they may go straight in. ...

Since most people keep their doors locked, entering without knocking will normally do some damage, a circumstance too common to require a heightened justification when a reasonable suspicion of exigency already justifies an unwarned entry. We have accordingly held that police in exigent circumstances may damage premises so far as necessary for a no-knock entrance without demonstrating the suspected risk in any more detail than the law demands for an unannounced intrusion simply by lifting the latch. United States v. Ramirez, 523 U.S. 65 (1998). Either way, it is enough that the officers had a reasonable suspicion of exigent circumstances....

Like *Ramirez*, this case turns on the significance of exigency revealed by circumstances known to the officers.... Although the police concededly arrived at Banks's door without reasonable suspicion of facts justifying a no-knock entry, they argue that announcing their presence started the clock running toward the moment of apprehension that Banks would flush away the easily disposable cocaine, prompted by knowing the police would soon be coming in....

Banks does not, of course, deny that exigency may develop in the period beginning when officers with a warrant knock to be admitted, and the issue comes down to whether it was reasonable to suspect imminent loss of evidence after the 15 to 20 seconds the officers waited prior to forcing their way. Though ... this call is a close one, we think that after 15 or 20 seconds without a response, police could fairly suspect that cocaine would be gone if they were reticent any longer.

[Each of Banks's] reasons for saying that 15 to 20 seconds was too brief rests on a mistake about the relevant enquiry: the fact that he was actually in the shower and did not hear the officers is not to the point, and the same is true of the claim that it might have taken him longer than 20 seconds if he had heard the knock and headed straight for the door. As for the shower, it is enough to say that the facts known to the police are what count in judging reasonable waiting time....

And the argument that 15 to 20 seconds was too short for Banks to have come to the door ignores the very risk that justified prompt entry. True, if the officers were to justify their timing here by claiming that Banks's failure to admit them fairly suggested a refusal to let them in, Banks could at least argue that no such suspicion can arise until an occupant has had time to get to the door, a time that will vary with the size of the establishment, perhaps five seconds to open a motel room door, or several minutes to move through a townhouse. In this case, however, the police claim exigent need to enter, and the crucial fact in examining their actions is not time to reach the door but the particular exigency claimed. On the record here, what matters is the opportunity to get rid of cocaine, which a prudent dealer will keep near a commode or kitchen sink. The significant circumstances include the arrival of the police during the day, when anyone inside would probably have been up and around, and the sufficiency of 15 to 20 seconds for getting to the bathroom or the kitchen to start flushing cocaine down the drain…. Once the exigency had matured, of course, the officers were not bound to learn anything more or wait any longer before going in, even though their entry entailed some harm to the building….

Our emphasis on totality analysis necessarily rejects positions taken on each side of this case. *Ramirez*, for example, cannot be read with the breadth the Government espouses, as "reflecting a general principle that the need to damage property in order to effectuate an entry to execute a search warrant should not be part of the analysis of whether the entry itself was reasonable." At common law, the knock-and-announce rule was traditionally justified in part by the belief that announcement generally would avoid "the destruction or breaking of any house … by which great damage and inconvenience might ensue." *Semayne's Case,* 5 Co. Rep. 91a, 91b, 77 Eng. Rep. 194, 196 (K.B. 1603). One point in making an officer knock and announce, then, is to give a person inside the chance to save his door. That is why, in the case with no reason to suspect an immediate risk of frustration or futility in waiting at all, the reasonable wait time may well be longer when police make a forced entry, since they ought to be more certain the occupant has had time to answer the door. It is hard to be more definite than that, without turning the notion of a reasonable time under all the circumstances into a set of sub-rules as the Ninth Circuit has been inclined to do. Suffice it to say that the need to damage property in the course of getting in is a good reason to require more patience than it would be reasonable to expect if the door were open. Police seeking a stolen piano may be able to spend more time to make sure they really need the battering ram.

On the other side, we disapprove of the Court of Appeals's four-part scheme for vetting knock-and-announce entries. [The] Court of Appeals's overlay of a categorical scheme on the general reasonableness analysis threatens to distort the "totality of the circumstances" principle, by replacing a stress on revealing facts with resort to pigeonholes. Attention to cocaine rocks and pianos tells a lot about the chances of their respective disposal and its bearing on reasonable time. Instructions couched in terms like "significant amount of time," and "an even more substantial amount of time," tell very little....

Last, there is Banks's claim that the entry violated 18 U.S.C. §3109. *Ramirez* held that the result should be the same under the Fourth Amendment and §3109, permitting an officer to enter by force "if, after notice of his authority and purpose, he is refused admittance." We explained the statute's requirement of prior notice before forcing entry as codifying a tradition embedded in Anglo-American law, and we held that §3109 implicates the exceptions to the common law knock-and-announce requirement that inform the Fourth Amendment itself. The upshot is that §3109 is subject to an exigent circumstances exception, which qualifies the requirement of refusal after notice, just as it qualifies the obligation to announce in the first place. Absent exigency, the police must knock and receive an actual refusal or wait out the time necessary to infer one. But in a case like this, where the officers knocked and announced their presence, and forcibly entered after a reasonable suspicion of exigency had ripened, their entry satisfied §3109 as well as the Fourth Amendment, even without refusal of admittance. The judgment of the Court of Appeals is reversed.

Darin Muehler v. Iris Mena
125 S. Ct. 1465 (2005)

REHNQUIST, C.J.

Respondent Iris Mena was detained in handcuffs during a search of the premises that she and several others occupied. Petitioners were lead members of a police detachment executing a search warrant of these premises. She sued the officers ... and the District Court found in her favor.... We hold that Mena's detention in handcuffs for the length of the search was consistent with our opinion in Michigan v. Summers, 452 U.S. 692 (1981), and that the officers' questioning during that detention did not violate her Fourth Amendment rights.

Based on information gleaned from the investigation of a gang-related, driveby shooting, petitioners Muehler and Brill had reason to believe at least one member of a gang—the West Side Locos—lived at 1363 Patricia Avenue. They also suspected that the individual was armed and dangerous, since he had recently been involved in the driveby shooting. As a result, Muehler obtained a search warrant for 1363

Patricia Avenue that authorized a broad search of the house and premises for, among other things, deadly weapons and evidence of gang membership. In light of the high degree of risk involved in searching a house suspected of housing at least one, and perhaps multiple, armed gang members, a Special Weapons and Tactics (SWAT) team was used to secure the residence and grounds before the search.

At 7 A.M. on February 3, 1998, petitioners, along with the SWAT team and other officers, executed the warrant. Mena was asleep in her bed when the SWAT team, clad in helmets and black vests adorned with badges and the word "POLICE," entered her bedroom and placed her in handcuffs at gunpoint. The SWAT team also handcuffed three other individuals found on the property. The SWAT team then took those individuals and Mena into a converted garage, which contained several beds and some other bedroom furniture. While the search proceeded, one or two officers guarded the four detainees, who were allowed to move around the garage but remained in handcuffs.

Aware that the West Side Locos gang was composed primarily of illegal immigrants, the officers had notified the Immigration and Naturalization Service (INS) that they would be conducting the search, and an INS officer accompanied the officers executing the warrant. During their detention in the garage, an officer asked for each detainee's name, date of birth, place of birth, and immigration status. The INS officer later asked the detainees for their immigration documentation. Mena's status as a permanent resident was confirmed by her papers.

The search of the premises yielded a .22 caliber handgun with .22 caliber ammunition, a box of .25 caliber ammunition, several baseball bats with gang writing, various additional gang paraphernalia, and a bag of marijuana. Before the officers left the area, Mena was released.

In her § 1983 suit against the officers she alleged that she was detained "for an unreasonable time and in an unreasonable manner" in violation of the Fourth Amendment. In addition, she claimed that the warrant and its execution were overbroad, that the officers failed to comply with the "knock and announce" rule, and that the officers had needlessly destroyed property during the search.... After a trial, a jury, pursuant to a special verdict form, found that Officers Muehler and Brill violated Mena's Fourth Amendment right to be free from unreasonable seizures by detaining her both with force greater than that which was reasonable and for a longer period than that which was reasonable. The jury awarded Mena $10,000 in actual damages and $20,000 in punitive damages against each petitioner for a total of $60,000....

In Michigan v. Summers, 452 U.S. 692 (1981), we held that officers executing a search warrant for contraband have the authority "to detain the occupants of the premises while a proper search is conducted." Such detentions are appropriate, we explained, because the character of the additional intrusion caused by detention is slight and because the justifications for detention are substantial. We made clear that the detention of an occupant is "surely less intrusive than the search itself," and the presence of a warrant assures that a neutral magistrate has determined that probable cause exists to search the home. Against this incremental intrusion, we posited three legitimate law enforcement interests that provide substantial justification for detaining an occupant: preventing flight in the event that incriminating evidence is found, minimizing the risk of harm to the officers, and facilitating the orderly completion of the search, as detainees' self-interest may induce them to open locked doors or locked containers to avoid the use of force.

Mena's detention was, under *Summers,* plainly permissible. An officer's authority to detain incident to a search is categorical; it does not depend on the quantum of proof justifying detention or the extent of the intrusion to be imposed by the seizure. Thus, Mena's detention for the duration of the search was reasonable under *Summers* because a warrant existed to search 1363 Patricia Avenue and she was an occupant of that address at the time of the search.

Inherent in *Summers'* authorization to detain an occupant of the place to be searched is the authority to use reasonable force to effectuate the detention.   See Graham v. Connor, 490 U.S. 386, 396 (1989) ("Fourth Amendment jurisprudence has long recognized that the right to make an arrest or investigatory stop necessarily carries with it the right to use some degree of physical coercion or threat thereof to effect it"). Indeed, *Summers* itself stressed that the risk of harm to officers and occupants is minimized "if the officers routinely exercise unquestioned command of the situation."

The officers' use of force in the form of handcuffs to effectuate Mena's detention in the garage, as well as the detention of the three other occupants, was reasonable because the governmental interests outweigh the marginal intrusion. The imposition of correctly applied handcuffs on Mena, who was already being lawfully detained during a search of the house, was undoubtedly a separate intrusion in addition to detention in the converted garage.[2] The detention was thus more intrusive than that which we upheld in *Summers.*

But this was no ordinary search. The governmental interests in not only detaining, but using handcuffs, are at their maximum when, as here, a warrant authorizes a search for weapons and a wanted gang member resides on the premises. In such inherently dangerous situations, the use of handcuffs minimizes the risk of harm to both officers and occupants. Though this safety risk inherent in executing a search warrant for weapons was sufficient to justify the use of handcuffs, the need to detain multiple occupants made the use of handcuffs all the more reasonable.

Mena argues that, even if the use of handcuffs to detain her in the garage was reasonable as an initial matter, the duration of the use of handcuffs made the detention unreasonable. The duration of a detention can, of course, affect the balance of interests.... However, the 2- to 3-hour detention in handcuffs in this case does not outweigh the government's continuing safety interests. As we have noted, this case involved the detention of four detainees by two officers during a search of a gang house for dangerous weapons. We conclude that the detention of Mena in handcuffs during the search was reasonable.

[Mena also argues that the officers violated her] Fourth Amendment rights by questioning her about her immigration status during the detention. This [contention is] premised on the assumption that the officers were required to have independent reasonable suspicion in order to question Mena concerning her immigration status because the questioning constituted a discrete Fourth Amendment event. But the premise is faulty. We have held repeatedly that mere police questioning does not constitute a seizure. "[E]ven when officers have no basis for suspecting a particular individual, they may generally ask questions of that individual; ask to examine the individual's identification; and request consent to search his or her luggage." Florida v. Bostick, 501 U.S. 429, 434 (1991). [Because the detention was not] prolonged by the questioning, there was no additional seizure within the meaning of the Fourth Amendment. Hence, the officers did not need reasonable

---

[2] In finding the officers should have released Mena from the handcuffs, the Court of Appeals improperly relied upon the fact that the warrant did not include Mena as a suspect. The warrant was concerned not with individuals but with locations and property....

suspicion to ask Mena for her name, date and place of birth, or immigration status....

[Mena] asserts that her detention extended beyond the time the police completed the tasks incident to the search. Because the [courts below] did not address this contention, we too decline to address it....

KENNEDY, J., concurring.

[It seems to me] important to add this brief statement to help ensure that police handcuffing during searches becomes neither routine nor unduly prolonged. The safety of the officers and the efficacy of the search are matters of first concern, but so too is it a matter of first concern that excessive force is not used on the persons detained, especially when these persons, though lawfully detained under Michigan v. Summers are not themselves suspected of any involvement in criminal activity. The use of handcuffs is the use of force, and such force must be objectively reasonable under the circumstances. Graham v. Connor, 490 U.S. 386 (1989).

The reasonableness calculation under *Graham* is in part a function of the expected and actual duration of the search. If the search extends to the point when the handcuffs can cause real pain or serious discomfort, provision must be made to alter the conditions of detention at least long enough to attend to the needs of the detainee. This is so even if there is no question that the initial handcuffing was objectively reasonable. The restraint should also be removed if, at any point during the search, it would be readily apparent to any objectively reasonable officer that removing the handcuffs would not compromise the officers' safety or risk interference or substantial delay in the execution of the search. The time spent in the search here, some two to three hours, certainly approaches, and may well exceed, the time beyond which a detainee's Fourth Amendment interests require revisiting the necessity of handcuffing in order to ensure the restraint, even if permissible as an initial matter, has not become excessive.

That said, under these circumstances I do not think handcuffing the detainees for the duration of the search was objectively unreasonable. As I understand the record, during much of this search 2 armed officers were available to watch over the 4 unarmed detainees, while the other 16 officers on the scene conducted an extensive search of a suspected gang safe house.... Where the detainees outnumber those supervising them, and this situation could not be remedied without diverting officers from an extensive, complex, and time-consuming search, the continued use of handcuffs after the initial sweep may be justified, subject to adjustments or temporary release under supervision to avoid pain or excessive physical discomfort....

STEVENS, J., concurring.

In my judgment ... the Court's discussion of the amount of force used to detain Iris pursuant to Michigan v. Summers is analytically unsound. [Given] the presumption that a reviewing court must draw all reasonable inferences in favor of supporting the verdict, I think it clear that the jury could properly have found that this 5-foot-2-inch young lady posed no threat to the officers at the scene, and that they used excessive force in keeping her in handcuffs for up to three hours. Although *Summers* authorizes the detention of any individual who is present when a valid search warrant is being executed, that case does not give officers *carte blanche* to keep individuals who pose no threat in handcuffs throughout a search, no matter how long it may last. On remand, I would therefore instruct the Court of Appeals to consider whether the evidence supports Mena's contention that the petitioners used excessive force in detaining her when it considers the length of the *Summers* detention.

[The] warrant in this case authorized the police to enter the Mena home to search for a gun belonging to Raymond Romero that may have been used in a gang-related driveby shooting. Romero, a known member of the West Side Locos gang, rented a room from the Mena family. The house, described as a "poor house," was home to several unrelated individuals who rented from the Menas. Each resident had his or her own bedroom, which could be locked with a padlock on the outside, and each had access to the living room and kitchen. In addition, several individuals lived in trailers in the back yard and also had access to the common spaces in the Mena home.

In addition to Romero, police had reason to believe that at least one other West Side Locos gang member had lived at the residence, although Romero's brother told police that the individual had returned to Mexico. The officers in charge of the search, petitioners Muehler and Brill, had been at the same residence a few months earlier on an unrelated domestic violence call, but did not see any other individuals they believed to be gang members inside the home on that occasion.

[Eight] members of the SWAT team forcefully entered the home at 7 A.M. In fact, Iris Mena was the only occupant of the house and she was asleep in her bedroom. The police woke her up at gunpoint, and immediately handcuffed her. At the same time, officers served another search warrant at the home of Romero's mother, where Romero was known to stay several nights each week. In part because Romero's mother had previously cooperated with police officers, they did not use a SWAT team to serve that warrant. Romero was found at his mother's house; after being cited for possession of a small amount of marijuana, he was released.

Meanwhile, after the SWAT team secured the Mena residence and gave the "all clear," police officers transferred Iris and three other individuals (who had been in trailers in the back yard) to a converted garage. [The other individuals included a 55-year-old Latina female, a 40-year-old Latino male who was later removed from the scene by the Immigration and Naturalization Service, and a white male who in his early 30s who was later charged with possession of a small amount of marijuana.] To get to the garage, Iris, who was still in her bedclothes, was forced to walk barefoot through the pouring rain. The officers kept her and the other three individuals in the garage for up to three hours while they searched the home. Although she requested them to remove the handcuffs, they refused to do so. For the duration of the search, two officers guarded Iris and the other three detainees.... With regard to the handcuffs, police may use them in different ways. Here, the cuffs kept Iris' arms behind her for two to three hours....

Police officers' legitimate concern for their own safety is always a factor that should weigh heavily in balancing the relevant ... factors. But, as Officer Brill admitted at trial, if that justification were always sufficient, it would authorize the handcuffing of every occupant of the premises for the duration of every *Summers* detention. [The] decision of what force to use must be made on a case-by-case basis. There is evidence in this record that may well support the conclusion that it was unreasonable to handcuff Iris Mena throughout the search. On remand, therefore, I would instruct the Ninth Circuit to consider that evidence, as well as the possibility that Iris was detained after the search was completed, when deciding whether the evidence in the record is sufficient to support the jury's verdict.

Page 185. Add the following material after the notes.

7. *Physical detentions during execution of warrant.* Can the police insist that those present at the location of a warranted search remain there while the search goes forward? Can they use force to prevent those present from moving about? Did the Supreme Court in Muehler v. Mena suggest that the police there had reached the outer limits of this power? See also Michigan v. Summers, 452 U.S. 692 (1981); Cotton v. State, 872 A.2d 87 (Md. 2005) (officers executing search warrant at residence used to sell drugs may detain person found standing outside the home); Commonwealth v. Charros, 824 N.E.2d 809 (Mass. 2005) (police executing search warrant of home may not stop owners in car one mile from home and return them to search location for frisk).

Problem 3-2A. Warrants and Grenades

On May 5, a man walked into a precinct station house in Harlem and told the police that he purchased drugs from a man named Boswell who lived on the ninth floor of a particular building in Harlem. The informant, who had never before worked with the police, told the officers that Boswell kept drugs and guns in a different location, Apartment 6F in the same building. The informer then described the layout of Apartment 6F and said that Boswell kept dogs there, and carried a pistol in his waistband. The police obtained a search warrant the next day and verified that Boswell had a long criminal record. Six days later, when police arrested Boswell elsewhere in Harlem on felony narcotics charges, he gave his home address as the building that the informant had named.

In an effort to obtain drugs and weapons as further evidence against Boswell, police officers executed the search warrant for Apartment 6F. At 6:10 A.M. on a weekday morning, thirteen police officers broke through the apartment door with a battering ram. They also threw a concussion grenade as they entered, meant to stun people nearby with loud noise and a flash.

When the officers arrived inside the apartment, however, they only found a 57-year-old woman, Alberta Spruill. The officers handcuffed Spruill, but a police captain soon realized the apartment's layout was different from the one the dealer had described, and released her from the handcuffs. When Spruill told the captain that she had a heart condition, he requested an ambulance. She went into cardiac arrest on the way to the hospital, where she died at 7:50 A.M. The city medical examiner ruled that Spruill died from the stress of the raid.

Relatives and neighbors called Ms. Spruill hardworking and devout, someone who minded her own business. She was a city employee for 29 years, who maintained lists of candidates for civil service jobs, including police officers.

Police Commissioner Raymond Kelly apologized to Spruill's family, ordered an investigation of the incident, and suspended the use of the grenades. Kelly said that the police executed more than 1,900 search warrants during the year; they went to the wrong address four times and used the grenades in 85 cases. Mayor Michael Bloomberg said that what had happened was tragic and "a terrible episode." State Assemblyman Keith Wright commented, "I'm sorry to say, but these things happen all too often in this neighborhood." Spruill's relatives planned to sue the city.

Later that week, the Police Department lifted the moratorium on the use of the grenades and announced it was developing a new system to track and store information on search warrants. The new Search Warrant Database compiles information for each warrant that the police request, including the names of the supervising officer, the judge who issued the warrant, the prosecutor assigned to the case, the location, building plans and possible hazards, and the results of the warrant. Under this new system, the number of "no knock" warrants fell dramatically.

Is the new database a sufficient or appropriate response to the death of Alberta Spruill? See William K. Rashbaum, Woman Dies After Police Mistakenly Raid Her Apartment, N.Y. Times, May 17, 2003.

The Spruill cases is dramatic, but even in New York in May of 2003, it does not appear to be unique. See Jim Dwyer, Police Raid Gone Awry: A Muddled Path to the Wrong Door, N.Y. Times, June 29, 2003 (raid with stun grenade on wrong apartment in Bronx involving both local and federal authorities two days before Spruill raid; victim Timothy Brockman was 68-year-old former Marine who uses a walker).

4.   So You Like Warrants?

Page 194.   Add the following material to note 4.

See State v. Larsen, 650 N.W.2d 144 (Minn. 2002) (conservation officer needed warrants to search recreational "ice fishing houses" on frozen lakes; court rejects analogy to closely-regulated industries); Scott E. Sundby, Protecting the Citizen "Whilst He Is Quiet": Suspicionless Searches, "Special Needs" and General Warrants, 74 Miss. L.J. 501-552 (2004).

D. *Consensual Searches*

1.   Components of a Voluntary Choice

Page 200.   Add the following material to note 1.

For a review of the empirical basis for consent doctrine, see Steven L. Chanenson, Get the Facts, Jack! Empirical Research and the Changing Constitutional Landscape of Consent Searches, 71 Tenn. L. Rev. 399 (2004).

Page 201.   Add the following material to note 4.

Compare State v. Brown, 156 S.W.3d 722 (Ark. 2004) (state constitution requires police officers conducting "knock and talk" to inform home dweller that consent may be refused); with State v. Johnston, 839 A.2d 830 (N.H. 2004) (refusing to impose standard requirement of rights advisory before knock and talk); State v. Mann, 857 A.2d 329 (Conn. 2004) (officers may frisk person who answers door during knock and talk procedure if behavior creates reasonable suspicion).

Page 202.   Add the following material to note 5.

See also State v. Collier, 612 S.E.2d 281 (Ga. 2005) (police may not obtain search warrant to compel driver to submit blood and urine samples for drug testing when driver invoked his right under implied consent statute law to refuse testing).

Page 202.   Add the following material to note 6.

See also "California Highway Patrol Settles Profiling Lawsuit," N.Y. Times, Feb. 27, 2003 (agency settles racial profiling lawsuit and bars officers from asking drivers for consent to search their cars or from using minor traffic violations as pretext for stopping car suspected of drug possession unless officers have probable cause of wrongdoing).

Page 203.   Add the following material to note 2.

From time to time, police investigating a crime will ask people to volunteer a DNA sample to exclude themselves as suspects. If a person who agrees to give such a DNA sample later changes his mind, can he "withdraw" his consent and demand that the police remove the DNA information from any database? See Lorraine Blackwell, Protests Curb Racial DNA Sampling, Chicago Tribune, May 4, 2004 (police searching for serial rapist stop nearly 200 black men resembling description of perpetrator to ask for DNA swabs; department agrees to inform men of right to refuse and to destroy existing samples).

2.   Third Party Consent

Page 206.   Add the following material to note 1.

State v. Randolph, 604 S.E.2d 835 (Ga. 2004) (two residents of home both present when police ask for consent to search; consent by one does not trump refusal by other resident).

Page 206.   Add the following material to note 2.

See Halsema v. State, 823 N.E.2d 668 (Ind. 2005) (resident's consent to home did not extend to bureau drawer reserved for exclusive use of defendant who was temporarily living at the home); State v. Licari, 659 N.W.2d 243 (Minn. 2003) (landlord's contractual right to inspect rented storage unit did not provide actual or apparent authority to consent to police search).

Chapter 4

Searches in Recurring Contexts

A.. *"Persons"*

1.   Searches Incident to Arrest

Page 218.   Add this material at the end of note 1.

See also State v. Lamay, 103 P.3d 448 (Idaho 2004) (suspect first encountered in hotel room lying on bed next to backpack on floor, then ordered to step into hallway outside hotel room, where he was arrested; later search of backpack not justified as incident to arrest).

Page 220.   Add this material at the end of note 6.

See State v. Spencer, 848 A.2d 1183 (Conn. 2004) (protective sweep not proper when resident of house containing several apartments accepted package containing marijuana addressed to neighbor and left package at neighbor's door, was arrested in hallway outside open door to his own apartment, and refused to answer police questions about presence of other persons in his apartment).

Page 221.   Add this material at the end of note 2.

See State v. Sykes, 695 N.W.2d 277 (Wis. 2005) (warrantless investigatory search that preceded arrest qualified as search incident to arrest even if officer at time of search did not intend to arrest suspect).

B.   *"Houses" and Other Places*

1.   The Outer Boundaries of Houses

Page 234.   Add this material at the end of note 1.

See People v. Pitman, 813 N.E.2d 93 (Ill. 2004) (defendant, through his mother who owned the farm, held a reasonable expectation of privacy in a barn even though it fell outside the curtilage of the home).

2.   Workplaces

Page 239.   Add this material at the end of note 1.

See People v. Galvadon, 103 P.3d 923 (Colo. 2005) (use of surveillance cameras in nonpublic room in back of liquor store did not undermine the reasonable expectation of privacy of the store's only night employer in the room).

Page 240.   Add this material at the end of note 2.

See Elizabeth E. Joh, The Paradox of Private Policing, 95 J. Crim. L. & Criminology 49 (2004).

3.   Schools and Prisons

Page 246.   Add this material at the end of note 3.

See State v. Jones, 666 N.W.2d 142 (Iowa 2003) (students maintain legitimate expectation of privacy in contents of their school lockers;

lockers may be searched without a warrant in furtherance of "special need" to maintain proper educational environment).

Page 247.   Add this material at the end of Problem 4-4.

Would your analysis change if you knew that the FBI estimates that nearly 100,000 students carry guns to school every day? See Rebecca N. Cordero, No Expectation of Privacy: Should School Officials Be Able to Search Students' Lockers Without Any Suspicion of Wrong Doing? A Study of *In Re Patrick Y* and Its Effect on Maryland Public School Students, 31 U. Balt. L. Rev. 305, n.1 (2002).

Page 253.   Add this material at the end of note 1.

See also Theodore v. Delaware Valley School District, 836 A.2d 76 (Pa. 2003) (random drug and alcohol testing for students who park at school or participate in extracurricular activities violates state constitution unless district presents evidence of existing drug or alcohol problem).

A study of 76,000 high school students published in 2003 found that drug testing in schools does not deter drug use among students. Thirty-seven percent of 12th graders in schools that tested for drugs said they had smoked marijuana in the last year, compared with 36 percent in schools that did not. The same pattern held true for other drugs and students at other grade levels. The study indicated that about 18 percent of the nation's high schools employed some type of drug testing. It does not differentiate between schools that use intensive screening and those that test only occasionally. See Greg Winter, "Study Finds No Sign That Testing Deters Students' Drug Use," N.Y. Times, May 17, 2003. Does this study suggest to you that schools should spend their limited funds on other forms of drug prevention, or that they should invest more in conducting more reliable and credible urinalysis tests?

Page 254.   Add this material in note 2 after the New York case.

Petersen v. Mesa, 83 35 (Ariz. 2004) (random, suspicionless drug testing of city firefighters violates Fourth Amendment, in absence of evidence that firefighters were acting under the influence).

D. *"Effects"*

1. Inventory Searches

Page 266.   Add this material at the end of note 1.

See also People v. Gipson, 786 N.E.2d 540 (Ill. 2003) (standardized procedures requiring search and inventory of impounded vehicles need not be in writing; if written, document need not be produced in court for prosecution to prove existence of procedures).

2. Cars and Containers

Page 272.   Add this material at the end of note 1.

The Supreme Court, in Thornton v. United States, 541 U.S. 615 (2004), decided that the constitution allows states to apply *Belton* to some occupants of automobiles even after they exit the vehicle. In that case, Thornton parked and got out of his car before a police officer who was following him could signal for him to pull over. The officer stopped Thornton on foot, arrested him after finding drugs in his pocket, and searched the nearby car incident to the arrest. He found a handgun in the car. The Court held that *Belton* governs even when an officer does not make contact until the person arrested has left the vehicle. Whether the officer orders a suspect out of a car or the suspect leaves the car by choice, the arrest of a suspect who is next to a vehicle presents identical concerns regarding officer safety and evidence destruction.

Chapter 5

Arrests

A. Stop or Arrest?

Page 289.   Add this material before the notes.

Robert Kaupp v. Texas
538 U.S. 626 (2003)

PER CURIAM.

This case turns on the Fourth Amendment rule that a confession obtained by exploitation of an illegal arrest may not be used against a criminal defendant. After a 14-year-old girl disappeared in January 1999, the Harris County Sheriff's Department learned she had had a sexual relationship with her 19-year-old half brother, who had been in the company of petitioner Robert Kaupp, then 17 years old, on the day of the girl's disappearance. On January 26th, deputy sheriffs questioned the brother and Kaupp at headquarters; Kaupp was cooperative and was permitted to leave, but the brother failed a polygraph examination (his third such failure). Eventually he confessed that he had fatally stabbed his half sister and placed her body in a drainage ditch. He implicated Kaupp in the crime.

Detectives immediately tried but failed to obtain a warrant to question Kaupp.[1] Detective Gregory Pinkins nevertheless decided (in his

---

[1] The detectives applied to the district attorney's office for a "pocket warrant," which they described as authority to take Kaupp into custody for questioning. The detectives did not seek a conventional arrest warrant, as they did not believe

words) to "get [Kaupp] in and confront him with what [the brother] had said." In the company of two other plain clothes detectives and three uniformed officers, Pinkins went to Kaupp's house at approximately 3 A.M. on January 27th. After Kaupp's father let them in, Pinkins, with at least two other officers, went to Kaupp's bedroom, awakened him with a flashlight, identified himself, and said, "we need to go and talk." Kaupp said "Okay." The two officers then handcuffed Kaupp and led him, shoeless and dressed only in boxer shorts and a T-shirt, out of his house and into a patrol car. The state points to nothing in the record indicating Kaupp was told that he was free to decline to go with the officers.

They stopped for 5 or 10 minutes where the victim's body had just been found, in anticipation of confronting Kaupp with the brother's confession, and then went on to the sheriff's headquarters. There, they took Kaupp to an interview room, removed his handcuffs, and advised him of his rights under Miranda v. Arizona, 384 U.S. 436 (1966). Kaupp first denied any involvement in the victim's disappearance, but 10 or 15 minutes into the interrogation, told of the brother's confession, he admitted having some part in the crime. He did not, however, acknowledge causing the fatal wound or confess to murder, for which he was later indicted. After moving unsuccessfully to suppress his confession as the fruit of an illegal arrest, Kaupp was convicted and sentenced to 55 years' imprisonment. . . .

A seizure of the person within the meaning of the Fourth and Fourteenth Amendments occurs when, "taking into account all of the circumstances surrounding the encounter, the police conduct would have communicated to a reasonable person that he was not at liberty to ignore the police presence and go about his business." Florida v. Bostick, 501 U.S. 429, 437 (1991). This test is derived from Justice Stewart's opinion in United States v. Mendenhall, 446 U.S. 544 (1980), which gave several "[e]xamples of circumstances that might indicate a seizure, even where the person did not attempt to leave," including "the threatening presence of several officers, the display of a weapon by an officer, some physical touching of the person of the citizen, or the use of language or tone of

---

they had probable cause for Kaupp's arrest. As the trial court later explained, the detectives had no evidence or motive to corroborate the brother's allegations of Kaupp's involvement; the brother had previously failed three polygraph examinations, while, only two days earlier, Kaupp had voluntarily taken and passed one, in which he denied his involvement.

voice indicating that compliance with the officer's request might be compelled."

Although certain seizures may be justified on something less than probable cause, see, *e.g.,* Terry v. Ohio, 392 U.S. 1 (1968), we have never sustained against Fourth Amendment challenge the involuntary removal of a suspect from his home to a police station and his detention there for investigative purposes . . . absent probable cause or judicial authorization." Such involuntary transport to a police station for questioning is sufficiently like arrest to invoke the traditional rule that arrests may constitutionally be made only on probable cause.

The state does not claim to have had probable cause here, and a straightforward application of the test just mentioned shows beyond cavil that Kaupp was arrested within the meaning of the Fourth Amendment, there being evidence of every one of the probative circumstances mentioned by Justice Stewart in *Mendenhall.* A 17-year-old boy was awakened in his bedroom at three in the morning by at least three police officers, one of whom stated "we need to go and talk." He was taken out in handcuffs, without shoes, dressed only in his underwear in January, placed in a patrol car, driven to the scene of a crime and then to the sheriff's offices, where he was taken into an interrogation room and questioned. This evidence points to arrest even more starkly than the facts in Dunaway v. New York, 442 U.S. 200, 212 (1979), where the petitioner "was taken from a neighbor's home to a police car, transported to a police station, and placed in an interrogation room." There we held it clear that the detention was "in important respects indistinguishable from a traditional arrest" and therefore required probable cause or judicial authorization to be legal. The same is, if anything, even clearer here.

Contrary reasons mentioned by the state courts are no answer to the facts. Kaupp's "Okay" in response to Pinkins's statement is no showing of consent under the circumstances. Pinkins offered Kaupp no choice, and a group of police officers rousing an adolescent out of bed in the middle of the night with the words "we need to go and talk" presents no option but "to go." There is no reason to think Kaupp's answer was anything more than a mere submission to a claim of lawful authority. If reasonable doubt were possible on this point, the ensuing events would resolve it: removal from one's house in handcuffs on a January night with nothing on but underwear for a trip to a crime scene on the way to an interview room at law enforcement headquarters. Even an initially consensual encounter . . . can be transformed into a seizure or detention within the meaning of the Fourth Amendment." It cannot seriously be suggested that when the detectives began to question Kaupp, a reasonable person in his situation would have thought he was sitting in the interview room as a matter of choice, free to change his mind and go home to bed.

Nor is it significant, as the state court thought, that the sheriff's department "routinely" transported individuals, including Kaupp on one prior occasion, while handcuffed for safety of the officers, or that Kaupp did not resist the use of handcuffs or act in a manner consistent with anything other than full cooperation. The test is an objective one, and stressing the officers' motivation of self-protection does not speak to how their actions would reasonably be understood. As for the lack of resistance, failure to struggle with a cohort of deputy sheriffs is not a waiver of Fourth Amendment protection, which does not require the perversity of resisting arrest or assaulting a police officer.

Since Kaupp was arrested before he was questioned, and because the state does not even claim that the sheriff's department had probable cause to detain him at that point, well-established precedent requires suppression of the confession unless that confession was "an act of free will [sufficient] to purge the primary taint of the unlawful invasion." Wong Sun v. United States, 371 U.S. 471 (1963). . . . Unless, on remand, the state can point to testimony undisclosed on the record before us, and weighty enough to carry the state's burden despite the clear force of the evidence shown here, the confession must be suppressed. . . .

Page 291.   Add this material at the end of note 5.

Cf. Devenpeck v. Alford, 125 S. Ct. 588 (2004) (officers pursuing a driver suspected of impersonating an officer arrested him for unlawful audio-taping of police conversation during stop, which was later determined not to be a crime; probable cause to arrest for impersonating an officer was sufficient to support arrest although not the crime the officers relied upon; warrantless arrest is reasonable so long as there exists probable cause to believe that a criminal offense has been or is being committed, on the basis of the reasonable conclusions to be drawn from the facts known to the arresting officer at the time of the arrest).

B. Arrest Warrants

Page 296.   Add this material at the end of note 1.

See State v. Maland, 103 P.3d 430 (Idaho 2004) (officers who have reasonable suspicion to believe that an individual who opened the door of a home is involved in criminal activity may not enter the home to conduct a stop and frisk).

C. Police Discretion in the Arrest Decision

Page 306.   Add this material in note 7 after the first paragraph.

Criminologists remain interested in this topic, and continue to generate new data and updated analyses. See Christopher D. Maxwell, Joel H. Garner & Jeffrey A. Fagan, The Preventive Effects of Arrest on Intimate Partner Violence: Research, Policy, and Theory, 2 Criminology & Pub. Pol. 51 (2002) (pooled data from Minneapolis and replication studies show positive effect of arrest).

D. Paper Arrests: Citations

Page 318.   Add this material in note 2 after the first paragraph.

See also State v. Brown, 792 N.E.2d 175 (Ohio 2003) (rejects *Atwater* under state constitution; officers may not make warrantless arrests for minor misdemeanors unless statutory exceptions are present); State v. Askerooth, 681 N.W.2d 353 (Minn. 2004) (same).

E. Use of Force in Making Arrests

Page 333.   Add this material at the end of note 3.

Police department policies restricting high speed chases often appear in the wake of tragic and highly visible incidents. For instance, in 2002, a police chase in Los Angeles caused the death of a 4-year-old girl. A report dealing with the incident noted that Los Angeles police led the nation in high speed chases in 2001, with 781 pursuits that resulted in 283 crashes and 139 injuries; 59 percent of the chases began when a driver committed a traffic violation. The report proposed that the Los Angeles police adopt a policy along the lines of the practice in Atlanta, Chicago, and Dallas. The police would abandon chases once motorists made clear they were not prepared to pull over, unless the police suspected a crime more serious than a traffic infraction has been committed. See Nick Madigan, Police Chases Scrutinized in Los Angeles After Death, N.Y. Times, Dec. 18, 2002.

Chapter 6

Remedies for Unreasonable Searches and Seizures

A. *Origins of the Exclusionary Rule*

Page 348.   Add this material at the end of note 3.

For an attempt to measure the effects of the exclusionary rule on crime rates (as opposed to conviction rates), see Raymond A. Atkins & Paul H. Rubin, Effects of Criminal Procedure on Crime Rates: Mapping Out the Consequences of the Exclusionary Rule, 46 J.L. & Econ. 157 (2003).

B. *Limitations on the Exclusionary Rule*

1.   Evidence Obtained in "Good Faith"

Page 358. Add this material at the end of note 2.

See also People v. Miller, 75 P.3d 1108 (Colo. 2003) (well-trained officer could not rely on month-old tip with no mention of ongoing activity as basis for probable cause in warrant; no good faith exception).

2.   Causation Limits: Inevitable Discovery and Independent Source

Page 368. Add this material at the end of note 2.

See also State v. Lee, 821 A.2d 922 (Md. 2003) (inevitable discovery and independent source exceptions cannot save evidence obtained in violation of constitutional knock and announce rule).

Page 369. Add this material at the end of note 4.

State v. Krukowski, 100 P.3d 1222 (Utah 2004) (officer's failure to disclose in search warrant application that he already conducted an illegal entry of premises cannot be basis for refusing to apply independent source doctrine).

Page 369. Add this material at the end of note 5.

Cf. People v. Jones, 810 N.E.2d 415 (N.Y. 2004) (police improperly arrested defendant in his home without arrest warrant; identification during lineup conducted while in custody was admissible).

3.   Standing to Challenge Illegal Searches and Seizures

Page 375. Add this material at the end of note 2.

See also State v. Cuntapay, 85 P.3d 634 (Haw. 2004) (when social host shares privacy of home with guest for card game, guest's expectations of privacy in home are reasonable under state constitution; rejects Minnesota v. Carter); State v. Smith, 97 P.3d 567 (Mont. 2004) (police responding to complaint of noise and marijuana aroma knocked on apartment door and were admitted by a party guest; officer heard vomiting from behind closed bathroom door, opened door to find another guest throwing up, officer noticed smell of alcohol; guest had expectation of privacy in closed bathroom).

C. Additions and Alternatives to the Exclusionary Rule

1. Administrative Remedies

Page 383.   Add this material at the end of note 5.

6. *Revocation of officer's license.* State and local police departments only hire individuals who are certified by state licensing authorities to serve as law enforcement officers. Administrative bodies in many states review allegations of police misconduct and sometimes revoke the license of an officer based on that misconduct; the licensing body in Florida is among the most active. See Fla. Stat. Ann. §943.395. The revocation of a license prevents other police forces in the same state from hiring an officer after he or she is fired for misconduct. One database, tracking the work of licensing authorities in eleven states going back to 1973, shows over 5,600 revocations during that time. See Roger L. Goldman, State Revocation of Law Enforcement Officers' Licenses and Federal Criminal Prosecution: An Opportunity for Cooperative Federalism, 22 St. Louis U. Pub. L. Rev. 121 (2003).

2. Tort Actions and Criminal Prosecutions

Page 390.   Add this material at the end of Problem 6-4.

See Vaughan v. Cox, 343 F.3d 1323 (11th Cir. 2003) (police officer not eligible for immunity).

Page 391.   Add this material at the end of note 3.

Brosseau v. Haugen, 125 S. Ct. 596 (2004) (police officer eligible for qualified immunity because no clearly established law warned officer that shooting suspect in vehicle to prevent high-speed chase was unconstitutional).

Chapter 7

The Impact of Technology

A. *Enhancement of the Senses*

Page 408. Add the following material to the end of note 1.

The Supreme Court has re-affirmed that a canine sniff does not amount to a separate "search" for purposes of federal law. In Illinois v. Caballes, 125 S. Ct. 834 (2005), the Court held that a dog sniff performed on the exterior of a vehicle during a valid traffic stop requires no justification because the dog only reveals the presence or absence of contraband and does not intrude on a reasonable expectation of privacy.

The development of a more nuanced dog-sniff caselaw among the states continues apace. Compare State v. Scheetz, 950 P.2d 722 (Mont. 1998) (dog sniff not a search because no reasonable expectation of privacy in the odors emanating from luggage at an airport; luggage was checked and the government's action was minimally intrusive and only revealed limited information about contraband), with State v. Tackitt, 67 P.3d 295 (Mont. 2003) (surveying cases, finding that "the better reasoned cases allow for a carefully drawn exception to the warrant requirement, but still require particularized suspicion when the area or object subject to the canine sniff is already exposed to the public"). See also State v. Ortiz, 600 N.W.2d 805 (Neb. 1999) (defendant had a legitimate expectation of some measure of privacy in the hallway outside his apartment, and anonymous tip did not give police officers reasonable suspicion to go to hallway outside of defendant's apartment for purpose of using drug detection dog to sniff for illegal drugs).

As of 2002, law enforcement agencies in North America used more than 7,000 dog and handler teams. After the terrorist attacks on the World Trade Center, federal agencies such as the U.S. Transportation Security Administration and the U.S. Customs Service planned to expand the use of canine teams by another 10,000. Because of the high costs of training a dog and handler, federal agencies are more likely than local enforcement agencies to add canine units. See Dave Hunter, Common Scents: Establishing a Presumption of Reliability for Detector Dog Teams Used in Airports in Light of the Current Terrorist Threat, 28 U. Dayton L. Rev. 89 (2002).

Page 410. Add the following material at the end of Problem 7-2.

Would it change your argument if you could demonstrate to the legislature that cameras at traffic intersections cause as many auto collisions as they prevent, because more drivers stop abruptly when a light turns yellow, resulting in more collisions from behind? How should a state legislature respond to the reality that traffic cameras generate large revenues, both for the local government installing the camera and the private contractor operating the cameras? Would a profit motive routinely affect the placement or use of the cameras? See Jonathan Miller, With Cameras on the Corner, Your Ticket Is in the Mail, N.Y. Times, Jan. 6, 2005. Does the sheer number of existing cameras make it easier or harder to justify further additions to the surveillance area? See Stephen Kinzer, Chicago Moving to "Smart" Surveillance Cameras, N.Y. Times, Sept. 21, 2004 ("Police specialists here can already monitor live footage from about 2,000 surveillance cameras around the city, so the addition of 250 cameras under the mayor's new plan is not a great jump").

Page 411. Add the following material at the end of note 1.

In 2002, the Nevada Supreme court held that the use of a beeper attached to a car to track a man suspected of voyeuristic activities was not a search and therefore did not require a warrant or other justification. Osburn v. State, 44 P.3d 523 (Nev. 2002). Two judges dissented:

> To best understand the extent of this intrusion, we should consider what the majority is now permitting law enforcement to do without any

oversight whatsoever. The police will be able to place a vehicle monitor on any vehicle, for any reason, and leave it there for as long as they want. There will be no requirement that the monitor be used only when probable cause—or even a reasonable suspicion—is shown, and there will be no time limit on how long the monitor will remain....

I fear that in some instances, the monitor will be used to continually monitor individuals only because law enforcement considers them "dirty." In the future, innocent citizens, and perhaps elected officials or even a police officer's girlfriend or boyfriend, will have their whereabouts continually monitored simply because someone in law enforcement decided to take such action.

One of the newest technological twists is the use of GPS to keep track of vehicle movement, and indeed to create a record of that movement. Would the precision and detail of GPS information lead to a different analysis than for radio beepers? See State v. Jackson 76 P.3d 217 (Wash. 2003) (requiring warrant under Washington State Const. Art. I, Sec. 7, providing that "[n]o person shall be disturbed in his private affairs, or his home invaded, without authority of law").

Page 412. Insert this material at the end of the notes.

Images from "spy satellites" have increased both in quantity and quality over the years. Commercial satellite imaging now supplements the government's satellite cameras, and they monitor domestic as well as foreign sites. The federal government now purchases these commercial images to supplement its own cameras. Given enough commercial and spy satellites, intelligence and law enforcement agencies could realistically achieve constant surveillance of the entire planet. James Bamford, Big Brother Is Tracking You. Without a Warrant. N.Y. Times, May 18, 2003. Do you expect the law that governs spy satellites to change as the presence of the cameras becomes more common and the access to the images gets broader?

B. *Wiretapping*

2.   Statutory Wiretapping Procedures

Page 423.   Insert this material at the end of note 1.

State v. Christensen, 102 P.3d 789 (Wash. 2004) (mother who secretly used speaker phone in base unit of cordless telephone to listen to daughter's conversation with defendant violated state wiretap law; no implied exception for parental eavesdropping on children).

Page 425. Add the following material at the end of note 6.

Professor Orin Kerr argues that, as with wiretapping, generally legislatures are better institutions than courts to deal with new technologies.

> Historically, the constitutional regulation of wiretapping is mostly a myth. Both before and after *Katz*, wiretapping has remained a predominantly statutory field of law. Modern courts generally have declined to use the Fourth Amendment to shape wiretapping law post-*Katz*, and have deferred to statutory wiretapping law instead. Nor is the dominance of statutory rules within wiretapping law unusual. In recent decades, Congress has enacted over a dozen laws that protect privacy in new technologies....
>
> Courts lack the institutional competence and knowledge to generate effective and nuanced rules in new technologies, whereas Congress is better suited to generate such rules. While courts can create effective privacy rules when technologies are stable and easily understood by generalist appellate judges, rapidly developing technologies leave courts poorly equipped to understand the impact of various rules....
>
> While criminal procedure scholars have focused primarily on constitutional protections, the real advances in protecting privacy in new technologies have come (and perhaps must come) from legislatures, not the courts. We are quickly moving toward a bifurcated privacy regime, in which constitutional rules govern privacy in traditional cases but legislative rules govern in cases involving developing technologies....

Orin Kerr, The Fourth Amendment and New Technologies: Constitutional Myths and the Case for Caution, 102 Mich. L. Rev. 801 (2004).

Page 430. Add the following material to note 9.

Federal and state authorities requested 1,358 wiretaps under Title III in 2002; that number climbed to 1,710 in 2004, a 25 percent increase in two years. Judges did not deny a single application. The 2004 report by the Administrative Office of the United States Courts offered more details:

> The number of applications for orders by federal authorities rose 26 percent to 730. The number of applications reported by state prosecuting officials grew 13 percent to 980, with 19 state jurisdictions providing reports, four fewer than in 2003, but equal to the number for 2002. Wiretaps installed were in operation an average of 43 days per wiretap in 2004 compared to 44 days in 2003. The average number of persons whose communications were intercepted increased from 116 per wiretap order in 2003 to 126 per order in 2004. The average percentage of intercepted communications that were incriminating was 21 percent in 2004, compared to 33 percent in 2003.

See Administrative Office of the United States Courts, 2003 Wiretap Report (April 2004).

3.   Bugs on Agents

Page 437.   Add this material to the end of the first paragraph in note 1.

More recently, Pennsylvania and Vermont have concluded that a warrant is required for secret taping by police of a conversation with a suspect. See State v. Geraw, 795 A.2d 1219 (Vt. 2002); Commonwealth v. Brion, 652 A.2d 287 (Pa. 1994) (confidential informant); C. Bast, What's Bugging You? Inconsistencies and Irrationalities of the Law of Eavesdropping, 47 DePaul L. Rev. 837 (1998) (discussing state law on surreptitious police monitoring and recording).

4.   Wiretaps to Fight Terrorism and Crime

Page 438. Insert this material before Problem 7-4.

In March 2004, the Bush Administration submitted a report to Congress on the use of intelligence wiretaps. In 2004, the government obtained 1,754 warrants to conduct the wiretaps and other intelligence-related searches, compared to 1,003 warrants in 2000 (a 75 percent increase over four years).

Page 440. Insert this material before part C.

Anti-USAPATRIOT Acts. Three states and more than 130 local governments have enacted "Anti-USAPATRIOT" resolutions and statutes. See Adam Clymer, In the Fight for Privacy, States Set Off Sparks, N.Y. Times, June 6, 2003. Some of these measures try to limit state involvement in PATRIOT Act investigations, while others request federal agents to share information with local authorities. Are these resolutions invalid under the Supremacy Clause? Will citizens of these jurisdictions enjoy more privacy than citizens elsewhere?

An Ordinance of the City Council to Defend the Bill of Rights and Civil Liberties
Arcata, California Ordinance No. 1339, April 2, 2003

§2190   Purposes.
The purposes of this ordinance are [to] ensure that local law enforcement continues to preserve and uphold residents' freedom of speech, assembly, association, and privacy, the right to counsel and due process in judicial proceedings, and protection from unreasonable searches and seizures, even if requested or authorized to infringe upon such rights by federal or state law enforcement agencies acting under new powers created by the USA PATRIOT Act, Homeland Security Act, or related Executive Orders....

§2191   No Unconstitutional Detentions or Profiling.
No management employee of the City shall officially engage in or permit unlawful detentions or profiling based on race, ethnicity, national

origin, gender, sexual orientation, or political or religious association that are in violation of individuals' civil rights or civil liberties....

§2192   No Unconstitutional Voluntary Cooperation.

No management employee of the City shall officially assist or voluntarily cooperate with investigations, interrogations, or arrest procedures, public or clandestine, that are in violation of individuals' civil rights or civil liberties....

§2193   Notification.

Management employees of the City shall promptly notify the City Manager when, in the course of City employment, [a] management employee of the City is contacted by another law enforcement agency and asked to cooperate or assist with an investigation, interrogation, or arrest procedure under provisions of the USA PATRIOT Act, Homeland Security Act, or related Executive Orders, or future enacted law, executive order or regulation, where such procedure is in violation of an individual's civil rights or civil liberties as specified in the Bill of Rights and Fourteenth Amendment of the United States Constitution.

Upon such notification from a management employee, the City Manager shall promptly report to the City Council, specifying the law enforcement agency seeking cooperation or assistance and the actions requested of the management employee.

§2194   Defense.

The City shall provide legal defense to any management employee who is criminally charged by another entity for his or her actions in compliance with this Ordinance....

Note

FISA Facts. Consider the following report of FISA applications for surveillance orders and the judgment of the FISA court.

Year	FISA Applications Presented	FISA Applications Approved	FISA Applications Rejected
1979	199	207	0
1980	319	322	0

1981	431	433	0
1982	473	475	0
1983	549	549	0
1984	635	635	0
1985	587	587	0
1986	573	573	0
1987	512	512	0
1988	534	534	0
1989	546	546	0
1990	595	595	0
1991	593	593	0
1992	484	484	0
1993	509	509	0
1994	576	576	0
1995	697	697	0
1996	839	839	0
1997	749	748	0
1998	796	796	0
1999	886	880	0
2000	1,005	1,012	0
2001	932	934	0
2002	1,228	1,228	0
2003	1,727	1,724	4
Totals	16,974	16,988	4

C. *Records in the Hands of Third Parties*

Page 445. Insert the following problem before the notes.

Problem 7-4A. Rush Limbo

On September 9, 1997, Lieutenant David Kenary, a commander of the Hartford Police Department's crimes against persons and property unit, called DEA investigator Marcus Brown to arrange a meeting at the Hartford Police Department. The purported purpose of the meeting was to exchange information about Santo Buccheri, a Hartford physician, and his issuance of prescriptions for controlled substances. At the meeting, Kenary informed Brown that he believed Buccheri was over-prescribing controlled substances and dispensing samples to his patients without maintaining proper records. Kenary asked Brown to notify him if

Nicholas Russo's name surfaced during any investigation of Buccheri and provided Brown with Russo's date of birth and home address.

Beginning on October 31, 1997, Brown went to pharmacies located near Buccheri's office and Russo's home and, without a search warrant, asked each of the pharmacies to provide him with Russo's prescription records. The records contained information about prescriptions that each pharmacy had filled for Russo, including the name of the prescribing physician, the date Russo submitted the prescription to the pharmacy, the type and quantity of drug prescribed and the price of the drug. The pharmacies complied with Brown's requests. Brown later returned to each pharmacy and, again by request, obtained copies of the actual prescription forms that Russo presented to the pharmacies.

The state filed an information charging Russo with thirty-two counts of obtaining Tylenol with codeine No. 3 (Tylenol 3), a controlled substance, by forging a prescription and thirty-two counts of forgery in the second degree.

The defendant moved to suppress the records of his prescriptions that the state obtained from the pharmacies without a warrant and without his consent. Russo contended that he has a reasonable expectation of privacy in his prescription records and, therefore, that the state obtained those records in violation of his rights under the federal and state constitutions. How would you rule? See State v. Russo, 790 A.2d 1132 (Conn. 2002).

Page 447. Insert this material at the end of Problem 7-5.

Early in 2003, Congress ordered the Department of Defense to report on its plans for the Total Information Awareness program. The report announced a name change for the program, henceforth to be called the "Terrorism Information Awareness" program because the old name "created in some minds the impression that TIA was a system to be used for developing dossiers on U.S. citizens." Despite the change in names, the description of the program remained mostly the same. Congress ultimately cut off most of the funding for the program.

Cybernovelist William Gibson had these reflections on privacy on the occasion of what would have been George Orwell's 100th birthday. See William Gibson, The Road to Oceania, N.Y. Times, June 25, 2003.

> [D]riven by the acceleration of computing power and connectivity and the simultaneous development of surveillance systems and tracking technologies, we are approaching a theoretical state of absolute informational transparency, one in which "Orwellian" scrutiny is no longer a strictly hierarchical, top-down activity, but to some extent a democratized one....
>
> Certain goals of the American government's Total (now Terrorist) Information Awareness initiative may eventually be realized simply by the evolution of the global information system — but not necessarily or exclusively for the benefit of the United States or any other government. This outcome may be an inevitable result of the migration to cyberspace of everything that we do with information....
>
> It is becoming unprecedentedly difficult for anyone, anyone at all, to keep a secret.

Gibson points to a tension that grows out of this information glut: the distinction between facts and meaning. Meaning, he observes, depends on contact.

> A world of informational transparency will necessarily be one of deliriously multiple viewpoints, shot through with misinformation, disinformation, conspiracy theories and a quotidian degree of madness. We may be able to see what's going on more quickly, but that doesn't mean we'll agree about it any more readily....

In the face of criticism of the Department of Defense's "Total Information Awareness" program, Secretary of Defense Donald Rumsfeld appointed a blue ribbon ad hoc "Technology and Privacy Advisory Committee" chaired by former Federal Communications Commission chair Newton Minnow, and peopled by seven major public legal figures—Floyd Abrams, Zoë Baird, Griffin Bell, Gerhard Casper, William T. Coleman, Jr., Lloyd N. Cutler and John O. Marsh, Jr. The Secretary asked TAPAC to answer four questions:

> 1. Should the goal of developing technologies that may help identify terrorists before they act be pursued?
> 2. What safeguards should be developed to ensure that the application of this or any like technology developed within DOD is carried out in accordance with U.S. law and American values related to privacy?
> 3. Which public policy goals are implicated by TIA and what steps should be taken to ensure that TIA does not frustrate those goals?

4. How should the Government ensure that the application of these technologies to global databases respects international and foreign domestic law and policy?

Excerpts of the March 2004 TAPAC report follow. Do reports like this ever have any impact on law, policy, or public debate? Will this one?

Safeguarding Privacy in the Fight Against Terrorism
Report of the Technology and Privacy Advisory Committee
March 2004

… As the murderous attacks of September 11 painfully demonstrated, this new threat is unlike anything the nation has faced before. The combination of coordinated, well-financed terrorists, willing to sacrifice their lives, potentially armed with weapons of mass destruction, capable of operating within our own borders poses extraordinary risks to our security, as well as to our constitutional freedoms, which could all too easily be compromised in the fight against this new and deadly terrorist threat.

To help guard against this, Secretary of Defense Donald Rumsfeld appointed the Technology and Privacy Advisory Committee ("TAPAC") in February 2003 to examine the use of "advanced information technologies to identify terrorists before they act." Secretary Rumsfeld charged the committee with developing safeguards "to ensure that the application of this or any like technology developed within [the Department of Defense] DOD is carried out in accordance with U.S. law and American values related to privacy." …

The decision to create TAPAC was prompted by the escalating debate over the Terrorism Information Awareness ("TIA") program. [In 2003], Congress terminated funding for the program with the exception of "processing, analysis, and collaboration tools for counterterrorism foreign intelligence," specified in a classified annex to the Act.…

The Scope of Government Data Mining

TIA was not unique in its potential for data mining, [which we define as searches of electronic databases for information concerning U.S. persons by or on behalf of an agency of the government]. TAPAC is aware of many other programs in use or under development both within DOD and elsewhere in the government that make similar uses of personal information concerning U.S. persons to detect and deter terrorist activities, including:

> • DOD programs to determine whether data mining can be used to identify individuals who pose a threat to U.S. forces abroad
> • the intelligence community's Advanced Research and Development Activity center, based in the National Security Agency ...
> • the Computer-Assisted Passenger Prescreening System in the Department of Homeland Security ("DHS")
> • the Treasury Department's Financial Crimes Enforcement Network ...
> • the "MATRIX" (Multi-State Anti-Terrorism Information Exchange) system to link law enforcement records with other government and private-sector databases in eight states and DHS
> • Congress' mandate in the Homeland Security Act that DHS "establish and utilize ... a secure communications and information technology infrastructure, including data mining and other advanced analytical tools," to "access, receive, and analyze data detect and identify threats of terrorism against the United States"

... TAPAC has reached four broad conclusions:

TIA was a flawed effort to achieve worthwhile ends. It was flawed by its perceived insensitivity to critical privacy issues, the manner in which it was presented to the public, and the lack of clarity and consistency with which it was described....

Data mining is a vital tool in the fight against terrorism, but when used in connection with personal data concerning U.S. persons, data mining can present significant privacy issues. Data mining tools, like most technologies, are inherently neutral: they can be used for good or ill. However, when those tools are used by the government to scrutinize personally identifiable data concerning U.S. persons who have done nothing to warrant suspicion, if they are conducted without an adequate predicate they run the risk of becoming the 21st-century equivalent of general searches, which the authors of the Bill of Rights were so concerned to protect against.

To be certain, data mining has many valuable and lawful uses in both the private and public sectors. In many settings it may prove less intrusive to privacy than other techniques for guarding against terrorist threats. Moreover, the same technologies that make data mining feasible

64

can be used to reduce the amount of personally identifiable data necessary, facilitate data mining with anonymized data, and create immutable audit trails and other protections against misuse.

However, when data mining involves the government accessing personally identifiable information about U.S. persons, it also raises privacy issues. The magnitude of those issues varies depending upon many factors, including: the sensitivity of the data being mined … and the number (or percentage) of U.S. persons identified in response to an inquiry who have not otherwise done anything to warrant government suspicion.

In developing and using data mining tools the government can and must protect privacy. Striking a balance between security and privacy is no easy task. Alexander Hamilton wrote in Federalist Paper 8 in 1787 that "safety from external danger is the most powerful director of national conduct. Even the ardent love of liberty will, after a time, give way to its dictates." "To be more safe," he concluded, nations "at length become willing to run the risk of being less free."…

This is precisely the challenge our nation faces today, a challenge made immediate and critical by the magnitude of the terrorist threat, its sustained nature, and the fact that it comes not from an identified enemy abroad but from a largely invisible enemy that may be operating within our borders.

Existing legal requirements applicable to the government's many data mining programs are numerous, but disjointed and often outdated, and as a result may compromise the protection of privacy, public confidence, and the nation's ability to craft effective and lawful responses to terrorism. … The legal protections that have historically applied in this context recognize distinctions between U.S. persons and non-U.S. persons, between law enforcement and national security, and between activities that take place in the United States as opposed to those that take place beyond our borders. This "line at the border" approach to privacy law and to national security is now increasingly inadequate because of the new threat from terrorists who may be operating within our borders, and advances in digital technologies, including the Internet, that have exponentially increased the volume of data available about individuals and greatly reduced the financial and other obstacles to retaining, sharing, and transferring those data across borders.…

RECOMMENDATION 2: The Secretary should establish a regulatory framework applicable to all data mining conducted by, or under the authority of, DOD, known or reasonably likely to involve personally identifiable information concerning U.S. persons.

The essential elements of that framework include a written finding by agency heads authorizing data mining; minimum technical requirements for data mining systems (including data minimization, data anonymization, creation of an audit trail, security and access controls, and training for personnel involved in data mining); special protections for data mining involving databases from other government agencies or from private industry; authorization from the Foreign Intelligence Surveillance Court before engaging in data mining with personally identifiable information concerning U.S. persons or reidentifying previously anonymized information concerning U.S. persons; and regular audits to ensure compliance.

We recommend *excluding* from these requirements data mining that is limited to foreign intelligence that does not involve U.S. persons; data mining concerning federal government employees in connection with their employment; and data mining that is based on particularized suspicion, including searches to identify or locate a specific individual (e.g., a suspected terrorist) from airline or cruise ship passenger manifests or other lists of names or other nonsensitive information about U.S. persons.

In addition, we recommend that data mining that is limited to information that is routinely available without charge or subscription to the public—on the Internet, in telephone directories, or in public records to the extent authorized by law—should be subject to only the requirements that it be conducted pursuant to the written authorization of the agency head ...) and auditing for compliance....

RECOMMENDATION 4: The Secretary should create a policy-level privacy officer....

RECOMMENDATION 5: The Secretary should create a panel of external advisors to advise the Secretary, the privacy officer, and other DOD officials on identifying and resolving informational privacy issues....

RECOMMENDATION 8: The Secretary should recommend that Congress and the President establish one framework of legal, technological, training, and oversight mechanisms necessary to guarantee the privacy of U.S. persons in the context of national security and law enforcement activities. A government-wide approach is desirable to address the significant privacy issues raised by the many programs under development, or already in operation....

We do not suggest that the resolution of informational privacy issues will be the same in every setting. Clearly, some modifications will be necessary. We believe, however, that government efforts to protect national security and fight crime and to protect privacy will be enhanced by the articulation of government-wide principles and a consistent system of laws and processes. National standards will also help provide clear models for state and local government efforts....

CONCLUSION

Our goal in these recommendations is to articulate a framework of law and technology to enable the government simultaneously to combat terrorism and safeguard privacy.... While these recommendations impose additional burdens on government officials before they employ some data mining tools, we believe that in the long-run they will enhance not only informational privacy, but national security as well. They are designed to help break down the barriers to information-sharing among agencies that have previously hampered national security efforts, ... and to ensure that scarce national security resources are deployed strategically and effectively....

We must not sacrifice liberty for security, because as Benjamin Franklin warned more than two centuries ago, "they that can give up essential liberty to purchase a little temporary safety deserve neither liberty nor safety." Franklin might well have added that those who trade liberty for safety all too often achieve neither....

SEPARATE STATEMENT OF WILLIAM T. COLEMAN, JR....

[Among] the reasons I file these respectful, separate views and recommendations are the following:

1. The report does not sufficiently reflect appreciation of the extent of the security and national defense problems—many novel and new—facing the Nation today in the early stages of the war on terrorism....

2. The report does not set forth or emphasize sufficiently the nature of the enemy facing us, not one of a foreign nation state, not one easily identified by uniform, but one who wears civilian clothes, one who purposely mixes with innocent U.S. persons, using their facilities (banks, airplanes, flying schools, etc.) and who otherwise immerses himself or herself in our free, open, friendly society, ... until he or she commits the terrorist acts, then often disappears again into our free, open, trusting, friendly society, living again in civilian clothes and assuming again his or her previous lifestyle.

3. The report directly, or at least by implication, wrongly elevates the concept of privacy and protection thereof—an important American civilized value ...—to the same constitutional level as the fundamental values of liberty, free speech, religion, the political process and racial discrimination issues, each expressly in the Constitution, and the report wrongly concludes that Government data mining runs the risk of "becoming the 21st-century equivalent of the general search" proscribed by the Bill of Rights. [Preserving] American lives from terrorist attack is as great if not a greater "American value," in fact, a constitutional duty of the President, the Secretary of Defense, and other Government officials and American soldiers....

4. The report pays little attention to the initial problem—use of "personally identifiable" information willingly supplied to the Government by such "personally identified" persons and legally in the Government's data files—at which the Secretary of Defense had asked TAPAC to look, but instead the report embarks upon many other issues....

6. The report does not emphasize that in the TIA program there was *no* collection of *new* personal information and that instead the TIA program was dealing only with information already lawfully collected by the Government or perhaps a third person who legally and willingly turned it over to the Government....

[There] are in the United States as of January 1, 2004 a population of over 285 million people. Of the 285 million people, 18 million are non-U.S. citizens. In addition there are millions of people in the United States each day who are non-U.S. persons. For example, Government and academic estimates indicate that there are 9–11 million illegal aliens living in the United States. Both U.S. borders, north and south, are porous by any standard of other nations. Each month over three million foreign people cross through these borders, most with legal right to do so, others not. In the year 2002, more than 27.9 million non-immigrant admissions were counted by the Immigration and Naturalization Service. Many persons stay beyond their legally authorized time....

There is fair evidence that *if* governmental officials, agents and employees *had real-time meaningful access* on September 10-11, 2001 to the *knowledge then in governmental files—all* such information being *originally obtained legally, and there was no statutory restriction of which governmental agents could look at it*—the terrorist attacks of September 11 probably could have been prevented....

When nation-states plan to attack another nation-state, usually there is some advance notice. We see armies, navies building up, equipment and uniformed human beings being moved. Here, ... in the main the wrongdoers were non-state actors, not nation-states.... Thus the public ought to appreciate and respect that responsible Government officials, agents and employees are trying to develop ways in which Government's officials, agents and employees get pre-notice in real time in an informative, useable way, free of clutter, and thus can thwart future such tragic events....

Page 448. Add the following material after note 1.

1a. *Financial, medical and other personal information held by third parties.* Government access to pharmaceutical records are just one important instance of a large range of personal information held by third parties. Major categories of information include banking records and other financial records, and health and medical records. The United States Supreme Court has been unwilling to find constitutional privacy limits on government access to such information. See United States v. Miller, 425 U.S. 435 (1976) (no reasonable expectation of privacy in bank records). State courts have divided on the question of constitutional privacy rights in banking records. See chapter 4, page 261, note 5. Both Congress and state legislatures have often stepped in where courts have hesitated to act. As financial, commercial, and medical habits, laws and procedures change, courts must confront new twists on existing case law and statutory frameworks. See, e.g., Commonwealth v. Duncan, 817 A.2d 455 (Pa. 2003) (no warrant required for name and address of ATM card holder, even though access to more detailed bank information subject to regulation). Another twist on the question of individual privacy rights in information held by third parties comes from the regulated status of many of the industries and entities that hold the information, such as banks, brokers, doctors, and pharmacists.

Page 450. Add the following material after note 3.

3a. *Prosaic information: airline passengers.* Sometimes the information sought by the government is far more prosaic than DNA and financial information. Several airlines have provided the federal government with lists of passengers who flew on particular flights at particular times. See Mathew Wald, Airline Gave Government Information on Passengers, N.Y. Times, Jan. 18, 2004. Should a willingness to provide such information to authorities be an explicit condition of using public transportation? After September 11, is the release of the names of people who purchase tickets or fly an implicit condition of travel, just like going through security procedures at airports?

D. *Nongovernmental Infringement of Privacy*

Page 460.   Insert this material at the end of note 3.

For another example of private industry acting voluntarily to protect the privacy of its customers, consider the U.S. automotive industry. It opposes a legal requirement that vehicles contain as standard equipment a "black box" to record information about crashes. See Matthew L. Wald, Automakers Block Crash Data Recorders, N.Y. Times, Dec. 29, 2002.

Chapter 8

Interrogations

A. *Voluntariness of Confessions*

1. Physical Abuse and Deprivations

Page 468.   Add this material to the end of note 2.

See State v. Harris, 105 P.3d 1258 (Kan. 2005) (detention of a suspect by shackling him to floor of interrogation room for seven hours did not render his subsequent confession involuntary; suspect was questioned for two and a half hours, denied access to telephone, but allowed to take bathroom breaks).

Page 469.   Add this material to the end of note 4.

Commonwealth v. Perez, 845 A.2d 779 (Pa. 2004) (disavowed state's bright-line rule that required suppression of inculpatory pre-arraignment statements made during a delay in arraignment that exceeded six hours; replaced with a totality of the circumstances test for determining the admissibility of statements made during delays in arraignment).

Page 470.   Add this material to the end of the notes.

During military operations in Afghanistan in 2001 and 2002, United States armed forces captured enemy combatants. Agents of the Central Intelligence Agency interrogated the detainees in locations near the fighting, and for months after their capture at the military detention facility at Guantanamo Bay in Cuba. The interrogators used "stress and duress" techniques. For instance, detainees who refused to cooperate were kept standing or kneeling for hours while wearing black hoods or spray-painted goggles. Some were allegedly held in awkward and painful positions, or were subjected to 24-hour lighting to disrupt their sleep. In some cases, the United States turned over captured combatants to foreign governments known to use torture during interrogations.

One official who supervised the capture and transfer of accused terrorists explained the tactics in these terms: "If you don't violate someone's human rights some of the time, you probably aren't doing your job.... I don't think we want to be promoting a view of zero tolerance on this. That was the whole problem for a long time with the CIA." Dana Priest & Barton Gellman, U.S. Decries Abuse But Defends Interrogations; "Stress and Duress" Tactics Used, Washington Post, Dec. 26, 2002. Do the techniques described above make any confessions of the detainees involuntary? Are such techniques acceptable so long as the government pursues no criminal charges against the detainee? So long as the interrogation takes place outside the territory of the United States?

2.   Promises and Threats

Page 475.   Add this material to the end of note 2.

See also Steven A. Drizin & Richard A. Leo, The Problem of False Confessions in the Post-DNA World, 82 N.C. L. Rev. 891 (2004) (analyzing pool of 125 cases).

3.   Police Lies

Page 480.   Add this material to the end of note 1.

State v. Burrell, 2005 WL 1175752 (Minn., May 19, 2005) (16-year-old suspect asked three times to speak with his mother; applying totality of circumstances test, denial of access to mother and misrepresentations of witnesses' statements about suspect's role in crime resulted in involuntary confession).

B. Miranda *Warnings*

1.   The *Miranda* Revolution

Page 496.   Add this material at the end of note 1.

See Mark A. Godsey, Rethinking the Involuntary Confession Rule: Toward a Workable Test for Identifying Compelled Self-Incrimination, 93 Calif. L. Rev. 465 (2005) (argues to replace voluntariness with self-incrimination as basic criterion for admission of confessions; proposes an "objective penalties" test, asking whether confession was obtained by using an objective penalty in any form on the suspect to punish silence or provoke speech).

2.   Triggering *Miranda* Warnings

Page 506.   Add this material at the end of note 1.

In Yarborough v. Alvarado, 541 U.S. 652 (2004), the Supreme Court considered whether a California state court made an "unreasonable application" of federal law when the state court determined that a 17-year-old, interviewed for 2 hours at the police station, was *not* in custody for purposes of *Miranda*. The issue arose in the procedural posture of federal habeas review of a state court conviction:

> Ignoring the deferential standard of §2254(d)(1) for the moment, it can be said that fair-minded jurists could disagree over whether Alvarado was in custody. On one hand, certain facts weigh against a finding that Alvarado was in custody. The police did not transport Alvarado to the station or require him to appear at a particular time. They did not threaten him or suggest he would be placed under arrest. Alvarado's parents remained in the lobby during the interview, suggesting that the interview would be brief. In fact, according to trial counsel for Alvarado, he and his parents were told that the interview was "not going to be long." During the interview, [Los Angeles County Sheriff's detective Cheryl] Comstock focused on [co-defendant] Soto's crimes rather than Alvarado's. Instead of pressuring Alvarado with the threat of arrest and prosecution, she appealed to his interest in telling the truth

and being helpful to a police officer. In addition, Comstock twice asked Alvarado if he wanted to take a break.

Other facts point in the opposite direction. Comstock interviewed Alvarado at the police station. The interview lasted two hours.... Comstock did not tell Alvarado that he was free to leave. Alvarado was brought to the police station by his legal guardians rather than arriving on his own accord, making the extent of his control over his presence unclear. Counsel for Alvarado alleges that Alvarado's parents asked to be present at the interview but were rebuffed, a fact that—if known to Alvarado—might reasonably have led someone in Alvarado's position to feel more restricted than otherwise. These facts weigh in favor of the view that Alvarado was in custody. These differing indications lead us to hold that the state court's application of our custody standard was reasonable.

The lower federal courts had reached a contrary result "by placing considerable reliance on Alvarado's age and inexperience with law enforcement." In a wonderful illustration of the pervasive legal puzzle of what is an "objective" or "subjective" factor, the majority emphasized the "objective circumstances of the interrogation" in determining the question of custody, and such "objective circumstances," the court then held, did not include the defendant's age or experience with law enforcement.

Page 512.   Add this material at the end of note 1.

State v. Sawyer, 156 S.W.3d 531 (Tenn. 2005) (reading arrest warrant affidavit to defendant amounted to interrogation; reading of warrant alone would not qualify).

3.   Form of Warnings

Page 522.   Add this material at the end of note 1.

Cf. State v. A.G.D. 835 A.2d 291 (N.J. 2003) (failure to inform suspect that warrant for his arrest had been issued invalided his waiver of state-law right against self-incrimination, deprived him of information necessary to a knowing and intelligent waiver).

C. Invocation and Waiver of Miranda Rights

Page 531.   Add this material at the end of note 3.

Garvey v. State, 2005 WL 1000542 (Del., April 28, 2005) (suspect who responded to *Miranda* advisory by saying, "Depends on what you ask me," unambiguously waived interrogation rights, indicating intent to selectively waive rights and an understanding of those rights); State v. DeWeese, 582 S.E.2d 786 (W.Va. 2003) (after seven-day lapse between waiver of rights custodial questioning, officers should have given defendant new round of warnings, even though suspect's attorney said warnings were not necessary).

Page 533.   Add this material at the end of note 7.

See also Saul M. Kassin & Rebecca J. Norwick, Why People Waive Their *Miranda* Rights: The Power of Innocence, 28 Law & Hum. Behav. 211 (2004).

D. Effect of Asserting Miranda Rights

Page 543.   Add this material at the end of note 1.

Cross v. State, 144 S.W.3d 521 (Tex. Crim. App. 2004) (after defendant invokes rights but then reinitiates further communications, police need not wait for another re-initiation to interview him again); McDougal v. State, 591 S.E.2d 788 (Ga. 2004) (request by suspect to speak to interrogating officers in his cell after previously invoking right to counsel does not amount to waiver; officers must ask why suspect summoned them before questioning him about crime).

E. Sixth Amendment Right to Counsel During Investigations

Page 551.   Add this material before the notes.

Problem 8-9A. Federal Lawyers, State Crimes

During the summer and fall of 2002, a series of murders occurred in suburban Washington, D.C. In each case, a person who was walking or standing in some public place was killed from long distance by a sniper's rifle.

In October 2002, law enforcement officials arrested two suspects in the shootings, John Allen Muhammad and Lee Boyd Malvo. Malvo was 17 years old at the time. Prosecutors charged both suspects with various crimes related to the shootings in federal court in Maryland. The federal Magistrate Judge appointed attorneys in Baltimore to represent Malvo and Muhammad. However, Attorney General Ashcroft decided to transfer the cases to Virginia, a jurisdiction where a death sentence was a stronger likelihood. Virginia authorities filed charges against the two suspects on November 6, and on November 7, federal marshals delivered Malvo to a detention center in Virginia and the federal government dropped its charges two days later.

When Malvo's attorneys, Robert Tucker and Joshua Treem, learned that Malvo was no longer in federal custody, they tried to learn his new location. Federal authorities refused to tell Tucker and Treem where Malvo was being held. The defense attorneys contacted the federal prosecutor in Virginia and requested in writing

> that no law enforcement officer make any attempt to interrogate our juvenile client unless we are present. In the event that the federal government intends to transfer our client's custody to state or local authorities, we request that you inform such authorities that we ask them not to interrogate our client unless we are present or other counsel appointed by the respective state or local jurisdiction is present.

That same day, the federal Magistrate Judge ordered Tucker and Treem to continue representing Malvo "until such time as other competent counsel have assumed responsibility for the representation of your clients."

Detective June Boyle was the lead homicide detective in Fairfax County, Virginia, assigned to the state case. When Malvo arrived at the detention center at 3:30 P.M., Boyle escorted him to her office. At 4:00, officers seated him, still handcuffed, in an interview room. Special Agent Brad Garrett of the FBI entered the room and asked Malvo if he wanted anything to eat or drink. Malvo asked for some veggie burgers and water. Garrett gave him a bottle of water right away and sent officers out to purchase veggie burgers. Then the following exchange occurred between Detective Boyle and Malvo:

> Boyle: "We want to talk to you."
> Malvo: "Do I get to talk to my attorneys?"
> Boyle: "Yes."
> Malvo: "Because the lawyers told me don't talk until they get here."

Boyle then told Malvo that the federal government had dropped the charges in Maryland, and that he was being charged in Virginia. She said "We need to get some information from you" and asked him some general background questions about his life before the time period of the alleged murders. Much of the discussion involved Malvo's vegetarian diet. Along the way, Malvo mentioned that he ate raisins—a fact with some possible relevance to the investigation because a box of raisins was found near the scene of one sniper shooting. Malvo answered these questions for about an hour until his veggie burgers arrived at 5:30 P.M.

At 5:55 P.M., Boyle advised Malvo of his *Miranda* rights, and told him he was being charged with homicide. She did not advise him about his right to have a parent or guardian present, because she knew that Malvo's parents were not in the area. Malvo replied that he understood his rights and that he wanted to talk to Boyle and Garrett without an attorney. He would not sign the consent form, however, because he said it would be "incriminating." Then the following exchange took place:

> Boyle: "Can we talk about the case now?"
> Malvo: "Yes."
> Boyle: "Do you want to talk without a lawyer present?"
> Malvo: "Yes."

> Boyle: "You mentioned an attorney earlier. Are you saying you want to talk
> to an attorney before you talk to us about this case?"
> Malvo: "No."
> Boyle: "Are you sure you want to talk to us without an attorney present?"
> Malvo: "Yes. If I don't want to answer, I won't."

Malvo went on to make incriminating statements about several of the sniper murders. When asked where he shot one of the victims, he laughed and pointed to his head. In discussing another of the killings, Malvo was amused by the fact that after he shot a man riding a lawn mower, "the lawn mower just kept going down the street." Malvo did refuse to answer some questions, saying on several occasions, "You figure it out. I'm not going to tell you." The interrogation lasted until 10:40 P.M.

During the interrogation, Boyle was unaware that the federal Magistrate Judge had ordered Treem and Tucker to continue representing Malvo; neither did she know about the written request they faxed to the federal prosecutor in Virginia. Boyle also did not know that at the time Malvo arrived at the detention center in Virginia on November 7, officials of the juvenile court appointed an attorney, Todd Petit, to represent Malvo. Petit did not know any interrogation was taking place that afternoon.

As a defense attorney for Malvo, what arguments would you present to exclude your client's statements from trial? Which are the strongest of your arguments? See www.co.fairfax.va.us/courts/cases/pdf/ 5603order.pdf.

Page 551.   Add this material to the end of note 1.

Fellers v. United States, 540 U.S. 519 (2004) (officer who went to home of indicted defendant to execute arrest violated right to counsel by discussing charge in absence of attorney; contact need not amount to an "interrogation" to violate Sixth Amendment).

F. Miranda: *Cures, Impacts, and Alternatives*

1. Cures and Remedies for *Miranda* Violations

Page 553.   Replace the Tennessee case and note 1 with the following material.

Can unwarned confessions that violate *Miranda* always be cured by later administration of *Miranda* warnings? In 2004, the Supreme Court of the United States clarified the federal law on this question.

Missouri v. Patrice Seibert
124 S. Ct. 2601 (2004)

SOUTER, J.

This case tests a police protocol for custodial interrogation that calls for giving no warnings of the rights to silence and counsel until interrogation has produced a confession. Although such a statement is generally inadmissible, since taken in violation of Miranda v. Arizona, 384 U.S. 436 (1966), the interrogating officer follows it with *Miranda* warnings and then leads the suspect to cover the same ground a second time. The question here is the admissibility of the repeated statement. Because this midstream recitation of warnings after interrogation and unwarned confession could not effectively comply with *Miranda's* constitutional requirement, we hold that a statement repeated after a warning in such circumstances is inadmissible.

Respondent Patrice Seibert's 12-year-old son Jonathan had cerebral palsy, and when he died in his sleep she feared charges of neglect because of bedsores on his body. In her presence, two of her teenage sons and two of their friends devised a plan to conceal the facts surrounding Jonathan's death by incinerating his body in the course of burning the family's mobile home, in which they planned to leave Donald Rector, a mentally ill teenager living with the family, to avoid any appearance that Jonathan had been unattended. Seibert's son Darian and a friend set the fire, and Donald died.

Five days later, the police awakened Seibert at 3 A.M. at a hospital where Darian was being treated for burns. In arresting her, Officer Kevin

Clinton followed instructions from Rolla, Missouri, officer Richard Hanrahan that he refrain from giving *Miranda* warnings. After Seibert had been taken to the police station and left alone in an interview room for 15 to 20 minutes, Hanrahan questioned her without *Miranda* warnings for 30 to 40 minutes, squeezing her arm and repeating "Donald was also to die in his sleep." After Seibert finally admitted she knew Donald was meant to die in the fire, she was given a 20-minute coffee and cigarette break. Officer Hanrahan then turned on a tape recorder, gave Seibert the *Miranda* warnings, and obtained a signed waiver of rights from her. He resumed the questioning with "Ok, 'trice, we've been talking for a little while about what happened on Wednesday the twelfth, haven't we?," and confronted her with her prewarning statements:

> Hanrahan: "Now, in discussion you told us, you told us that there was a[n] understanding about Donald."
> Seibert: "Yes."
> Hanrahan: "Did that take place earlier that morning?"
> Seibert: "Yes."
> Hanrahan: "And what was the understanding about Donald?"
> Seibert: "If they could get him out of the trailer, to take him out of the trailer."
> Hanrahan: "And if they couldn't?"
> Seibert: "I, I never even thought about it. I just figured they would."
> Hanrahan: " 'Trice, didn't you tell me that he was supposed to die in his sleep?"
> Seibert: "If that would happen, 'cause he was on that new medicine, you know...."
> Hanrahan: "The Prozac? And it makes him sleepy. So he was supposed to die in his sleep?"
> Seibert: "Yes."

After being charged with first-degree murder for her role in Donald's death, Seibert sought to exclude both her prewarning and postwarning statements. At the suppression hearing, Officer Hanrahan testified that he made a "conscious decision" to withhold *Miranda* warnings, thus resorting to an interrogation technique he had been taught: question first, then give the warnings, and then repeat the question "until I get the answer that she's already provided once." He acknowledged that Seibert's ultimate statement was "largely a repeat of information ... obtained" prior to the warning.

The trial court suppressed the prewarning statement but admitted the responses given after the *Miranda* recitation. A jury convicted Seibert of second-degree murder....

Miranda conditioned the admissibility at trial of any custodial confession on warning a suspect of his rights: failure to give the prescribed warnings and obtain a waiver of rights before custodial questioning generally requires exclusion of any statements obtained. Conversely, giving the warnings and getting a waiver has generally produced a virtual ticket of admissibility; maintaining that a statement is involuntary even though given after warnings and voluntary waiver of rights requires unusual stamina, and litigation over voluntariness tends to end with the finding of a valid waiver. To point out the obvious, this common consequence would not be common at all were it not that *Miranda* warnings are customarily given under circumstances allowing for a real choice between talking and remaining silent.

The technique of interrogating in successive, unwarned and warned phases raises a new challenge to *Miranda.* Although we have no statistics on the frequency of this practice, it is not confined to Rolla, Missouri. An officer of that police department testified that the strategy of withholding *Miranda* warnings until after interrogating and drawing out a confession was promoted not only by his own department, but by a national police training organization and other departments in which he had worked. Consistently with the officer's testimony, the Police Law Institute, for example, instructs that "officers may conduct a two-stage interrogation.... At any point during the pre-*Miranda* interrogation, usually after arrestees have confessed, officers may then read the *Miranda* warnings and ask for a waiver. If the arrestees waive their *Miranda* rights, officers will be able to repeat any *subsequent* incriminating statements later in court." Police Law Institute, Illinois Police Law Manual 83 (Jan. 2001 - Dec. 2003), http://www. illinoispolicelaw.org/training/lessons/ILPLMIR.pdf (hereinafter Police Law Manual).[2] The upshot of all this advice is a question-first practice

---

[2] Emphasizing the impeachment exception to the *Miranda* rule approved by this Court, Harris v. New York, 401 U.S. 222 (1971), some training programs advise officers to omit *Miranda* warnings altogether or to continue questioning after the suspect invokes his rights. See also Weisselberg, Saving *Miranda*, 84 Cornell L. Rev. 109 (1998) (collecting California training materials encouraging questioning "outside *Miranda*"). This training is reflected in the reported cases

of some popularity, as one can see from the reported cases describing its use, sometimes in obedience to departmental policy.

When a confession so obtained is offered and challenged, attention must be paid to the conflicting objects of *Miranda* and question-first. *Miranda* addressed "interrogation practices [likely to disable an individual] from making a free and rational choice" about speaking and held that a suspect must be "adequately and effectively" advised of the choice the Constitution guarantees. The object of question-first is to render *Miranda* warnings ineffective by waiting for a particularly opportune time to give them, after the suspect has already confessed.

[It] would be absurd to think that mere recitation of the litany suffices to satisfy *Miranda* in every conceivable circumstance. The inquiry is simply whether the warnings reasonably convey to a suspect his rights as required by *Miranda.* The threshold issue when interrogators question first and warn later is thus whether it would be reasonable to find that in these circumstances the warnings could function "effectively" as *Miranda* requires. Could the warnings effectively advise the suspect that he had a real choice about giving an admissible statement at that juncture? Could they reasonably convey that he could choose to stop talking even if he had talked earlier? For unless the warnings could place a suspect who has just been interrogated in a position to make such an informed choice, there is no practical justification for accepting the formal warnings as compliance with *Miranda,* or for treating the second stage of interrogation as distinct from the first, unwarned and inadmissible segment.

There is no doubt about the answer that proponents of question-first give to this question about the effectiveness of warnings given only after successful interrogation, and we think their answer is correct. By any objective measure, applied to circumstances exemplified here, it is likely

---

involving deliberate questioning after invocation of *Miranda* rights. Scholars have noted the growing trend of such practices. See, *e.g.,* Leo, Questioning the Relevance of *Miranda* in the Twenty-First Century, 99 Mich. L. Rev. 1000 (2001); Weisselberg, In the Stationhouse After *Dickerson,* 99 Mich. L. Rev. 1121 (2001)....

It is not the case, of course, that law enforcement educators en masse are urging that *Miranda* be honored only in the breach. Most police manuals do not advocate the question-first tactic, because they understand that Oregon v. Elstad, 470 U.S. 298 (1985), involved an officer's good-faith failure to warn.

that if the interrogators employ the technique of withholding warnings until after interrogation succeeds in eliciting a confession, the warnings will be ineffective in preparing the suspect for successive interrogation, close in time and similar in content. After all, the reason that question-first is catching on is as obvious as its manifest purpose, which is to get a confession the suspect would not make if he understood his rights at the outset; the sensible underlying assumption is that with one confession in hand before the warnings, the interrogator can count on getting its duplicate, with trifling additional trouble.... What is worse, telling a suspect that "anything you say can and will be used against you," without expressly excepting the statement just given, could lead to an entirely reasonable inference that what he has just said will be used, with subsequent silence being of no avail. Thus, when *Miranda* warnings are inserted in the midst of coordinated and continuing interrogation, they are likely to mislead and deprive a defendant of knowledge essential to his ability to understand the nature of his rights and the consequences of abandoning them....

Missouri argues that a confession repeated at the end of an interrogation sequence envisioned in a question-first strategy is admissible on the authority of Oregon v. Elstad, 470 U.S. 298 (1985), but the argument disfigures that case. In *Elstad,* the police went to the young suspect's house to take him into custody on a charge of burglary. Before the arrest, one officer spoke with the suspect's mother, while the other one joined the suspect in a "brief stop in the living room," where the officer said he "felt" the young man was involved in a burglary. The suspect acknowledged he had been at the scene. This Court noted that the pause in the living room "was not to interrogate the suspect but to notify his mother of the reason for his arrest," and described the incident as having "none of the earmarks of coercion." The Court, indeed, took care to mention that the officer's initial failure to warn was an "oversight" that "may have been the result of confusion as to whether the brief exchange qualified as 'custodial interrogation' or ... may simply have reflected ... reluctance to initiate an alarming police procedure before [an officer] had spoken with respondent's mother." At the outset of a later and systematic station house interrogation going well beyond the scope of the laconic prior admission, the suspect was given *Miranda* warnings and made a full confession. In holding the second statement admissible and voluntary, *Elstad* rejected the "cat out of the bag" theory that any short, earlier admission, obtained in arguably innocent neglect of *Miranda,* determined the character of the later, warned confession; on the facts of that case, the Court thought any causal connection between the first and second responses to the police was "speculative and attenuated." Although the *Elstad* Court expressed no explicit conclusion about either officer's state of mind, it is fair to read *Elstad* as treating the living room conversation as a good-faith *Miranda* mistake, not only open to correction by careful warnings before systematic questioning in that particular case, but posing no threat to warn-first practice generally.

The contrast between *Elstad* and this case reveals a series of relevant facts that bear on whether *Miranda* warnings delivered midstream could be effective enough to accomplish their object: the completeness and detail of the questions and answers in the first round of interrogation, the overlapping content of the two statements, the timing and setting of the first and the second, the continuity of police personnel, and the degree to which the interrogator's questions treated the second round as continuous with the first. In *Elstad,* it was not unreasonable to see the occasion for questioning at the station house as presenting a markedly different experience from the short conversation at home; since a reasonable person in the suspect's shoes could have seen the station house questioning as a new and distinct experience, the *Miranda* warnings could have made sense as presenting a genuine choice whether to follow up on the earlier admission.

At the opposite extreme are the facts here, which by any objective measure reveal a police strategy adapted to undermine the *Miranda* warnings.[6] The unwarned interrogation was conducted in the station house, and the questioning was systematic, exhaustive, and managed with psychological skill. When the police were finished there was little, if anything, of incriminating potential left unsaid. The warned phase of questioning proceeded after a pause of only 15 to 20 minutes, in the same place as the unwarned segment. [The] police did not advise that her prior statement could not be used. Nothing was said or done to dispel the oddity of warning about legal rights to silence and counsel right after the police had led her through a systematic interrogation.... The impression

---

[6] Because the intent of the officer will rarely be as candidly admitted as it was here (even as it is likely to determine the conduct of the interrogation), the focus is on facts apart from intent that show the question-first tactic at work.

that the further questioning was a mere continuation of the earlier questions and responses was fostered by references back to the confession already given. It would have been reasonable to regard the two sessions as parts of a continuum, in which it would have been unnatural to refuse to repeat at the second stage what had been said before....

Strategists dedicated to draining the substance out of *Miranda* cannot accomplish by training instructions what Dickerson v. United States, 530 U.S. 428 (2000), held Congress could not do by statute. Because the question-first tactic effectively threatens to thwart *Miranda's* purpose of reducing the risk that a coerced confession would be admitted, and because the facts here do not reasonably support a conclusion that the warnings given could have served their purpose, Seibert's postwarning statements are inadmissible....

BREYER, J., concurring.

In my view, the following simple rule should apply to the two-stage interrogation technique: Courts should exclude the "fruits" of the initial unwarned questioning unless the failure to warn was in good faith. I believe this is a sound and workable approach to the problem this case presents. Prosecutors and judges have long understood how to apply the "fruits" approach, which they use in other areas of law. And in the workaday world of criminal law enforcement the administrative simplicity of the familiar has significant advantages over a more complex exclusionary rule.

I believe the plurality's approach in practice will function as a "fruits" test. The truly "effective" *Miranda* warnings on which the plurality insists will occur only when certain circumstances—a lapse in time, a change in location or interrogating officer, or a shift in the focus of the questioning—intervene between the unwarned questioning and any postwarning statement....

KENNEDY, J., concurring in the judgment.

The interrogation technique used in this case is designed to circumvent *Miranda*. It undermines the *Miranda* warning and obscures its meaning. The plurality opinion is correct to conclude that statements obtained through the use of this technique are inadmissible....

The *Miranda* rule has become an important and accepted element of the criminal justice system. At the same time, not every violation of the rule requires suppression of the evidence obtained. Evidence is admissible when the central concerns of *Miranda* are not likely to be implicated and when other objectives of the criminal justice system are best served by its introduction....

Oregon v. Elstad, 470 U.S. 298 (1985), reflects this approach.... In my view, *Elstad* was correct in its reasoning and its result.... An officer may not realize that a suspect is in custody and warnings are required. The officer may not plan to question the suspect or may be waiting for a more appropriate time. Skilled investigators often interview suspects multiple times, and good police work may involve referring to prior statements to test their veracity or to refresh recollection. In light of these realities it would be extravagant to treat the presence of one statement that cannot be admitted under *Miranda* as sufficient reason to prohibit subsequent statements preceded by a proper warning. That approach would serve "neither the general goal of deterring improper police conduct nor the Fifth Amendment goal of assuring trustworthy evidence would be served by suppression of the ... testimony."

This case presents different considerations. The police used a two-step questioning technique based on a deliberate violation of *Miranda*. The *Miranda* warning was withheld to obscure both the practical and legal significance of the admonition when finally given.... The technique used in this case distorts the meaning of *Miranda* and furthers no legitimate countervailing interest....

The plurality concludes that whenever a two-stage interview occurs, admissibility of the postwarning statement should depend on "whether the *Miranda* warnings delivered midstream could have been effective enough to accomplish their object" given the specific facts of the case. This test envisions an objective inquiry from the perspective of the suspect, and applies in the case of both intentional and unintentional two-stage interrogations. In my view, this test cuts too broadly. *Miranda's* clarity is one of its strengths, and a multifactor test that applies to every two-stage interrogation may serve to undermine that clarity. I would apply a narrower test applicable only in the infrequent case, such as we have here, in which the two-step interrogation technique was used in a calculated way to undermine the *Miranda* warning....

O'CONNOR, J., dissenting.

The plurality devours Oregon v. Elstad, 470 U.S. 298 (1985), even as it accuses petitioner's argument of "disfiguring" that decision. I believe that we are bound by *Elstad* to reach a different result, and I would vacate the judgment of the Supreme Court of Missouri.... I would analyze the two-step interrogation procedure under the voluntariness standards central to the Fifth Amendment and reiterated in *Elstad*....

Problem 8-9B. Hot Load

Officers Mike Hannan and Terry Thomas of the Tennessee Highway Patrol stopped a speeding vehicle driven by Kellie Alisha Jones. When Jones was unable to find the vehicle's registration, Officer Hannan asked her to accompany him to his squad car while he wrote out a traffic citation. While Jones went to the squad car, the passenger, Hosie Smith, looked in the glove compartment for the vehicle's registration. Officer Thomas, who was on the passenger's side of the car, asked Smith questions regarding ownership of the car and the couple's destination. After this brief conversation with Smith, Thomas returned to the squad car and sat in the back seat. While waiting for radio verification of Jones's license and the vehicle's registration, both officers continued to question Jones about the ownership of the car and her destination. When asked who her passenger was, Jones stated that it was her boyfriend, but she could only give the name "Pumpkin" when asked about his name. Because Smith and Jones appeared to be extremely nervous, and had given inconsistent answers to the questions about their destination and the ownership of the car, the officers became suspicious and asked Jones if she was carrying any illegal items, weapons, or contraband. Jones denied knowledge of such cargo, and consented to a search of the car.

Officer Thomas re-approached the station wagon on the passenger side and asked Smith if there were any illegal items in the car. Smith denied knowledge of any such contraband. Thomas then told Smith that he had permission to look through the vehicle, and asked again about any illegal items in the car. Smith said, "Yes, it was probably a hot load." Thomas then asked, "By a hot load, do you mean cash, marijuana, or cocaine, one of the three?" Smith responded, "Probably." Thomas searched the car and found 22 pounds of pure cocaine in the locked glove compartment. At 6:25 P.M., the officers placed both Smith and Jones under arrest, read them their *Miranda* rights, and transported them to Highway Patrol Headquarters.

At 9:45 P.M., Smith was questioned by Officer Lonnie Hood. Before he was questioned, Smith was read his *Miranda* rights again and signed a written waiver of those rights. During the course of the interrogation, Smith gave Officer Hood an incriminating account of his employment to drive the station wagon with Jones from Oklahoma City, Oklahoma, to Fayetteville, North Carolina. This statement was reduced to writing by Officer Hood and signed by Smith.

Smith filed a motion to suppress the cocaine found in the car, his statements to Thomas beside the road, and to Hood at Highway Patrol Headquarters.

Instead of following *Elstad* under state law, the court (like about 15 other state courts) embraced the earlier "cat out of the bag" theory of United States v. Bayer, 331 U.S. 532 (1947). In *Bayer,* the Court recognized:

> Of course, after an accused has once let the cat out of the bag by confessing, no matter what the inducement, he is never thereafter free of the psychological and practical disadvantages of having confessed. He can never get the cat back in the bag. The secret is out for good. In such a sense, a later confession always may be looked upon as fruit of the first.

The Tennessee court rejected the idea that all subsequent warnings could cure prior invalid confessions, but it also rejected the idea that all invalid confessions tainted all later confessions. State v. Smith, 834 S.W.2d 915 (Tenn. 1992). The Tennessee court held that unwarned confessions raised a "rebuttable presumption" that a subsequent confession is tainted by the initial illegality." The prosecution can overcome that presumption by establishing that "the taint is so attenuated as to justify admission of the subsequent confession."

Under the state constitution, the "crucial inquiry" for the courts is "whether the events and circumstances surrounding and following the initial, illegal conduct of the law enforcement officers prevented the accused from subsequently (1) making a free and informed choice to waive the State constitutional right not to provide evidence against one's self, and (2) voluntarily confessing his involvement in the crime." In addressing these questions, Tennessee courts examine the following factors:

> 1. The use of coercive tactics to obtain the initial, illegal confession and the causal connection between the illegal conduct and the challenged, subsequent confession;
> 2. The temporal proximity of the prior and subsequent confessions;
> 3. The reading and explanation of *Miranda* rights to the defendant before the subsequent confession;
> 4. The circumstances occurring after the arrest and continuing up until the making of the subsequent confession including, but not limited to, the length of the detention and the deprivation of food, rest, and bathroom facilities;
> 5. The coerciveness of the atmosphere in which any questioning took place including, but not limited to, the place where the questioning occurred, the identity of the interrogators, the form of the questions, and the repeated or prolonged nature of the questioning;
> 6. The presence of intervening factors including, but not limited to, consultations with counsel or family members, or the opportunity to consult with counsel, if desired;
> 7. The psychological effect of having already confessed, and whether the defendant was advised that the prior confession may not be admissible at trial;
> 8. Whether the defendant initiated the conversation that led to the subsequent confession; and
> 9. The defendant's sobriety, education, intelligence level, and experience with the law, as such factors relate to the defendant's ability to understand the administered *Miranda* rights.

If you were arguing this motion for Smith, how would you try to persuade the trial court that the state constitutional standard is more protective of *Miranda* rights than the more recent *Seibert* case? What would be the outcome of the *Smith* facts under *Seibert*? Will states like Tennessee now revert to the new federal position?

Notes

1. *Out-of-court statements obtained after earlier* Miranda *violations: majority position.* Unlike illegal searches and seizures, an

unwarned interrogation will not necessarily require a later court to exclude all the evidence derived from the tainted statement. Although any statement made during an unwarned interrogation must not come into evidence, later statements of the suspect might still be admissible— even though the statements appear to be the "fruit of the poisonous tree."

In Oregon v. Elstad, 470 U.S. 298 (1985), the Supreme Court held that the state could use as evidence a subsequent confession. According to the Court, when the initial unwarned statement was given voluntarily,

> a careful and thorough administration of Miranda warnings serves to cure the condition that rendered the unwarned statement inadmissible. The warning conveys the relevant information and thereafter the suspect's choice whether to exercise his privilege to remain silent should ordinarily be viewed as an act of free will.

470 U.S. at 310. Before *Seibert* was decided, a significant minority of states (around 15) rejected the *Elstad* decision, placing a burden on the government to overcome a presumption of compulsion for subsequent confessions. See, e.g., Commonwealth v. Smith, 593 N.E.2d 1288 (Mass. 1992). Would you expect those states to revise their state constitutional doctrine in light of *Seibert*?

In Missouri v. Seibert, 124 S. Ct. 2601 (2004), a plurality decision limited *Elstad*, rejecting a subsequent warned (and therefore "cured") confession in the face of strategic behavior by police who started with an unwarned (and therefore illegal and inadmissible) statement. The plurality found that the later warnings did not "reasonably convey ... to a suspect his rights as required by *Miranda*" and interpreted *Elstad* to apply only after original statements obtained in good faith. Justice Breyer concurred, suggesting that subsequent warnings should be inadmissible as tainted "fruit" unless the earlier statement was obtained in good faith. Justice Kennedy would apply *Elstad* to reject only if "the two-step interrogation technique was used in a calculated way to undermine the Miranda warning." Will trial courts be able to make reliable factual findings on the question of intent in future cases?

As is so often the case with plurality decisions (and a good bit of the time with majority or even unanimous decisions!), *Seibert* leaves for later litigation to determine how the holding might apply to situations where suspects make short, unwarned statements.

Page 558.   Add this material at the end of note 5.

6. *Section 1983 and coercive questioning.* In Chavez v. Martinez, 538 U.S. 760 (2003), the Court rejected the claim that an interrogation in a hospital room given to an injured suspect shot by police violated either the defendant's Fifth or Fourteenth Amendment rights. The majority found no Fifth Amendment violation since the defendant "was never prosecuted for a crime, let alone compelled to be a witness against himself in a criminal case." The Court held there was no Fourteenth Amendment violation since there was "no evidence that Chavez acted with a purpose to harm Martinez by intentionally interfering with his medical treatment. Medical personnel were able to treat Martinez throughout the interview, and Chavez ceased his questioning to allow tests and other procedures to be performed. Nor is there evidence that Chavez's conduct exacerbated Martinez's injuries or prolonged his stay in the hospital." Because the court held that none of Martinez's rights were violated, it found that the officers were entitled to the defense of qualified immunity.

Page 559.   Add this material at the end of note 1.

In United States v. Patane, 124 S. Ct. 2620 (2004), the court held that physical evidence produced through unwarned but voluntary statements was admissible. Are state courts likely to follow *Patane*? Page 559, note 1. Commonwealth v. Martin, 827 N.E.2d 198 (Mass. 2005) (rejects *Patane*, state constitution requires suppression of physical evidence derived from unwarned statements).

3.   Alternatives to *Miranda*

Page 575.   Add this material to the end of note 5.

Matthews v. Commonwealth, 2005 WL 923601 (Ky., Apr. 21, 2005) (police interrogators may lie to suspect about whether they are recording his statements); Commonwealth v. DiGiambattista, 813 N.E.2d 516 (Mass. 2004) (admission of confession that resulted from an unrecorded custodial interrogation detention entitles defendant to jury instruction concerning the need to evaluate his statement or confession with "particular caution").

Page 575.   Add this material to the end of note 6.

See Christopher Slobogin, Toward Taping, 1 Ohio St. J. Crim. Law 309 (2003) (reviews cases from Alaska and Minnesota; because *Miranda* regime has failed, voluntariness should once again be the focal point of interrogation regulation, and taping is most likely way to move in that direction).

Chapter 9

Identifications

A. *Risks of Mistaken Identification*

Page 585.   Add this material after note 5.

6. *Words and memory.* Some memory problems arise simply from the fact that investigators ask the witness to express the memory in words. Laboratory studies found that memories for a mock criminal's face were much poorer among eyewitnesses who had described what the perpetrator looked like shortly after seeing him, compared with those who had not formulated a description in words. The problem is known as "verbal overshadowing of visual memories." Bruce Bower, Words Get in the Way: Talk Is Cheap, But It Can Tax Your Memory, Science News, Apr. 19, 2003.

B. *Exclusion of Identification Evidence*

2.   Exclusion on Due Process Grounds

Page 598.   Replace the second full paragraph with this material.

For more than a generation, courts have insisted that due process will prevent the use of the least reliable identification procedures, regardless of the presence or absence of counsel. In Stovall v. Denno, 388 U.S. 293 (1967), decided the same day as United States v. Wade, the Supreme Court refused to exclude evidence of a pretrial identification under the due process clause because the identification was unduly "suggestive." While investigating a stabbing case, the police entered the victim's hospital room with the suspect handcuffed to an officer, and asked the victim if the suspect was the person who had committed the crime. Because the police had no viable alternative to the procedure used here it was not "unnecessarily suggestive."

Page 606.   Add this material at the end of note 3.

See Nancy Steblay, Jennifer Dysart, Solomon Fulero & R.C.L. Lindsay, Eyewitness Accuracy Rates in Police Showup and Lineup Presentations: A Meta-Analytic Comparison, 27 Law & Hum. Behav. 523 (2003) (in target present conditions, showups and lineups yield approximately equal hit rates, while in target absent conditions, showups produce higher level of correct rejections; false identifications are more numerous for showups when innocent suspect resembles perpetrator).

C. Other Remedies for Improper Identification Procedures

Page 618.   Add this material at the end of note 2.

See also Commonwealth v. Christie, 98 S.W.3d 485 (Ky. 2002) (trial courts have discretion under Evidence Rule 702 to admit expert witness testimony about risk of erroneous eyewitness identifications; error to reject such testimony as categorically inadmissible).

Chapter 10

Complex Investigations

A. Selection and Pursuit of Targets

2. Entrapment Defenses

Page 642.   Add this material at the end of note 3.

See Alexandra Natapoff, Snitching: The Institutional and Communal Consequences, 73 Univ. Cincinnati L. Rev. 645 (2004) (use of informants is usually framed as a threat to accuracy, but practice is understood through its connections to plea bargaining, prosecutorial discretion, administrative nature of American criminal justice; all of these realities threaten principles of accountability, consistency, predictability, and other rule of law precepts).

B. The Investigative Grand Jury

1. Grand Jury Secrecy

Page 650.   Add this material after note 7.

8.   *Material grand jury witnesses.* Soon after the terrorist attacks of September 11, 2001, Attorney General Ashcroft announced that "aggressive detention of material witnesses" was a vital part of the government's plan to prevent further attacks. A federal statute, 18 U.S.C.

§3144, allows the government to detain witnesses as a means to obtaining their grand jury testimony:

> If it appears from an affidavit filed by a party that the testimony of a person is material in a criminal proceeding, and if it is shown that it may become impracticable to secure the presence of the person by subpoena, a judicial officer may order the arrest of the person and treat the person in accordance with the provisions of §3142 of this title [dealing with pretrial detention of defendants charged with a crime]. No material witness may be detained because of inability to comply with any condition of release if the testimony of such witness can adequately be secured by deposition, and if further detention is not necessary to prevent a failure of justice. Release of a material witness may be delayed for a reasonable period of time until the deposition of the witness can be taken....

Prior to 2001, the typical use of this statute was to hold reluctant or fearful witnesses for a few days to obtain a deposition or grand jury testimony. After the September 11 attacks, the government obtained judicial warrants under this statute to detain more people for longer periods of time than before. The detentions were not founded on probable cause that the people had committed any crimes. Many non-citizens identified during the investigation of the bombing were held for weeks or months, and only about half the detainees ultimately testified before a grand jury. See Michael Greenberger, "Indefinite Material Witness Detention Without Probable Cause: Thinking Outside the Fourth Amendment," in At War with Civil Rights and Liberties (Thomas E. Baker & John F. Stack, Jr., eds., 2004).

Does the material witness statute require any revisions in light of its use in this new context? Should the statute specify a time limit for obtaining grand jury testimony? Should it require that any person detained under the statute must actually appear before a grand jury? Should the secrecy rules for grand juries be altered for these witnesses?

9. *Target testimony.* New York law allows defendants the right to have an attorney present during grand jury testimony and the right to testify themselves before the grand jury. At one time, attorneys virtually never advised their clients to testify before a grand jury considering an indictment of the client, but now they are more commonly advising clients to testify. It appears that the tactic has increased the number of "no true bills." See William Glaberson, New Trend Before Grand Juries:

Meet the Accused, N.Y. Times, June 20, 2004. What might account for this change in defense practices? Under what circumstances should a suspect testify before a grand jury?

2. Immunity for Witnesses

Page 657. Add this material to the end of note 4.

For an assessment of the effect of the self-incrimination privilege in modern practice, where most cases do not go to trial, see Stephanos Bibas, The Right to Remain Silent Helps Only the Guilty, 88 Iowa L. Rev. 421 (2003).

Chapter 11

Defense Counsel

A. When Will Counsel Be Provided?

2. Point in Proceedings

Page 700.   Add this material at the end of note 1.

Although most jurisdictions do no provide counsel to defendants during bail hearings, a recent pilot project in Baltimore made defense attorneys available at the bail hearing. A study of the project compared two groups of defendants charged with similar non-violent offenses; the authors concluded that two and a half times as many represented defendants were released on recognizance as unrepresented defendants. More than twice as many represented defendants had their bail reduced to affordable amounts. The Study also found that detainees believed they were treated more fairly and were more willing to accept the legitimacy of the judicial process. See Douglas L. Colbert, Ray Paternoster & Shawn D. Bushway, Do Attorneys Really Matter? The Empirical and Legal Case for the Right of Counsel at Bail, 23 Cardozo L. Rev. 1719 (2002).

Page 700.   Replace note 2 with this material.

2. *Defense counsel for DWI examinations: majority position.* In most states, there is no constitutional or statutory right to counsel for DWI examinations if they precede formal charging. Roughly a

dozen high state courts have granted a person arrested on DWI charges the right to consult with retained counsel before performing sobriety tests. See State v. Spencer, 750 P.2d 147 (Or. 1988). Does this position create a special rule for DWI defendants not applicable to most criminal defendants? Are DWI defendants as a class different from other criminal defendants? Will the lawyer be able to persuade a problem drinker to seek treatment?

Page 702.   Add this material after note 7.

8. *What happens when funds dry up?* Economic downturns lead to reduced tax revenues, and ultimately to less public funding available for defense counsel. If the state does not pay for the defense lawyer in cases where the state has an obligation to furnish one, the case cannot go forward. Prosecutions must be postponed and ultimately dismissed. As a prosecutor or trial judge facing such a quandary, which cases would you delay or dismiss? The least serious cases? All cases scheduled from Fridays? All cases on the calendar for November and December? For a survey of different responses to this dilemma, see Lisa Stansky, The Big Squeeze, Nat'l L.J., May 23, 2003 (Oregon prosecutors met budget shortfall by declining prosecutions for car theft, prostitutions, trespassing, shoplifting; judges closed courthouse on Fridays from March through June).

B. Selection and Rejection of Counsel

Page 707.   Add this material at the end of note 1.

The law in some states allows a defendant to partially waive the right to counsel; the defendant may rely on an appointed counsel for some purposes, but also serve as co-counsel and examine some witnesses himself or herself. See Hill v. Commonwealth, 125 S.W.3d 221 (Ky. 2004) (judge must hold *Faretta* hearing before granting defendant's request to waive a portion of right to counsel and serve as co-counsel at trial).

Page 708.   Add this material at the end of note 2.

See Partin v. Commonwealth, 2005 WL 1183158 (Ky., May 19, 2005) (rights to self-representation and confrontation satisfied even though trial court prohibited defendant from personally cross-examining his wife during trial on domestic violence charges, cross-examination conducted by standby counsel).

Page 708.   Add this material at the end of note 3.

See People v. Carson, 104 P.3d 837 (Cal. 2005) (trial court may terminate a defendant's self-representation based on out-of-court misconduct, such as witness tampering, that "seriously threatens the core integrity of the trial").

Page 708.   Add this material at the end of note 4.

See Brooks v. McCaughtry 380 F.3d 1009 (7th Cir. 2004) (Posner, J.) (distinguishes *Godinez*; finding that defendant is competent to stand trial does not by itself mean that defendant is competent waive right to counsel; no habeas relief for defendant who was forced to accept counsel).

C. *Adequacy of Counsel*

Page 716.   Add this material before *Michael Bruno v. State*.

For observers who believe that appellate courts in general, and the United States Supreme Court in particular, too rarely see counsel conduct that falls below the standards of effectiveness presented in *Strickland*, consider the following 7-2 decision in a death penalty case. Does the case mark a new approach to applying the *Strickland* standard, even in non-capital cases?

Kevin Wiggins v. Sewall Smith
539 U.S. 510 (2003)

O'CONNOR, J.

Petitioner, Kevin Wiggins, argues that his attorneys' failure to investigate his background and present mitigating evidence of his unfortunate life history at his capital sentencing proceedings violated his Sixth Amendment right to counsel. In this case, we consider whether the United States Court of Appeals for the Fourth Circuit erred in upholding the Maryland Court of Appeals' rejection of this claim.

On September 17, 1988, police discovered 77-year-old Florence Lacs drowned in the bathtub of her ransacked apartment in Woodlawn, Maryland. The State indicted petitioner for the crime on October 20, 1988, and later filed a notice of intention to seek the death penalty. Two Baltimore County public defenders, Carl Schlaich and Michelle Nethercott, assumed responsibility for Wiggins' case. In July 1989, petitioner elected to be tried before a judge in Baltimore County Circuit Court. On August 4, after a 4-day trial, the court found petitioner guilty of first-degree murder, robbery, and two counts of theft.

After his conviction, Wiggins elected to be sentenced by a jury, and the trial court scheduled the proceedings to begin on October 11, 1989. On September 11, counsel filed a motion for bifurcation of sentencing in hopes of presenting Wiggins' case in two phases. Counsel intended first to prove that Wiggins did not act as a "principal in the first degree,"— *i.e.*, that he did not kill the victim by his own hand. See Md. Ann. Code, Art. 27, §413 (requiring proof of direct responsibility for death eligibility). Counsel then intended, if necessary, to present a mitigation case. In the memorandum in support of their motion, counsel argued that bifurcation would enable them to present each case in its best light; separating the two cases would prevent the introduction of mitigating evidence from diluting their claim that Wiggins was not directly responsible for the murder.

On October 12, the court denied the bifurcation motion, and sentencing proceedings commenced immediately thereafter. In her opening statement, Nethercott told the jurors they would hear evidence suggesting that someone other than Wiggins actually killed Lacs. Counsel then explained that the judge would instruct them to weigh Wiggins' clean record as a factor against a death sentence. She concluded: "You're going to hear that Kevin Wiggins has had a difficult life. It has not been easy for him. But he's worked. He's tried to be a productive citizen, and he's reached the age of 27 with no convictions for prior crimes of violence and no convictions, period.... I think that's an important thing for you to consider." During the proceedings themselves, however, counsel introduced no evidence of Wiggins' life history.

Before closing arguments, Schlaich made a proffer to the court, outside the presence of the jury, to preserve bifurcation as an issue for appeal. He detailed the mitigation case counsel would have presented had the court granted their bifurcation motion. He explained that they would have introduced psychological reports and expert testimony demonstrating Wiggins' limited intellectual capacities and childlike emotional state on the one hand, and the absence of aggressive patterns in his behavior, his capacity for empathy, and his desire to function in the world on the other. At no point did Schlaich proffer any evidence of petitioner's life history or family background. On October 18, the court instructed the jury on the sentencing task before it, and later that afternoon, the jury returned with a sentence of death.

[In state post-conviction proceedings, Wiggins] presented testimony by Hans Selvog, a licensed social worker certified as an expert by the court. Selvog testified concerning an elaborate social history report he had prepared containing evidence of the severe physical and sexual abuse petitioner suffered at the hands of his mother and while in the care of a series of foster parents. Relying on state social services, medical, and school records, as well as interviews with petitioner and numerous family members, Selvog chronicled petitioner's bleak life history.

According to Selvog's report, petitioner's mother, a chronic alcoholic, frequently left Wiggins and his siblings home alone for days, forcing them to beg for food and to eat paint chips and garbage. Wiggins' abusive behavior included beating the children for breaking into the kitchen, which she often kept locked. She had sex with men while her children slept in the same bed and, on one occasion, forced petitioner's hand against a hot stove burner—an incident that led to petitioner's hospitalization. At the age of six, the State placed Wiggins in foster care. Petitioner's first and second foster mothers abused him physically, and, as petitioner explained to Selvog, the father in his second foster home repeatedly molested and raped him. At age 16, petitioner ran away from his foster home and began living on the streets. He returned intermittently to additional foster homes, including one in which the foster mother's sons allegedly gang-raped him on more than one occasion. After leaving the foster care system, Wiggins entered a Job Corps program and was allegedly sexually abused by his supervisor.

During the postconviction proceedings, Schlaich testified that he did not remember retaining a forensic social worker to prepare a social history, even though the State made funds available for that purpose. He explained that he and Nethercott, well in advance of trial, decided to focus their efforts on "retrying the factual case" and disputing Wiggins' direct responsibility for the murder. In April 1994, at the close of the proceedings, the judge observed from the bench that he could not remember a capital case in which counsel had not compiled a social history of the defendant, explaining, "not to do a social history, at least to see what you have got, to me is absolute error. I just—I would be flabbergasted if the Court of Appeals said anything else." In October 1997, however, the trial court denied Wiggins' petition for postconviction relief. The court concluded that "when the decision not to investigate ... is a matter of trial tactics, there is no ineffective assistance of counsel."

[The 1996 federal habeas corpus statute, 28 U.S.C. §2254(d), governs the available standard of review. That statute provides that a federal court may overturn a state criminal conviction if the petitioner presents a legal claim "adjudicated on the merits in State court proceedings" and the state court's decision "was contrary to, or involved an unreasonable application of, clearly established Federal law, as determined by the Supreme Court of the United States." Federal habeas courts can also overturn state decisions "based on an unreasonable determination of the facts."]

We have made clear that the "unreasonable application" prong of §2254(d)(1) permits a federal habeas court to "grant the writ if the state court identifies the correct governing legal principle from this Court's decisions but unreasonably applies that principle to the facts" of petitioner's case. In other words, a federal court may grant relief when a state court has misapplied a "governing legal principle" to a set of facts different from those of the case in which the principle was announced. In order for a federal court to find a state court's application of our precedent "unreasonable," the state court's decision must have been more than incorrect or erroneous. The state court's application must have been "objectively unreasonable."

We established the legal principles that govern claims of ineffective assistance of counsel in Strickland v. Washington, 466 U.S. 668 (1984). An ineffective assistance claim has two components: A petitioner must show that counsel's performance was deficient, and that the deficiency prejudiced the defense....

In this case, as in *Strickland,* petitioner's claim stems from counsel's decision to limit the scope of their investigation into potential mitigating evidence. Here, as in *Strickland,* counsel attempt to justify their limited investigation as reflecting a tactical judgment not to present mitigating evidence at sentencing and to pursue an alternate strategy instead. In rejecting Strickland's claim, we defined the deference owed such strategic judgments in terms of the adequacy of the investigations supporting those judgments:

> [S]trategic choices made after thorough investigation of law and facts relevant to plausible options are virtually unchallengeable; and strategic choices made after less than complete investigation are reasonable precisely to the extent that reasonable professional judgments support the limitations on investigation. In other words, counsel has a duty to make reasonable investigations or to make a reasonable decision that makes particular investigations unnecessary. In any ineffectiveness case, a particular decision not to investigate must be directly assessed for reasonableness in all the circumstances, applying a heavy measure of deference to counsel's judgments.

Our opinion in Williams v. Taylor, 529 U.S. 362 (2000), is illustrative of the proper application of these standards. In finding Williams' ineffectiveness claim meritorious, we applied *Strickland* and concluded that counsel's failure to uncover and present voluminous mitigating evidence at sentencing could not be justified as a tactical decision to focus on Williams' voluntary confessions, because counsel had not "fulfilled their obligation to conduct a thorough investigation of the defendant's background." 529 U.S., at 396 (citing 1 ABA Standards for Criminal Justice 4-4.1, commentary, p. 4-55 (2d ed. 1980))....

In light of these standards, our principal concern in deciding whether Schlaich and Nethercott exercised "reasonable professional judgment" is not whether counsel should have presented a mitigation case. Rather, we focus on whether the investigation supporting counsel's decision not to introduce mitigating evidence of Wiggins' background *was itself reasonable.* In assessing counsel's investigation, we must conduct an objective review of their performance, measured for "reasonableness under prevailing professional norms," which includes a context-dependent consideration of the challenged conduct as seen from counsel's perspective at the time ("Every effort must be made to eliminate the distorting effects of hindsight").

The record demonstrates that counsel's investigation drew from three sources. Counsel arranged for William Stejskal, a psychologist, to conduct a number of tests on petitioner. Stejskal concluded that petitioner had an IQ of 79, had difficulty coping with demanding situations, and exhibited features of a personality disorder. These reports revealed nothing, however, of petitioner's life history.

With respect to that history, counsel had available to them the written PSI, which included a one-page account of Wiggins' "personal history" noting his "misery as a youth," quoting his description of his own background as "disgusting," and observing that he spent most of his life in foster care. Counsel also "tracked down" records kept by the Baltimore City Department of Social Services (DSS) documenting petitioner's various placements in the State's foster care system....

Counsel's decision not to expand their investigation beyond the PSI and the DSS records fell short of the professional standards that prevailed in Maryland in 1989. As Schlaich acknowledged, standard practice in Maryland in capital cases at the time of Wiggins' trial included the preparation of a social history report. Despite the fact that the Public Defender's office made funds available for the retention of a forensic social worker, counsel chose not to commission such a report. Counsel's conduct similarly fell short of the standards for capital defense work articulated by the American Bar Association (ABA)— standards to which we long have referred as "guides to determining what is reasonable." The ABA Guidelines provide that investigations into mitigating evidence "should comprise efforts to discover *all reasonably available* mitigating evidence and evidence to rebut any aggravating evidence that may be introduced by the prosecutor." ABA Guidelines for the Appointment and Performance of Counsel in Death Penalty Cases 11.4.1(C), p. 93 (1989). Despite these well-defined norms, however, counsel abandoned their investigation of petitioner's background after having acquired only rudimentary knowledge of his history from a narrow set of sources. Cf. *id.,* 11.8.6, p. 133 (noting that among the topics counsel should consider presenting are medical history, educational history, employment and training history, *family and social history,* prior adult and juvenile correctional experience, and religious and cultural influences) (emphasis added); 1 ABA Standards for Criminal Justice 4-4.1, commentary, p. 4-55 ("The lawyer also has a substantial and important role to perform in raising mitigating factors both to the prosecutor initially and to the court at sentencing.... Investigation is essential to fulfillment of these functions").

The scope of their investigation was also unreasonable in light of what counsel actually discovered in the DSS records. The records revealed several facts: Petitioner's mother was a chronic alcoholic; Wiggins was shuttled from foster home to foster home and displayed some emotional difficulties while there; he had frequent, lengthy absences from school; and, on at least one occasion, his mother left him and his siblings alone for days without food. [Any] reasonably competent attorney would have realized that pursuing these leads was necessary to making an informed choice among possible defenses, particularly given the apparent absence of any aggravating factors in petitioner's background. Indeed, counsel uncovered no evidence in their investigation to suggest that a mitigation case, in its own right, would have been counterproductive, or that further investigation would have been fruitless; this case is therefore distinguishable from our precedents in which we have found limited investigations into mitigating evidence to be reasonable. Had counsel investigated further, they may well have discovered the sexual abuse later revealed during state postconviction proceedings.

The record of the actual sentencing proceedings underscores the unreasonableness of counsel's conduct by suggesting that their failure to investigate thoroughly resulted from inattention, not reasoned strategic judgment. [Prior] to sentencing, counsel never actually abandoned the possibility that they would present a mitigation defense. Until the court denied their motion, then, they had every reason to develop the most powerful mitigation case possible.

What is more, during the sentencing proceeding itself, counsel did not focus exclusively on Wiggins' direct responsibility for the murder. After introducing that issue in her opening statement, Nethercott entreated the jury to consider not just what Wiggins "is found to have done," but also "who [he] is." Though she told the jury it would "hear that Kevin Wiggins has had a difficult life," counsel never followed up on that suggestion with details of Wiggins' history. At the same time, counsel called a criminologist to testify that inmates serving life sentences tend to adjust well and refrain from further violence in prison—testimony with no bearing on whether petitioner committed the murder by his own hand. Far from focusing exclusively on petitioner's direct responsibility, then, counsel put on a halfhearted mitigation case.... When viewed in this light, the "strategic decision" the state courts and respondents all invoke to justify counsel's limited pursuit of mitigating evidence resembles more a *post-hoc* rationalization of counsel's conduct than an accurate description of their deliberations prior to sentencing.

In rejecting petitioner's ineffective assistance claim, the Maryland Court of Appeals appears to have assumed that because counsel had *some* information with respect to petitioner's background—the information in the PSI and the DSS records—they were in a position to make a tactical choice not to present a mitigation defense. In assessing the reasonableness of an attorney's investigation, however, a court must consider not only the quantum of evidence already known to counsel, but also whether the known evidence would lead a reasonable attorney to investigate further. Even assuming Schlaich and Nethercott limited the scope of their investigation for strategic reasons, *Strickland* does not establish that a cursory investigation automatically justifies a tactical decision with respect to sentencing strategy. Rather, a reviewing court must consider the reasonableness of the investigation said to support that strategy.... In light of what the PSI and the DSS records actually revealed, [Wiggins's attorneys] chose to abandon their investigation at an unreasonable juncture, making a fully informed decision with respect to sentencing strategy impossible....

The dissent insists that this Court's hands are tied, under §2254(d), "by the state court's factual determinations that Wiggins' trial counsel *did* investigate and *were* aware of Wiggins' background." But as we have made clear, the Maryland Court of Appeals' conclusion that the *scope* of counsel's investigation into petitioner's background met the legal standards set in *Strickland* represented an objectively unreasonable application of our precedent.... The requirements of §2254(d) thus pose no bar to granting petitioner habeas relief....

In finding that Schlaich and Nethercott's investigation did not meet *Strickland* 's performance standards, we emphasize that *Strickland* does not require counsel to investigate every conceivable line of mitigating evidence no matter how unlikely the effort would be to assist the defendant at sentencing. Nor does *Strickland* require defense counsel to present mitigating evidence at sentencing in every case. Both conclusions would interfere with the "constitutionally protected independence of counsel" at the heart of *Strickland.* We base our conclusion on the much more limited principle that "strategic choices made after less than complete investigation are reasonable" only to the extent that "reasonable professional judgments support the limitations on investigation." A decision not to investigate thus "must be directly assessed for reasonableness in all the circumstances." ...

In order for counsel's inadequate performance to constitute a Sixth Amendment violation, petitioner must show that counsel's failures prejudiced his defense. In *Strickland,* we made clear that, to establish prejudice, a "defendant must show that there is a reasonable probability that, but for counsel's unprofessional errors, the result of the proceeding would have been different. A reasonable probability is a probability sufficient to undermine confidence in the outcome." In assessing prejudice, we reweigh the evidence in aggravation against the totality of available mitigating evidence....

The mitigating evidence counsel failed to discover and present in this case is powerful. As Selvog reported based on his conversations with Wiggins and members of his family, Wiggins experienced severe privation and abuse in the first six years of his life while in the custody of his alcoholic, absentee mother. He suffered physical torment, sexual molestation, and repeated rape during his subsequent years in foster care. The time Wiggins spent homeless, along with his diminished mental capacities, further augment his mitigation case. Petitioner thus has the kind of troubled history we have declared relevant to assessing a defendant's moral culpability. Penry v. Lynaugh, 492 U.S. 302 (1989) ("Evidence about the defendant's background and character is relevant because of the belief, long held by this society, that defendants who commit criminal acts that are attributable to a disadvantaged background ... may be less culpable than defendants who have no such excuse").

Given both the nature and the extent of the abuse petitioner suffered, we find there to be a reasonable probability that a competent attorney, aware of this history, would have introduced it at sentencing in an admissible form. While it may well have been strategically defensible upon a reasonably thorough investigation to focus on Wiggins' direct responsibility for the murder, the two sentencing strategies are not necessarily mutually exclusive. Moreover, given the strength of the available evidence, a reasonable attorney may well have chosen to prioritize the mitigation case over the direct responsibility challenge, particularly given that Wiggins' history contained little of the double edge we have found to justify limited investigations in other cases....

We further find that had the jury been confronted with this considerable mitigating evidence, there is a reasonable probability that it would have returned with a different sentence....

Wiggins' sentencing jury heard only one significant mitigating factor—that Wiggins had no prior convictions. Had the jury been able to place petitioner's excruciating life history on the mitigating side of the scale, there is a reasonable probability that at least one juror would have struck a different balance.

Moreover, in contrast to the petitioner in Williams v. Taylor, Wiggins does not have a record of violent conduct that could have been introduced by the State to offset this powerful mitigating narrative. [The] mitigating evidence in this case is stronger, and the State's evidence in support of the death penalty far weaker, than in *Williams,* where we found prejudice as the result of counsel's failure to investigate and present mitigating evidence. We thus conclude that the available mitigating evidence, taken as a whole, "might well have influenced the jury's appraisal" of Wiggins' moral culpability....

SCALIA, J., dissenting.

The Court today vacates Kevin Wiggins' death sentence on the ground that his trial counsel's investigation of potential mitigating evidence was "incomplete." Wiggins' trial counsel testified under oath, however, that he was aware of the basic features of Wiggins' troubled childhood that the Court claims he overlooked. The Court chooses to disbelieve this testimony for reasons that do not withstand analysis. Moreover, even if this disbelief could plausibly be entertained, that would certainly not establish (as 28 U.S.C. §2254(d) requires) that the

Maryland Court of Appeals was *unreasonable* in believing it, and in therefore concluding that counsel adequately investigated Wiggins' background.

[In post-conviction] proceedings, Carl Schlaich (one of Wiggins' two trial attorneys) testified that, although he did not retain a social worker to assemble a "social history" report, he nevertheless had detailed knowledge of Wiggins' background.... In light of this testimony, the Maryland Court of Appeals found that "counsel *did* investigate and *were* aware of Wiggins' background," (emphasis in original), and, specifically, that "counsel were aware that Wiggins had a most unfortunate childhood." These state-court determinations of factual issues are binding on federal habeas courts, including this Court, unless rebutted by clear and convincing evidence.

[Wiggins also] must establish that he was "prejudiced" by his counsel's alleged "error." Specifically, Wiggins must demonstrate that, if his trial attorneys had retained a licensed social worker to assemble a "social history" of their client, there is a "reasonable probability" that (1) his attorneys would have chosen to present the social history evidence to the jury, *and* (2) upon hearing that evidence, the jury would have spared his life. The Court's analysis on these points continues its disregard for the record in a determined procession towards a seemingly preordained result.

Wiggins has not shown that the incremental information in Hans Selvog's social-history report would have induced counsel to change this course. Schlaich testified under oath that presenting the type of evidence in Selvog's report would have conflicted with his chosen defense strategy to raise doubts as to Wiggins' role as a principal, and that he wanted to avoid a "shotgun approach" with the jury.[4]... It is irrelevant whether a hypothetical "reasonable attorney" might have introduced evidence of alleged sexual abuse; *Wiggins'* attorneys would *not* have done so.... There is simply *nothing* to show (and the Court does not even

---

[4] Introducing evidence that Wiggins suffered semiweekly (or perhaps daily) sexual abuse as a child, for example, could have led the jury to conclude that this horrible experience made Wiggins precisely the type of person who could perpetrate this bizarre crime—in which a 77-year-old woman was found drowned in the bathtub of her apartment, clothed but missing her underwear, and sprayed with Black Flag Ant and Roach Killer.

dare to *assert*) that there is a "reasonable probability" this evidence would have been introduced *in this case....*

Today's decision is extraordinary—even for our "death is different" jurisprudence. It fails to give effect to §2254(e)(1)'s requirement that state court factual determinations be presumed correct.... I dissent.

Page 723.   Add this material at the end of Problem 11-3.

Florida v. Nixon, 125 S. Ct. 551 (2004).

Page 724.   Add this material at the end of note 2.

How should the standard for prejudice change when the defendant pleads guilty rather than going to trial? The majority of courts declare that a defendant can be prejudiced by an attorney's failure to explain a potential defense during consultations about a guilty plea, even if the defense would not have succeeded. See Grosvenor v. State, 874 So. 2d 1176 (Fla. 2004).

Page 725.   Add this material in note 4, after citation to Maryland case.

Cf. People v. Morales, 808 N.E.2d 510 (Ill. 2004) (dual representation of defendant and potential witness does not establish per se conflict; retained counsel for defendant charged with first-degree murder in connection with drug-related shooting also represented defendant's boss in drug gang in a federal drug prosecution, and alleged murder victim was a courier sent by the boss to collect money from defendant).

Page 726.   Add this material at the end of note 4.

See also Florida v. Nixon, 125 S. Ct. 551 (2004) (attorney predicted that prosecution's evidence of guilt in murder trial would be virtually impossible to refute, proposed to defendant a strategy of conceding guilt to focus on urging leniency at penalty phase, but defendant did not respond; no presumption of prejudice under *Cronic* for conceding guilt under these circumstances).

Page 729.   Add this material at the end of note 3.

In re Rantz, 109 P.3d 132 (Colo. 2005) (defendant does not have to obtain post-conviction relief before suing defense counsel for malpractice, but issue preclusion may prevent a defendant who lost an ineffective assistance of counsel claim in post-conviction proceeding from raising a civil malpractice claim; collects cases).

D. Systems for Providing Counsel

Page 732.   Replace the Louisiana case with the following materials.

Louisiana offers a fascinating study in the practical politics of funding for criminal defense attorneys. The state Supreme Court took the national spotlight in 1993, when it decided the remarkable case of State v. Peart, 621 So. 2d 780, 785 (La. 1993). In that case, Leonard Peart was charged with armed robbery, aggravated rape, aggravated burglary, attempted armed robbery, and first degree murder. Because he was indigent, the trial court appointed public defender Rick Teissier to defend Peart.

Louisiana statutes provided for local funding of individual districts' indigent defender systems. Almost all of the funds for indigent defense came from criminal violation assessments, mostly traffic tickets. This system produced unstable funding for criminal defense: for instance, when the City of East Baton Rouge ran out of pre-printed traffic tickets in 1990, the indigent defender program's sole source of income was suspended while more tickets were being printed. The general pattern was chronic underfunding of indigent defense programs in most areas of the state.

At the time of his appointment to defend Peart, Teissier was handling 70 active felony cases. In the period between January 1 and August 1, 1991, Teissier represented 418 defendants. Of these, he entered 130 guilty pleas at arraignment. His clients were routinely incarcerated 30 to 70 days before he met with them. He had at least one serious case set for trial for every trial date during that period. The public defender's office in Orleans Parish had only enough funds to hire three investigators, who were supposed to assist defense attorneys in more than 7,000 cases per year in Criminal District Court, plus cases in

Juvenile Court, Traffic Court, and Magistrates' Court. There were no funds for expert witnesses.

These caseloads convinced the Louisiana Supreme Court that indigent defendants "are not likely to receive the reasonably effective assistance of counsel the constitution guarantees." As the trial judge put it, "not even a lawyer with an S on his chest could effectively handle this docket." Consequently, the court adopted a "rebuttable presumption" of ineffective assistance:

> we remand this case to the trial court and instruct the judge ... when hearing Leonard Peart's case and others in which similar claims are asserted by indigent defendants pre-trial, to hold individual hearings for each defendant and apply a rebuttable presumption that indigents are not receiving assistance of counsel sufficiently effective to meet constitutionally required standards. If the trial judge, applying this presumption and weighing all evidence presented, finds that Leonard Peart or any other defendant ... is not likely receiving reasonably effective assistance of counsel, then he shall not permit the trial of such cases to be conducted.

The Louisiana Supreme Court's opinion in *Peart* was not the last word on the subject. The state legislature restructured the funding mechanism for indigent defense in 1994, but complaints continued about the high caseloads and poor investigative and clerical support that limited the effectiveness of defense attorneys. The following case picks up the story over a decade later.

State v. Adrian Citizen
898 So. 2d 325 (La. 2005)

VICTORY, J.

These consolidated cases present the issue of funding for indigent defendants in criminal cases in the State of Louisiana. In particular, the legislature has enacted statutes which require the State to provide the funds for indigent defense through the Louisiana Indigent Defense Assistance Board and statewide indigent defender boards in each judicial district but has at the same time failed to provide adequate appropriation to support these services. Further, the legislature has exempted local governmental entities from the payment of such expenses.

The instant direct appeal arises out of two unrelated Calcasieu Parish killings. After a Calcasieu Parish grand jury returned a first degree murder indictment on April 11, 2002 against Benjamin Tonguis, the trial court appointed the Chief Public Defender for the parish, Ronald Ware, to represent him. Ware informed the court of his prohibitive caseload, and the court removed him from the case and sought to appoint solo practitioner Phyllis E. Mann. On December 10, 2003, counsel filed a document captioned as a Motion to Determine Source of Funds to Provide Competent Defense.... On January 30, 2004, the trial court consolidated the *Tonguis* case with that of Adrian Shannondoah Citizen, another Calcasieu Parish first-degree murder defendant indicted on October 10, 2002, seeking to be represented by appointed counsel Phyllis Mann. Also on that date, the trial court held a hearing on the funding issues raised by Mann. At this hearing, counsel for the Calcasieu Parish Police Jury (the "CPPJ") filed a motion to dismiss his client as a party to Mann's motion, as in his view La. R.S. 15:304 [forbids] local funding for the representation of indigent defendants. The court then explored the possibility with prosecutors of amending the charges against each defendant to second-degree murder and, after receiving no favorable response, considered [testimony] regarding the financial status of the CPPJ, with an eye toward using it as a funding source.

[Counsel] for the CPPJ explained that the current system for maintaining the criminal justice system in Calcasieu Parish ... evolved in 1985 after voters in the parish approved an *ad valorem* tax specifically dedicated to maintaining the Criminal Court Fund. [In] 2000, the tax, as supplemented by fines and forfeitures, put into the Criminal Court Fund $3,500,000, by far the largest portion of the total amount of $5,300,000, which also included funds from other sources such as grant programs. By agreement, 20% of the Fund portion generated by the *ad valorem* tax and fines and forfeitures goes into the witness and juror fee account, 60% to the D.A.'s office, and 40% to the district courts. Any surplus remaining in the witness and jury fee account at the end of the year does not revert to the general parish fund but is split on a 50/50 basis between the courts and the D.A.'s office. In 2000, that surplus amounted to some $440,000, an average figure over a seven year period....

The parish attorney explained that ... since voters in Calcasieu Parish had approved the *ad valorem* tax, by far the biggest component of the Criminal Court Fund, specifically for the purpose of maintaining the court system and the District Attorney's Office, the CPPJ had no obligation, or even the authority, to divert some of that tax money to criminal defense. Chief Public Defender Ware underscored the problem facing the court by stating that his office currently owed close to $47,000 for capital defense and expected to owe at least an additional $150,000 in upcoming cases which he had already committed to fund. He further informed the court that his office generated approximately $5,550 per month. Despite the apparent intransigence of the CPPJ, Prosecutor Wayne Frey suggested that the court pay defense counsel from the surplus monies contained in the CPPJ's Criminal Court Fund (provided the parties agreed upon a funding cap), and the court agreed to propose the idea to his fellow judges and to go before the CPPJ with a funding proposal. However, an increase in jury and witness fees had reduced the surplus in the Fund from a previous average of $450,000 to approximately $300,000. The court expressed its frustration with the continued lack of funding and the fact that it faces some version of the same funding dilemma in virtually every criminal case before it.

[After] meeting no success with the judges and district attorney, the court found that the CPPJ was the only possible source of adequate funding. The court went on to find [that La. R.S. 15:304 unconstitutionally deprives] the defendants of their right to a fair and speedy trial and their right to counsel. Finally, the court ordered the CPPJ to place $200,000 into the court registry to be distributed to the attorneys representing Tonguis and Citizen. In its ensuing written reasons, the court also ordered the CPPJ to place into an escrow account $75,000 for expert witness fees and case related expenses....

A defendant is entitled to the assistance of counsel in criminal proceedings. Specifically, La. Const. Art. I § 13 provides that "at each stage of the proceedings, every person is entitled to assistance of counsel ... appointed by the court if he is indigent and charged with an offense punishable by imprisonment. The legislature shall provide for a uniform system for securing and compensating qualified counsel for indigents."

... The current legislative system set out in an attempt to meet the constitutional command of La. Const. Art. I § 13 to provide a uniform system for securing and compensating qualified counsel for indigents appears in La. R.S. 15:144 *et seq.* (Title XIV: Right to Counsel). These statutes require each judicial district to create an indigent defender board, which shall maintain lists of volunteer and non-volunteer attorneys licensed to practice law in Louisiana. Each board must then select the procedure for providing counsel to indigents, whether it be through court selection of volunteer attorneys (or non-volunteer attorneys if needed), through employment of a chief indigent defender and supporting assistants, through contracting with available attorneys, or through any combination of the above. Title XIV further creates an indigent defender fund in each judicial district, sets out proceedings to determine indigency, and authorizes partial reimbursement from indigents. Finally, La. R.S. 15:151 *et seq.* establish a statewide Indigent Defense Assistance Board to provide for supplementary funds in certain cases, and to "cause counsel to be enrolled" to represent a defendant sentenced to death on direct appeal and in post-conviction proceedings.

[The trial court heard extensive testimony that the state, the local Indigent Defender's Office, and the Indigent Defense Assistance Board have no money to spare. In fact, the board's director, Edward Greenlee, testified that the state reduced his agency's funding by 25% after its first year of existence, then failed to restore funding to previous levels in the seven subsequent years. Additionally, Greenlee testified that the state prohibits the board from running a deficit. Accordingly, when the local parish police jury's justice fund runs an average surplus of several hundred thousand dollars per year, the trial court's decision to tap these funds proves tempting.]

In 1993, this Court addressed the issue of indigent defense funding in State v. Peart, 621 So. 2d 780, 785 (La. 1993). At the time *Peart* was decided, La. R.S. 15:304 required all parishes and the City of New Orleans to pay "all expenses … whatever attending criminal proceedings." In *Peart,* the Court … held that an inmate may raise certain ineffective assistance claims pretrial when judicial economy demands it…. The Court then determined that defendants assigned counsel in a particular section of Orleans Parish Criminal District Court received constitutionally deficient counsel, and thus found the existence of a rebuttable presumption of counsel's ineffectiveness in cases arising out of that section of court. Finally, the Court noted that:

> If legislative action is not forthcoming and indigent defense reform does
> not take place, this Court, in the exercise of its constitutional and
> inherent power and supervisory jurisdiction, may find it necessary to
> employ the more intrusive and specific measures it has thus far avoided

to ensure that indigent defendants receive reasonably effective assistance of counsel.

Also in 1993, the Court decided State v. Wigley, 624 So. 2d 425, 426 (La. 1993), wherein we held that uncompensated representation of indigents, when reasonably imposed, is a professional obligation burdening the privilege of practicing law in this state and does not violate the constitutional rights of attorneys. However, we also held that "any assignment of counsel [from the private] bar to defend an indigent defendant must provide for reimbursement to the assigned attorney of properly incurred and reasonable out-of-pocket expenses and overhead costs."[8] Finally, in order to appoint private counsel in indigent defendant cases, the Court set out the following requirements:

> We fully appreciate that the sources of funds from which appointed counsel may be reimbursed are limited. In future cases it will therefore be the district judge's responsibility to determine before he appoints counsel that funds sufficient to cover the anticipated expenses and overhead are likely to be available to reimburse counsel in the manner outlined above, whether the funds come from the Indigent Defender Board, from the state, from one court fund or another, from the local government subdivision pursuant to La. Rev. Stat. Ann. § 15:304, or from any other available source. If the district judge determines that funds are not available to reimburse appointed counsel, he should not appoint members of the private bar to represent indigents....

[In 1994], the legislature amended La. R.S. 15:304 to add a proviso that "nothing in this Section shall be construed to make the parishes or the city of New Orleans responsible for the expenses associated with the

---

[8] In *Wigley*, we [found] that in order to be reasonable and not oppressive, any assignment of counsel to defend an indigent defendant must provide for reimbursement to the assigned attorney of properly incurred and reasonable out-of-pocket expenses and overhead costs. However, a fee for services need not be paid, as long as the time the attorney must devote to cases for which he does not receive a fee does not reach unreasonable levels. What is unreasonable in this context is to be determined by the trial judge in the exercise of his discretion. Such a system will strike a balance between the attorney's ethical duty to provide services *pro bono publico* and his or her practical need to continue to perform his or her other obligations....

costs, expert fees, or attorney fees of a defendant in a criminal proceeding." ... La. R.S. 15:304, as amended in 1994, now provides:

> All expenses incurred in the different parishes of the state or in the city of New Orleans by the arrest, confinement, and prosecution of persons accused or convicted of crimes, their removal to prison, the pay of witnesses specifically provided for by law, jurors and all prosecutorial expenses whatever attending criminal proceedings shall be paid by the respective parishes in which the offense charged may have been committed or by the city of New Orleans, as the case may be.... Nothing in this Section shall be construed to make the parishes or the city of New Orleans responsible for the expenses associated with the costs, expert fees, or attorney fees of a defendant in a criminal proceeding....

[The defense attorney argued that this statute deprives her of] "her property interest in both her license to practice law and the financial interest of her law firm without due process of law in violation of the Fourth and Fourteenth Amendments to the United States Constitution and Article 1, Section 4 of the Louisiana Constitution of 1974 as amended." ... The trial court rejected counsel's argument regarding counsel's own due process claim, but agreed with counsel's argument regarding the most recent changes to La. R.S. 15:304 ... and their effect on the rights of the instant indigent defendants.

[The] trial court's ruling that La. R.S. 15:304 [violates] the defendants' rights of due process, right to counsel, and equal protection is erroneous. The constitution requires that indigent defendants are entitled to the assistance of counsel and that the legislature provide for a uniform system for securing and compensating qualified counsel. The statutes at issue clearly meet the constitutional requirements because they ... specifically provide the medium in which to seek funding for indigent defense. The statutes do not declare that indigent defense costs will not be paid, they simply place this burden on the state. The fact that the legislature has not adequately funded the programs it has created to meet its constitutional mandate does not make the statutes themselves unconstitutional. Further, while the statutes prohibit the parishes from being required to pay for indigent defense, nothing in the statutes prohibit the parishes from paying these expenses if they so chose....

As we have found that the statutes are not unconstitutional, the next issue is whether the trial court exceeded the constitutional function of the judiciary in ordering the police jury to set aside funding for indigent defendants. As a general matter, as mentioned above, La. Const. Art. I § 13 explicitly states that "the legislature shall provide for a uniform system for securing and compensating qualified counsel for indigents." Additionally, La. Const. Art. II § 2 states that "except as otherwise provided by this constitution, no one of these branches, nor any person holding office in one of them, shall exercise power belonging to either of the others." *Cf.* La. Const. Art. III § 1 ("The legislative power of the state is vested in the legislature").

Given the above, the constitution explicitly places the duty of providing a working system for securing the representation of indigent defendants squarely on the shoulders of the legislature. Accordingly, while the legislature may be in breach of that duty, in one view at least, a trial court may not reach into a local parish's accounts when constitutionally prohibited by the legislature.

The legislature has clearly determined through statutory enactments that the State, not the parishes, will pay for indigent defense pursuant to the constitutional mandate of La. Const. Art. I, § 13.... Thus, we find that the trial court erred in ordering the CPPJ to place $200,000 in the court registry for the court appointed attorneys and to place $75,000 in escrow for other case-related expenses.

However, we have often expressed in indigent defendant funding cases that budget exigencies cannot serve as an excuse for the oppressive and abusive extension of attorneys' professional responsibilities, and that this Court, in the exercise of its constitutional and inherent power and supervisory jurisdiction, has the power to take corrective measures to ensure that indigent defendants are provided with their constitutional and statutory rights. In fact, in *Peart,* we specifically warned the legislature that we would undertake more intrusive measures if the legislature failed to act.

The legislature has taken steps to remedy the critical state of indigent criminal defense in Louisiana since our warnings in *Peart.* For instance, it created the statewide Indigent Defense Assistance Board in 1997. In 2003, the legislature, by separate but identical House and Senate Resolutions, created the Louisiana Task Force on Indigent Defense Services, effective January 12, 2004, to study the problem and make an initial report no later than March 1, 2004. The legislature has constituted the Task Force as a blue ribbon committee whose members range from the Governor to the Chief Justice of this Court. It is not clear whether the 2003 Task Force ever made its report, but this year, by concurrent resolution, the legislature voted to continue the Task Force, directing it to report on its findings together with specific recommendations no later than April 1, 2005. We assume that, given the obvious deficiencies in funding from the State to satisfy its constitutional mandate in La. Const. Art. I, § 13, this Task Force will work diligently to formulate specific recommendations on April 1, 2005, to address these problems and that the legislature will act quickly to promulgate these, or other, appropriate solutions.

However, even assuming that these steps will lead to sweeping reform of the system and to adequate funding for indigent defense, reform will not likely come in any reasonable time to help the present defendants. Until the legislature takes remedial action, this Court must address the immediate problems of the instant defendants in securing constitutionally adequate counsel (in a constitutionally and statutorily required timely manner) in their forthcoming capital prosecutions. We are very much cognizant of the lengths to which other state courts have gone to ensure that the indigents' constitutional rights are protected, in spite of legislative inaction.[12] This is particularly appropriate in cases

---

[12] For example, the Supreme Judicial Court of Massachusetts confronted a lack of legislative funding in Lavallee v. Justices in the Hampden Superior Court, 812 N.E.2d 895 (Mass. 2004). In that case, certain judicial districts lacked the funding to woo competent attorneys to represent the indigent. Additionally, the state agency charged with providing court-appointed counsel in most circumstances had no staff available to represent petitioners. [The court held that] "on a showing that no counsel is available to represent a particular indigent defendant despite good faith efforts, such a defendant may not be held more than seven days and the criminal case against such a defendant may not continue beyond forty-five days." The court ... noted that several State courts have temporarily deferred in the first instance, and only temporarily, to legislative action to ensure that the system for compensation for indigent representation meets constitutional standards (citing *Peart*; State ex rel. Stephan v. Smith, 747 P.2d 816, 848-50 (Kan. 1987); Smith v. State, 394 A.2d 834, 839 (N.H. 1978)).

The *Lavallee* court also recognized that some state courts of last resort have granted preliminary relief in the form of increased compensation rates, but have simultaneously directed their Legislatures to amend permanently the

involving indigent defense in our state courts, as this is an area over which the Court has supervisory jurisdiction and the duty to ensure that the criminal justice system is functioning in a constitutional manner.

In this case, Mr. Citizen, was indicted for first-degree murder on October 10, 2002, and he remains in jail with no funds available for the attorney appointed to represent him and, under current circumstances, may remain there indefinitely[13] unless funds are provided for his

---

compensation rates for indigent representation (citing State ex rel. Wolff v. Ruddy, 617 S.W.2d 64, 67-68 (Mo. 1981); State v. Lynch, 796 P.2d 1150, 1164 (Okla. 1990)). Along these lines, a New York trial court recently issued a permanent injunction directing that counsel be paid $90 per hour, and removed the statutory fee cap until the Legislature changed the rates and increased its appropriation for compensation for indigent representation. New York County Lawyers' Ass'n v. State, 196 Misc. 2d 761, 763 N.Y.S.2d 397 (N.Y. Sup. Ct. 2003)....

In contemplating more dramatic action should the need arise, the Court in *Peart* pointed to cases such as Arnold v. Kemp, 813 S.W.2d 770, 776-77 (Ark. 1991) ($1,000 cap on fees constitutionally unacceptable because burden imposed on attorneys was excessive to the extent that it constituted a taking; court also found that system of appointing attorneys, based on where attorney lives and his ability to provide effective assistance of counsel, violated the appellants' right to equal protection); *Lynch, supra* (applauding *pro bono* legal representation, court nevertheless holds that "voluntary services are insufficient to accommodate the right of indigent citizens to the effective assistance of counsel"); *Stephan, supra,* (ordering the dismissal of charges against certain defendants if the state cannot make available funds for their defense).

At least one indigent defender has prompted a trial court to take the extreme measure of threatening to hold a legislative body reluctant to release funds in contempt. When Kentucky cut the budget for his office, indigent defender Dan Goyette responded with a corresponding cut in services. Specifically, his office refused to provide attorneys for people facing involuntary mental hospitalization. The chief judge in Goyette's District reportedly ordered the official in charge of the state budget to restore Goyette's funding or face contempt. Other judges in the district ordered the release of four unrepresented persons hospitalized against their will.

[13] There are time limitations imposed by the Code of Criminal Procedure for bringing indicted defendants to trial. There is no time limitation for the institution of prosecution for first degree murder. However, no trial shall be commenced in a capital case after three years from the date of institution of the prosecution and in other felony cases after two years from the date of institution of the prosecution. La. C.Cr.P. art. 578. Additionally, all defendants have a right to a speedy trial. La. Const. Art. 1, § 16; La. C.Cr.P. art. 701.

defense. Mr. Tonguis, was indicted for the first-degree murder of his infant child on April 11, 2002, and though he is not incarcerated, no funds are available for the attorney appointed to represent him. Implicit in these defendants' constitutional right to assistance of counsel is the State's inability to proceed with their prosecution until it provides adequate funds for their defense. While La. R.S. 15:304 ... cannot be construed to force the CPPJ to pay for the costs of these indigents' defenses, nothing ... prohibits the CPPJ from paying these expenses, and these funds may come from the Criminal Court Fund upon agreement of the legal entities responsible for its administration under La. R.S. 15:571.11.

In order to assure timely representation, we now alter one of the rules previously laid down in *Wigley, supra.* A district judge should appoint counsel to represent an indigent defendant from the time of the indigent defendant's first appearance in court, even if the judge cannot then determine that funds sufficient to cover the anticipated expenses and overhead are likely to be available to reimburse counsel. The appointed attorney may then file a motion to determine funding, as was done in this case, and if the trial judge determines that adequate funding is not available, the defendant may then file, at his option, a motion to halt the prosecution of the case until adequate funding becomes available. The judge may thereafter prohibit the State from going forward with the prosecution until he or she determines that appropriate funding is likely to be available....

Page 746.   Add this material at the end of note 3.

See Lavallee v. Justices in the Hampden Superior Court, 812 N.E.2d 895 (Mass. 2004) (indigent defendants lacked representation due to shortage of lawyers in county bar advocates program, many were arraigned without benefit of counsel, judge set bail or ordered preventive detention for each unrepresented petitioner; appellate court held that on showing that no counsel was available to represent defendant despite good-faith efforts to obtain counsel, defendant may not be held more than seven days and criminal case against him may not continue beyond 45 days); Leonard Post, Montana Upgrades Indigency Defense System, Nat'l L.J. June 6, 2005 (describing legislation that establishes statewide indigent criminal defense system that meets national standards for delivering high-quality representation; legislation passed in response to lawsuit filed by ACLU).

E. The Ethics of Defending Criminals

Page 757.   Add this material at the end of note 3.

See John W. Stanford, The Christian Lawyer: Defending Apparently Guilty Defendants and Using Deceptive Courtroom Strategies and Tactics: An Evangelical Biblical View, 16 Regent U. L. Rev. 275 (2003-2004).

Chapter 12

Pretrial Release and Detention

B. Pretrial Detention

Page 788.   Add this material at the end of note 1.

See also People v. Purcell, 778 N.E.2d 695 (Ill. 2002) (strikes down law requiring defendant to show that guilt is not evident, because allocation of burden to accused is inconsistent with state constitution's presumption of bail).

Page 791.   Add this new section heading after the breaker rule.

C. Detention of Excludable Aliens and Enemy Combatants

Page 795.   Add this material at the end of the chapter.

What follows is an excerpt from a report of the Inspector General of the United States Department of Justice, reviewing the extended detention of excludable aliens rounded up in the days and months following September 11. The report both recognizes the extraordinary and critical circumstances of terrorist threats to the United States and criticizes the actions and decisions of federal agencies. With the benefit of a few years' hindsight, does this criticism now appear well grounded?

The September 11th Detainees:
A Review of the Treatment of Aliens Held on
Immigration Charges in Connection With the
Investigation of the September 11 Attacks
U.S. Dep't of Justice, Office of the Inspector General, April 2003

On September 11, 2001, terrorists hijacked four airplanes and flew two of them into the World Trade Center Towers in New York City and one into the Pentagon in Arlington, Virginia. The fourth plane crashed into a field in southwestern Pennsylvania before it could strike a target in Washington, D.C. The attacks killed more than 3,100 people, including all 246 people aboard the airplanes.

The Federal Bureau of Investigation immediately initiated a massive investigation, called "PENTTBOM," into this coordinated terrorist attack. The FBI investigation focused on identifying the terrorists who hijacked the airplanes and anyone who aided their efforts. In addition, the FBI worked with other federal, state, and local law enforcement agencies to prevent follow-up attacks in this country and against U.S. interests abroad.

One of the principal responses by law enforcement authorities after the September 11 attacks was to use the federal immigration laws to detain aliens suspected of having possible ties to terrorism. Within two months of the attacks, law enforcement authorities had detained, at least for questioning, more than 1,200 citizens and aliens nationwide. Many of these individuals were questioned and subsequently released without being charged with a criminal or immigration offense. Many others, however, were arrested and detained for violating federal immigration law.

Our review determined that the Immigration and Naturalization Service (INS) detained 762 aliens as a result of the PENTTBOM investigation. Of these 762 aliens, 24 were in INS custody on immigration violations prior to the September 11 attacks. The remaining 738 aliens were arrested between September 11, 2001, and August 6, 2002, as a direct result of the FBI's PENTTBOM investigation. All 762 detainees were placed on what became known as an "INS Custody List" because of the FBI's assessment that they may have had a connection to the September 11 attacks or terrorism in general, or because the FBI was unable, at least initially, to determine whether they were connected to terrorism. The Government held these aliens in a variety of federal, local, and private detention facilities across the United States while the FBI investigated them for ties to the September 11 attacks or terrorism in general....

Soon after these detentions began, the media began to report allegations of mistreatment of the detainees. For example, detainees and their attorneys alleged that the detainees were not informed of the charges against them for extended periods of time; were not permitted contact with attorneys, their families, and embassy officials; remained in detention even though they had no involvement in terrorism; or were physically abused, verbally abused, and mistreated in other ways while detained.

Several individual detainees and non-profit organizations filed lawsuits against the Department of Justice protesting the lack of public information about the detainees and the length and conditions of the detainees' confinement. For example, [five] detainees filed a class action lawsuit alleging they were physically abused, verbally abused, and held without a legitimate immigration or law enforcement purpose long after they received final removal or voluntary departure orders. In addition, advocacy organizations such as Amnesty International and the Lawyers Committee for Human Rights issued reports asserting mistreatment of the detainees or mishandling of their cases.

[T]he Department of Justice Office of the Inspector General (OIG) initiated this review to examine the treatment of detainees arrested in connection with the Department's September 11 terrorism investigation. Specifically, the OIG's review focused on:

- Issues affecting the length of the detainees' confinement, including the process undertaken by the FBI and others to clear individual detainees of a connection to the September 11 attacks or terrorism in general;
- Bond determinations for detainees;
- The removal process and the timing of removal; and
- Conditions of confinement experienced by detainees, including their access to legal counsel....

Our review did not seek to examine all aspects of the Department's terrorism investigation, including the specific investigative techniques involved in the September 11 investigation or the decisions made by federal, state, and local law enforcement on why to detain specific individuals. Additional issues beyond the scope of this review include the reasons and justifications for the Department's decision to limit public release of information concerning arrests related to the ongoing terrorism investigation, its decision to close immigration proceedings to the public, and its use of voluntary interviews for certain categories of aliens.[8]... In addition, our review did not examine the Department's use of material witness warrants to detain certain individuals in connection with its terrorism investigation, another issue currently being litigated in the courts.[9]...

In conducting our review, we were mindful of the circumstances confronting the Department and the country as a result of the September 11 attacks, including the massive disruptions they caused.... It is also important to note that nearly all of the 762 aliens we examined violated immigration laws, either by overstaying their visas, by entering the country illegally, or some other immigration violation....

Within a week of the attacks, the FBI had assigned more than 7,000 employees to the task of tracking down anyone who had aided the terrorists and attempting to prevent additional attacks. In the ensuing weeks, ... law enforcement officers across the country arrested hundreds of illegal aliens they encountered while pursuing PENTTBOM leads, whether or not they were the subjects of the leads....

The Department instituted a policy that all aliens in whom the FBI had interest in connection with the PENTTBOM investigation, no matter how tangential the connection, required clearance by the FBI of any connection to terrorism before they could be removed or released. Therefore, determining which of these aliens was "of interest" to the FBI's terrorism investigation became the first of a series of critical decision points. We found that often the FBI could not state whether or

---

[8] For example, on November 9, 2001, the Department and the FBI sought voluntary interviews with approximately 5,000 male visitors or foreign nationals between the ages of 18 and 33 who had entered the United States after January 2000 from countries "where there have been strong al Qaeda presences."

[9] A material witness warrant can be obtained from a judge upon a showing that the testimony of a person is material to a criminal proceeding and that it may become impracticable to secure the presence of the person by subpoena. See 18 U.S.C. §3144....

not it had an interest in a particular alien and therefore, out of an abundance of caution, the FBI labeled the alien of interest or of unknown interest, and consequently the INS treated the alien as a September 11 detainee who required clearance from the FBI before he could be released.

In fact, in New York City we found that the FBI and the INS made little attempt to distinguish between aliens arrested as subjects of a PENTTBOM lead and those encountered coincidentally. This lack of precision had important ramifications for many aliens in the time they spent confined and the conditions of that confinement....

We do not criticize the decision to require FBI clearance of aliens to ensure they had no connection to the September 11 attacks or terrorism in general. However, we criticize the indiscriminate and haphazard manner in which the labels of "high interest," "of interest," or "of undetermined interest" were applied to many aliens who had no connection to terrorism. Even in the hectic aftermath of the September 11 attacks, we believe the FBI should have taken more care to distinguish between aliens who it actually suspected of having a connection to terrorism as opposed to aliens who, while possibly guilty of violating federal immigration law, had no connection to terrorism but simply were encountered in connection with a PENTTBOM lead. Alternatively, by early November 2001, when it was clear that the clearances could not be accomplished in a matter of days (or even weeks), the Department should have permitted the FBI and INS to review the cases and keep on the list only those detainees for whom there was some factual basis to suspect a connection to terrorism or to the PENTTBOM investigation....

Moreover, the FBI failed to provide adequate field office staff to quickly conduct the detainee clearance investigations and failed to provide adequate FBI Headquarters staff to effectively coordinate and monitor the detainee clearance process. This contributed to the slow pace of the FBI's clearance process, which meant the FBI's initial determination of its "interest" had enormous consequences for the detained aliens.... The average time from arrest to clearance was 80 days and less than 3 percent of the detainees were cleared within 3 weeks of their arrest....

In the aftermath of the September 11 attacks, 184 aliens arrested on immigration charges were confined in high-security federal prisons, as opposed to less restrictive INS detention facilities. Eighty-four of these aliens were held at the MDC in Brooklyn, New York. These MDC detainees were held under "the most restrictive conditions possible," which included "lockdown" for at least 23 hours per day, extremely limited access to telephones, and restrictive escort procedures any time the detainees were moved outside their cells.

[Our] review raises serious questions about the treatment of the September 11 detainees housed at the MDC in several regards. First, BOP officials imposed a "communications blackout" specifically for September 11 detainees within a week of the terrorist attacks. During this blackout period, detainees were not permitted to receive any telephone calls, visitors, or mail, or to place any telephone calls or send mail. While we were unable to determine the exact length of this communications blackout, it appears to have lasted several weeks, after which time the September 11 detainees were permitted limited attorney and social contacts. During this time, attorneys and family members were unable to receive any information about these detainees, including where they were being held. While such a policy was within the BOP's discretion, we question the justification for a total communications blackout on all these individuals, particularly for the length of time that it was imposed....

The detainees were placed in restraints whenever they were outside their cells, including handcuffs, leg irons, and heavy chains. Four staff members were required to be present each time a detainee was placed into restraints and escorted from a cell. The detainees also were required to remain in restraints during their non-contact visits with their attorneys or family members.

[With] regard to allegations of physical and verbal abuse, we concluded that the evidence indicates a pattern of abuse by some correctional officers against some September 11 detainees, particularly during the first months after the attacks. Most detainees we interviewed at the MDC alleged that MDC staff physically abused them. Many also told us that that MDC staff verbally abused them with such taunts as "Bin Laden Junior" or with threats such as "you will be here for the next 20-25 years like the Cuban people."...

In sum, we recognize the uncertainties and confusion surrounding the initial policies and treatment relating to these September 11 detainees. Much about these detainees was unknown, and the BOP had to accept the FBI's loosely applied assessment of these detainees as "of interest" to the terrorism investigation. However, while we fault the FBI for the slowness of the clearance process, we believe the blackout and the initial [high security] designation that the BOP imposed for several weeks was excessive, particularly because many of these detainees had no counsel or any contact with families....

While the chaotic situation and the uncertainties surrounding the detainees' role in the September 11 attacks and the potential for additional terrorism explain some of these problems, they do not explain or justify all of them. We believe that the Department and the BOP should consider these issues carefully in an effort to avoid similar problems in the future....

Notes

1. *Detention of excludable aliens.* In Zadvydas v. Davis, 533 U.S. 678 (2001), the Supreme Court invalidated a statute allowing an alien who is subject to a final order of removal to be detained beyond a 90-day statutory "removal period" at the discretion of the attorney general. The Court held that as a matter of due process aliens could not be detained indefinitely following a final order of removal and that the attorney general had to justify continued detention. Two years later, however, the Court in Demore v. Kim, 538 U.S. 510 (2003), upheld a statute requiring mandatory detention for deportable criminal aliens, as applied to a lawful permanent resident who entered the United States at age six and was convicted of burglary and "petty theft with priors." Is it significant that *Zadvydas* was decided shortly before September 11 and *Demore* a year and a half after September 11?

2. *Detention of material witnesses.* Federal law empowers the government to detain "material witnesses" who might have information relating to the commission of a federal crime. The traditional use of the federal material witness statute was to hold reluctant or fearful witnesses for a short time (typically a few days) to obtain their grand jury testimony. During terrorism investigations since 2001, FBI agents have obtained judicial approval for warrants allowing them to detain material witnesses, and then have held them for several months; only about half the witnesses ever testified before a grand jury. See Adam Liptak, For Post-9/11 Material Witness, It Is a Terror of a Different Kind, N.Y.

Times, Aug. 19, 2004 (recounts experience of former college football player arrested in March 2003 as a material witness in a terrorism investigation; held "in a small cell for hours and hours and hours buck naked"; federal judge ordered him to move in with his in-laws in Las Vegas; witness was never charged with a crime and never asked to testify as a witness; 16 months after his arrest, court said he was free to resume his life).

3. *Detention of terrorism suspects.* The Inspector General report both recognized the critical circumstances of terrorist threats to the United States and criticized the actions of federal officials in identifying suspects for detention and in extending the length of those detentions. Shortly thereafter, a Justice Department spokesperson defended the department's actions: "We make no apologies for finding every legal way possible to protect the American public from further terrorist attacks." Would you expect an internal executive branch report like the one by the inspector general to have an impact on law and policy?

Chapter 13

Charging

B. *Prosecutorial Screening*

1. Declination and Diversion

Page 808. **Add this material before the notes.**

The United States Department of Justice issued the following revised guidelines for charging and plea bargaining with corporate entity defendants. The Department may have been responding to the national focus on corporate crime spawned in part by the Enron debacle and various allegations of improper securities business. The following policies highlight the interwoven decisions about declination, charging, plea bargaining, and sentencing that make it hard to look at charging policies standing alone.

Federal Prosecution of Business Organizations
United States Attorney Manual §9-162, February 2003

I. Charging a Corporation: General

A. General Principle: Corporations should not be treated leniently because of their artificial nature nor should they be subject to harsher treatment. Vigorous enforcement of the criminal laws against corporate wrongdoers, where appropriate, results in great benefits for law enforcement and the public, particularly in the area of white collar crime. Indicting corporations for wrongdoing enables the government to address and be a force for positive change of corporate culture, alter corporate behavior, and prevent, discover, and punish white collar crime.

B. Comment: [Corporations] are likely to take immediate remedial steps when one is indicted for criminal conduct that is pervasive throughout a particular industry, and thus an indictment often provides a unique opportunity for deterrence on a massive scale. In addition, a corporate indictment may result in specific deterrence by changing the culture of the indicted corporation and the behavior of its employees. Finally, certain crimes that carry with them a substantial risk of great public harm, e.g., environmental crimes or financial frauds, are by their nature most likely to be committed by businesses, and there may, therefore, be a substantial federal interest in indicting the corporation.

Charging a corporation, however, does not mean that individual directors, officers, employees, or shareholders should not also be charged. Prosecution of a corporation is not a substitute for the prosecution of criminally culpable individuals within or without the corporation. Because a corporation can act only through individuals, imposition of individual criminal liability may provide the strongest deterrent against future corporate wrongdoing. Only rarely should provable individual culpability not be pursued, even in the face of offers of corporate guilty pleas....

II.   Charging a Corporation: Factors to Be Considered

A.   General Principle: Generally, prosecutors should apply the same factors in determining whether to charge a corporation as they do with respect to individuals. See United States Attorneys' Manual §9-27.220, et seq. Thus, the prosecutor should weigh all of the factors normally considered in the sound exercise of prosecutorial judgment: the sufficiency of the evidence; the likelihood of success at trial; the probable deterrent, rehabilitative, and other consequences of conviction; and the adequacy of noncriminal approaches. However, due to the nature of the corporate "person," some additional factors are present. In conducting an investigation, determining whether to bring charges, and negotiating plea agreements, prosecutors should consider the following factors in reaching a decision as to the proper treatment of a corporate target:

1. the nature and seriousness of the offense, including the risk of harm to the public, and applicable policies and priorities, if any, governing the prosecution of corporations for particular categories of crime;

2. the pervasiveness of wrongdoing within the corporation, including the complicity in, or condonation of, the wrongdoing by corporate management;

3. the corporation's history of similar conduct, including prior criminal, civil, and regulatory enforcement actions against it;

4. the corporation's timely and voluntary disclosure of wrongdoing and its willingness to cooperate in the investigation of its agents, including, if necessary, the waiver of corporate attorney-client and work product protection;

5. the existence and adequacy of the corporation's compliance program;

6. the corporation's remedial actions, including any efforts to implement an effective corporate compliance program or to improve an existing one, to replace responsible management, to discipline or terminate wrongdoers, to pay restitution, and to cooperate with the relevant government agencies;

7. collateral consequences, including disproportionate harm to shareholders, pension holders and employees not proven personally culpable and impact on the public arising from the prosecution;

8. the adequacy of the prosecution of individuals responsible for the corporation's malfeasance; and

9. the adequacy of remedies such as civil or regulatory enforcement actions....

VI. Cooperation and Voluntary Disclosure

A. General Principle: In determining whether to charge a corporation, that corporation's timely and voluntary disclosure of wrongdoing and its willingness to cooperate with the government's investigation may be relevant factors. In gauging the extent of the corporation's cooperation, the prosecutor may consider the corporation's willingness to identify the culprits within the corporation, including senior executives; to make witnesses available; to disclose the complete results of its internal investigation; and to waive attorney-client and work product protection.

B. Comment: In investigating wrongdoing by or within a corporation, a prosecutor is likely to encounter several obstacles resulting from the nature of the corporation itself. It will often be difficult to determine which individual took which action on behalf of the corporation. Lines of authority and responsibility may be shared among operating divisions or departments, and records and personnel may be spread throughout the United States or even among several countries. Where the criminal conduct continued over an extended period of time, the culpable or knowledgeable personnel may have been promoted, transferred, or fired, or they may have quit or retired. Accordingly, a corporation's cooperation may be critical in identifying the culprits and locating relevant evidence.

In some circumstances, therefore, granting a corporation immunity or amnesty or pretrial diversion may be considered in the course of the government's investigation. In such circumstances, prosecutors should refer to the principles governing non-prosecution agreements generally. See U.S. Attorneys' Manual §9-27.600-650. These principles permit a non-prosecution agreement in exchange for cooperation when a corporation's "timely cooperation appears to be necessary to the public interest and other means of obtaining the desired cooperation are unavailable or would not be effective." ...

[Prosecution policies] specific to the industry or statute may require prosecution notwithstanding a corporation's willingness to cooperate. For example, the Antitrust Division offers amnesty only to the first corporation to agree to cooperate. This creates a strong incentive for corporations participating in anti-competitive conduct to be the first to cooperate. In addition, amnesty, immunity, or reduced sanctions may not be appropriate where the corporation's business is permeated with fraud or other crimes.

One factor the prosecutor may weigh in assessing the adequacy of a corporation's cooperation is the completeness of its disclosure including, if necessary, a waiver of the attorney-client and work product protections, both with respect to its internal investigation and with respect to communications between specific officers, directors and employees and counsel. Such waivers permit the government to obtain statements of possible witnesses, subjects, and targets, without having to negotiate individual cooperation or immunity agreements. In addition, they are often critical in enabling the government to evaluate the completeness of a corporation's voluntary disclosure and cooperation. Prosecutors may, therefore, request a waiver in appropriate circumstances. The Department does not, however, consider waiver of a corporation's attorney-client and work product protection an absolute requirement, and prosecutors should consider the willingness of a corporation to waive such protection when necessary to provide timely and complete information as one factor in evaluating the corporation's cooperation.

Another factor to be weighed by the prosecutor is whether the corporation appears to be protecting its culpable employees and agents. Thus, while cases will differ depending on the circumstances, a corporation's promise of support to culpable employees and agents, either through the advancing of attorneys fees, through retaining the employees without sanction for their misconduct, or through providing information to the employees about the government's investigation pursuant to a joint defense agreement, may be considered by the prosecutor in weighing the extent and value of a corporation's cooperation. By the same token, the prosecutor should be wary of attempts to shield corporate officers and employees from liability by a willingness of the corporation to plead guilty.

Another factor to be weighed by the prosecutor is whether the corporation, while purporting to cooperate, has engaged in conduct that impedes the investigation (whether or not rising to the level of criminal obstruction). Examples of such conduct include: overly broad assertions of corporate representation of employees or former employees; inappropriate directions to employees or their counsel, such as directions not to cooperate openly and fully with the investigation including, for example, the direction to decline to be interviewed; making presentations or submissions that contain misleading assertions or omissions; incomplete or delayed production of records; and failure to promptly disclose illegal conduct known to the corporation....

VII. Corporate Compliance Programs

A. General Principle: Compliance programs are established by corporate management to prevent and to detect misconduct and to ensure that corporate activities are conducted in accordance with all applicable criminal and civil laws, regulations, and rules. The Department encourages such corporate self-policing, including voluntary disclosures to the government of any problems that a corporation discovers on its own. However, the existence of a compliance program is not sufficient, in and of itself, to justify not charging a corporation for criminal conduct undertaken by its officers, directors, employees, or agents. Indeed, the commission of such crimes in the face of a compliance program may suggest that the corporate management is not adequately enforcing its program....

B. Comment: [The] critical factors in evaluating any program are whether the program is adequately designed for maximum effectiveness in preventing and detecting wrongdoing by employees and whether corporate management is enforcing the program or is tacitly encouraging or pressuring employees to engage in misconduct to achieve business objectives.

The Department has no formal guidelines for corporate compliance programs. The fundamental questions any prosecutor should ask are: "Is the corporation's compliance program well designed?" and "Does the corporation's compliance program work?" In answering these questions, the prosecutor should consider the comprehensiveness of the compliance program; the extent and pervasiveness of the criminal conduct; the number and level of the corporate employees involved; the seriousness, duration, and frequency of the misconduct; and any remedial actions taken by the corporation, including restitution, disciplinary action, and revisions to corporate compliance programs. Prosecutors should also consider the promptness of any disclosure of wrongdoing to the government and the corporation's cooperation in the government's investigation.

[Prosecutors should determine] whether a corporation's compliance program is merely a "paper program" or whether it was designed and implemented in an effective manner. In addition, prosecutors should determine whether the corporation has provided for a staff sufficient to audit, document, analyze, and utilize the results of the corporation's compliance efforts. In addition, prosecutors should determine whether the corporation's employees are adequately informed about the compliance program and are convinced of the corporation's commitment to it. This will enable the prosecutor to make an informed decision as to whether the corporation has adopted and implemented a truly effective compliance program that, when consistent with other federal law enforcement policies, may result in a decision to charge only the corporation's employees and agents....

VIII. Restitution and Remediation

A. General Principle: Although neither a corporation nor an individual target may avoid prosecution merely by paying a sum of money, a prosecutor may consider the corporation's willingness to make restitution and steps already taken to do so. A prosecutor may also consider other remedial actions, such as implementing an effective corporate compliance program, improving an existing compliance program, and disciplining wrongdoers, in determining whether to charge the corporation.

B. Comment: … A corporation's response to misconduct says much about its willingness to ensure that such misconduct does not recur. Thus, corporations that fully recognize the seriousness of their misconduct and accept responsibility for it should be taking steps to implement the personnel, operational, and organizational changes necessary to establish an awareness among employees that criminal conduct will not be tolerated. Among the factors prosecutors should consider and weigh are whether the corporation appropriately disciplined the wrongdoers and disclosed information concerning their illegal conduct to the government….

XI. Selecting Charges

A. General Principle: Once a prosecutor has decided to charge a corporation, the prosecutor should charge, or should recommend that the grand jury charge, the most serious offense that is consistent with the nature of the defendant's conduct and that is likely to result in a sustainable conviction.

B. Comment: Once the decision to charge is made, the same rules as govern charging natural persons apply….

XII. Plea Agreements with Corporations

A. General Principle: In negotiating plea agreements with corporations, prosecutors should seek a plea to the most serious, readily provable offense charged. In addition, the terms of the plea agreement should contain appropriate provisions to ensure punishment, deterrence, rehabilitation, and compliance with the plea agreement in the corporate context. Although special circumstances may mandate a different conclusion, prosecutors generally should not agree to accept a corporate guilty plea in exchange for non-prosecution or dismissal of charges against individual officers and employees.

B. Comment: Prosecutors may enter into plea agreements with corporations for the same reasons and under the same constraints as apply to plea agreements with natural persons. See U.S. Attorneys' Manual §§9-27.400-500. This means, inter alia, that the corporation should be required to plead guilty to the most serious, readily provable offense charged. As is the case with individuals, the attorney making this determination should do so on the basis of an individualized assessment of the extent to which particular charges fit the specific circumstances of the case, are consistent with the purposes of the federal criminal code, and maximize the impact of federal resources on crime....

A corporation should be made to realize that pleading guilty to criminal charges constitutes an admission of guilt and not merely a resolution of an inconvenient distraction from its business. As with natural persons, pleas should be structured so that the corporation may not later "proclaim lack of culpability or even complete innocence." See U.S. Attorneys' Manual §§9-27.420(b)(4), 9-27.440, 9-27.500. Thus, for instance, there should be placed upon the record a sufficient factual basis for the plea to prevent later corporate assertions of innocence.

A corporate plea agreement should also contain provisions that recognize the nature of the corporate "person" and ensure that the principles of punishment, deterrence, and rehabilitation are met. In the corporate context, punishment and deterrence are generally accomplished by substantial fines, mandatory restitution, and institution of appropriate compliance measures, including, if necessary, continued judicial oversight or the use of special masters. In addition, where the corporation is a government contractor, permanent or temporary debarment may be appropriate. Where the corporation was engaged in government contracting fraud, a prosecutor may not negotiate away an agency's right to debar or to list the corporate defendant....

Page 819.   Add this material at the end of note 3.

See also Flynt v. Commonwealth, 105 S.W.3d 415 (Ky. 2003) (court must have prosecutor's approval to admit defendant into diversion program; separation of powers doctrine requires this reading of statute).

Page 820.   Add this material after note 6.

Problem 13-0. Youth Court

There are approximately 500 "Youth Courts" in the United States. These courts are intended to provide prosecutors, police and schools with an alternative to juvenile courts. Often the "judges" in youth courts are not lawyers; sometimes they are not even adults, but the offender's peers. Does the creation of diversion courts (as opposed to diversion programs) exacerbate, undermine, or sidestep concerns about prosecutorial power and discretion? Consider the Utah statutes reprinted below, which provide for the creation and operation of youth courts. Youth courts had been created on an ad hoc basis prior to the statute's enactment. Youth court jurisdiction in Utah extends to "status offenses" (offenses that would not be a crime if committed by an adult), lesser misdemeanors, infractions, and violation of municipal and county ordinances. Youth court jurisdiction in Utah does not extend to felonies, Class A misdemeanors, controlled substances, any offenses committed as part of gang activity, or any offense where a dangerous weapon is used. Youth courts can be established by non-profit entities.

If you are a district attorney, would you encourage the development and use of Youth Courts in your state? What other kinds of offenders or offenses might be handled with similar group diversion models?

Utah Code Ann. §78-57-103

(1) Youth Court is a diversion program which provides an alternative disposition for cases involving juvenile offenders in which youth participants, under the supervision of an adult coordinator, may serve in various capacities within the courtroom, acting in the role of jurors, lawyers, bailiffs, clerks, and judges.

(a) Youth who appear before youth courts have been identified by law enforcement personnel, school officials, a prosecuting attorney, or the juvenile court as having committed acts which indicate a need for intervention to prevent further development toward juvenile delinquency, but which appear to be acts that can be appropriately addressed outside the juvenile court process.

(b) Youth Courts may only hear cases as provided for in this chapter.

(c) Youth Court is a diversion program and not a court established under the Utah Constitution....

(2) Any person may refer youth to a Youth Court for minor offenses. Once a referral is made, the case shall be screened by an adult coordinator to determine whether it qualifies as a Youth Court case.

(3) Youth Courts have authority over youth:

(a) referred for a minor offense or offenses, or who are granted permission for referral under this chapter;

(b) who, along with a parent, guardian, or legal custodian, voluntarily and in writing, request Youth Court involvement;

(c) who admit having committed the referred offense;

(d) who, along with a parent, guardian, or legal custodian, waive any privilege against self-incrimination and right to a speedy trial; and

(e) who, along with their parent, guardian, or legal custodian, agree to follow the Youth Court disposition of the case....

(5) Youth Courts may exercise authority over youth described in Subsection (4), and over any other offense with the permission of the juvenile court and the prosecuting attorney in the county or district that would have jurisdiction if the matter were referred to juvenile court....

(7) Youth Courts may decline to accept a youth for Youth Court disposition for any reason and may terminate a youth from Youth Court participation at any time.

(8) A youth or the youth's parent, guardian, or custodian may withdraw from the Youth Court process at any time. The Youth Court shall immediately notify the referring source of the withdrawal.

(9) The Youth Court may transfer a case back to the referring source for alternative handling at any time.

(10) Referral of a case of Youth Court may not prohibit the subsequent referral of the case to any court.

Utah Code Ann. §78-57-105

(1) Youth Court dispositional options include:

(a) community service;

(b) participation in law-related educational classes, appropriate counseling, treatment, or other educational programs;

(c) providing periodic reports to the Youth Court;

(d) participating in mentoring programs;

(e) participation by the youth as a member of a Youth Court;

(f) letters of apology;

(g) essays; and

(h) any other disposition considered appropriate by the Youth Court and adult coordinator.

(2) Youth Courts may not impose a term of imprisonment or detention and may not impose fines.

(3) Youth Court dispositions shall be completed within 180 days from the date of referral.

(4) Youth Court dispositions shall be reduced to writing and signed by the youth and a parent, guardian, or legal custodian indicating their acceptance of the disposition terms.

(5) Youth Court shall notify the referring source if a participant fails to successfully complete the Youth Court disposition. The referring source may then take any action it considers appropriate.

2. Encouraging or Mandating Criminal Charges

Page 825.   Add this material at the end of note 3.

See also Robert C. Davis, Barbara E. Smith & Bruce Taylor, Increasing the Proportion of Domestic Violence Arrests that Are Prosecuted: A Natural Experiment in Milwaukee, 2 Criminology & Pub. Pol. 263 (2003).

4. Selection of Charges and System

Page 841.   Add this material at the end of note 1.

See also Johnson v. State, 61 P.3d 1234 (Wyo. 2003) (availability of two criminal statutes for prosecuting same course of conduct did not implicate state or federal constitutional equal protection clauses; life prison term for felony murder and five-year term for felony child abuse were both available).

Chapter 14

Jeopardy and Joinder

A. Double Jeopardy

1. Multiple Sovereigns

Page 888. Add the following material at the end of note 1.

See also United States v. Lara, 541 U.S. 193 (2004) (dual sovereignty doctrine permits federal government to prosecute Native Americans for offenses after they have already been convicted of similar offenses in tribal courts).

2. "Same Offence"

Page 890. Add the following material after note 5.

6. *Double jeopardy in Europe.* The European Union (EU) Convention implementing the Schengen Agreement of 1985 states in Article 54 that "[a] person who has been finally judged by a Contracting Party may not be prosecuted by another Contracting Party for the same offences provided that, where he is sentenced, the sentence has been served or is currently being served or can no longer be carried out under the sentencing laws of the Contracting Party." In two consolidated cases, the European Court of Justice held in 2003 that under this provision a person cannot be prosecuted in another member state even if 1) his case was discontinued by the prosecution after payment of a certain amount

of money (based on a procedure of discontinuation) or 2) the case was settled out-of-court through a monetary payment (also based on national procedure). C-187/01 *Hüseyin Gözütok* and C-385/01 *Klaus Brügge* (Feb. 11, 2003). Article 54 sweeps far more broadly than internal United States double jeopardy barriers. The decision is noteworthy because it equates the discontinuation of procedures through a decision by the public prosecutor with a trial (or other judicial action).

Page 901.   Add the following material after note 6.

7. *Double jeopardy after mistrial.* Typically mistrials do not bar a retrial, even though double jeopardy protections have attached, so long as the retrial was a "manifest necessity." To allow a mistrial to bar subsequent prosecution would invite a moral hazard on the part of attorneys if a case turns against them during trial. A significant minority of state courts view federal constitutional limits on prosecutorial misbehavior as insufficient to protect defendants' double jeopardy rights. See also Commonwealth v. Martorano, 741 A.2d 1221 (Pa. 1999) (expanding scope of double jeopardy in like of "Machiavellian" prosecutorial misconduct in a murder case). See generally George C. Thomas III, Solving the Double Jeopardy Mistrial Riddle, 69 S. Cal. L. Rev. 1551 (1996). While the "prosecutorial misconduct" exception to the "manifest necessity" exception to double jeopardy protections may seem like angels searching for the pin to dance on, the relative frequency of mistrials in complex cases makes the scope of double jeopardy protections in this setting significant.

B. Joinder

1.   Discretionary Joinder and Severance of Offenses

Page 922. Add the following material at the end of note 1.

See also State v. Ramos, 818 A.2d 1228 (N.H. 2003) (adopts ABA Standards for joinder, because former more permissive approach produced inconsistent results; when two or more unrelated offenses are joined for trial, both prosecution and defense have absolute right to severance).

Chapter 15

Discovery and Speedy Trial

A. Discovery

1. Prosecution Disclosures

Page 934.   Replace the last two paragraphs preceding Problem 15-1 with this material.

The criminal discovery rules show remarkable variety from jurisdiction to jurisdiction. Federal Rule of Criminal Procedure 16 and the South Carolina rule reprinted below are typical of the more restrictive rules, which give the defendant access to only a handful of documents and tangible objects before trial. Most states go beyond these limited categories to allow defense discovery of a wider range of prosecution information. The ABA Standards for Criminal Justice have been an influential model for those states moving in the direction of wider discovery. The New Jersey rule reprinted below illustrates the greater scope of documents and other information that some states consider essential to the preparation of a defense.

Use the following problem as a setting for applying the New Jersey and South Carolina rules. Under each of these approaches to criminal discovery, what information gets exchanged, and what types of evidence go unmentioned? How will a plea negotiation or a trial progress if the defense lawyer does not have access to such information before trial? Can defense counsel develop the same information through different avenues?

Page 935.   Replace the first sentence after the bullet points with this material.

Anticipate how the prosecutors might respond if the relevant discovery rules are similar to those in South Carolina.

Page 936.   Replace the North Carolina statute with this material.

South Carolina Rule of Criminal Procedure 5(a)

(1) *Information Subject to Disclosure.*

(A) *Statement of Defendant.* Upon request by a defendant, the prosecution shall permit the defendant to inspect and copy or photograph: any relevant written or recorded statements made by the defendant, or copies thereof, within the possession, custody or control of the prosecution, the existence of which is known, or by the exercise of due diligence may become known, to the attorney for the prosecution; the substance of any oral statement which the prosecution intends to offer in evidence at the trial made by the defendant whether before or after arrest in response to interrogation by any person then known to the defendant to be a prosecution agent.

(B) *Defendant's Prior Record.* Upon request of the defendant, the prosecution shall furnish to the defendant such copy of his prior criminal record, if any, as is within the possession, custody, or control of the prosecution, the existence of which is known, or by the exercise of due diligence may become known, to the attorney for the prosecution.

(C) *Documents and Tangible Objects.* Upon request of the defendant the prosecution shall permit the defendant to inspect and copy books, papers, documents, photographs, tangible objects, buildings or places, or copies or portions thereof, which are within the possession, custody or control of the prosecution, and which are material to the preparation of his defense or are intended for use by the prosecution as evidence in chief at the trial, or were obtained from or belong to the defendant.

(D) *Reports of Examinations and Tests.* Upon request of a defendant the prosecution shall permit the defendant to inspect and copy any results or reports of physical or mental examinations, and of scientific tests or experiments, or copies thereof, which are within the possession, custody, or control of the prosecution, the existence of which is known, or by the exercise of due diligence may become known, to the attorney for the prosecution, and which are material to the preparation of the defense or are intended for use by the prosecution as evidence in chief at the trial.

(2) *Information Not Subject to Disclosure.* Except as provided in paragraphs (A), (B), and (D) of subdivision (a)(1), this rule does not authorize the discovery or inspection of reports, memoranda, or other internal prosecution documents made by the attorney for the prosecution or other prosecution agents in connection with the investigation or prosecution of the case, or of statements made by prosecution witnesses or prospective prosecution witnesses provided that after a prosecution witness has testified on direct examination, the court shall, on motion of the defendant, order the prosecution to produce any statement of the witness in the possession of the prosecution which relates to the subject matter as to which the witness has testified; and provided further that the court may upon a sufficient showing require the production of any statement of any prospective witness prior to the time such witness testifies.

(3) *Time for Disclosure.* The prosecution shall respond to the defendant's request for disclosure no later then thirty days after the request is made, or within such other time as may be ordered by the court.

Page 949.   Add this case before the Hawaii procedure rule.

Delma Banks v. Doug Dretke
540 U.S. 668 (2004)

GINSBURG, J.

Petitioner Delma Banks, Jr., was convicted of capital murder and sentenced to death. Prior to trial, the State advised Banks's attorneys there would be no need to litigate discovery issues, representing: "We will, without the necessity of motions, provide you with all the discovery to which you are entitled."... Ultimately, through discovery and an evidentiary hearing authorized in a federal habeas corpus proceeding, [some] long-suppressed evidence came to light. The District Court granted Banks relief from the death penalty, but the Court of Appeals reversed. In the latter court's judgment, Banks had documented his claims of prosecutorial misconduct too late and in the wrong forum; therefore he did not qualify for federal-court relief. We reverse that judgment. When police or prosecutors conceal significant exculpatory or impeaching material in the State's possession, it is ordinarily incumbent on the State to set the record straight.

I.

On April 14, 1980, police found the corpse of 16-year-old Richard Whitehead in Pocket Park, east of Nash, Texas, a town in the vicinity of Texarkana. A preliminary autopsy revealed that Whitehead had been shot three times. Bowie County Deputy Sheriff Willie Huff, lead investigator of the death, learned from two witnesses that Whitehead had been in the company of petitioner, 21-year-old Delma Banks, Jr., late on the evening of April 11. On April 23, Huff received a call from a confidential informant reporting that "Banks was coming to Dallas to meet an individual and get a weapon." That evening, Huff and other officers followed Banks to South Dallas, where Banks visited a residence. Police stopped Banks's vehicle en route from Dallas, found a handgun in the car, and arrested the car's occupants. Returning to the Dallas residence Banks had visited, Huff encountered and interviewed Charles Cook and recovered a second gun, a weapon Cook said Banks had left with him several days earlier. Tests later identified the second gun as the Whitehead murder weapon.

In a May 21, 1980, pretrial hearing, Banks's counsel sought information from Huff concerning the confidential informant who told Huff that Banks would be driving to Dallas. Huff was unresponsive. Any information that might reveal the identity of the informant, the prosecution urged, was privileged. The trial court sustained the State's objection. Several weeks later, in a July 7, 1980, letter, the prosecution advised Banks's counsel that "[the State] will, without necessity of motions provide you with all discovery to which you are entitled."

The guilt phase of Banks's trial spanned two days in September 1980. Witnesses testified to seeing Banks and Whitehead together on April 11 in Whitehead's green Mustang, and to hearing gunshots in Pocket Park at 4 A.M. on April 12. Charles Cook testified that Banks arrived in Dallas in a green Mustang at about 8:15 A.M. on April 12, and stayed with Cook until April 14. Cook gave the following account of Banks's visit. On the morning of his arrival, Banks had blood on his leg and told Cook "he [had] got into it on the highway with a white boy." That night, Banks confessed to having "kill[ed] the white boy for the hell of it and take[n] his car and come to Dallas." During their ensuing conversation, Cook first noticed that "[Banks] had a pistol." Two days later, Banks left Dallas by bus. The next day, Cook abandoned the Mustang in West Dallas and sold Banks's gun to a neighbor. Cook further testified that, shortly before the police arrived at his residence to question him, Banks had revisited him and requested the gun....

In addition to Cook, Robert Farr was a key witness for the prosecution. Corroborating parts of Cook's account, Farr testified to traveling to Dallas with Banks to retrieve Banks's gun. On cross-examination, defense counsel asked Farr whether he had "ever taken any money from some police officers," or "given any police officers a statement." Farr answered no to both questions; he asserted emphatically that police officers had not promised him anything and that he had "talked to no one about this case" until a few days before trial. These answers were untrue, but the State did not correct them. Farr was the paid informant who told Deputy Sheriff Huff that Banks would travel to Dallas in search of a gun. In a 1999 affidavit, Farr explained:

> I assumed that if I did not help Huff with his investigation of Delma that he would have me arrested for drug charges. That's why I agreed to help Huff. I was afraid that if I didn't help him, I would be arrested.... Willie Huff asked me to help him find Delma's gun. I told Huff that he would have to pay me money right away for my help on the case. I think altogether he gave me about $200 for helping him. He paid me some of the money before I set Delma up. He paid me the rest after Delma was arrested and charged with murder.... In order to help Willie Huff, I had to set Delma up. I told Delma that I wanted to rob a pharmacy to get drugs and that I needed his gun to do it. I did not really plan to commit a robbery but I told Delma this so that he would give me his gun.... I convinced Delma to drive to Dallas with me to get the gun.

The defense presented no evidence. Banks was convicted of murder committed in the course of a robbery [and the] penalty phase ran its course the next day. Governed by the Texas statutory capital murder scheme applicable in 1980, the jury decided Banks's sentence by answering three "special issues."... The critical question at the penalty phase in Banks's case was: "Do you find from the evidence beyond a reasonable doubt that there is a probability that the defendant, Delma Banks, Jr., would commit criminal acts of violence that would constitute a continuing threat to society?"

On this question, the State offered two witnesses, Vetrano Jefferson and Robert Farr. Jefferson testified that, in early April 1980, Banks had struck him across the face with a gun and threatened to kill him. Farr's testimony focused once more on the trip to Dallas to fetch Banks's gun. The gun was needed, Farr asserted, because "we [Farr and Banks] were going to pull some robberies." According to Farr, Banks "said he would take care of it" if "there was any trouble during these burglaries." When the prosecution asked: "How did [Banks] say he would take care of it?", Farr responded: "[Banks] didn't go into any specifics, but he said it would be taken care of."

On cross-examination, defense counsel twice asked whether Farr had told Deputy Sheriff Huff of the Dallas trip. The State remained silent as Farr twice perjuriously testified: "No, I did not." Banks's counsel also inquired whether Farr had previously attempted to obtain prescription drugs by fraud, and, "up tight over that," would "testify to anything anybody wanted to hear." Farr first responded: "Can you prove it?" Instructed by the court to answer defense counsel's questions, Farr again said: "No, I did not."

Two defense witnesses impeached Farr, but were, in turn, impeached themselves. James Kelley testified to Farr's attempts to obtain drugs by fraud; the prosecution impeached Kelley by eliciting his close relationship to Banks's girlfriend. Later, Kelley admitted to being drunk while on the stand. Former Arkansas police officer Gary Owen testified that Farr, as a police informant in Arkansas, had given false information; the prosecution impeached Owen by bringing out his pending application for employment by defense counsel's private investigator....

Urging Farr's credibility, the prosecution called the jury's attention to Farr's admission, at trial, that he used narcotics. Just as Farr had been truthful about his drug use, the prosecution suggested, he was also "open and honest with [the jury] in every way" in his penalty-phase testimony. Farr's testimony, the prosecution emphasized, was "of the utmost significance" because it showed "[Banks] is a danger to friends and strangers, alike." Banks's effort to impeach Farr was ineffective, the prosecution further urged, because defense witness "Kelley knew nothing about the murder," and defense witness Owen "wished to please his future employers."

The jury answered yes to the three special issues, and the judge sentenced Banks to death. The Texas Court of Criminal Appeals denied Banks's direct appeal. [A] postconviction motion, filed January 13, 1992, presented questions later advanced in federal court and reiterated in the petition now before us. Banks alleged "upon information and belief" that "the prosecution knowingly failed to turn over exculpatory evidence as required by Brady v. Maryland, 373 U.S. 83 (1963); the withheld evidence, Banks asserted, "would have revealed Robert Farr as a police informant and Mr. Banks' arrest as a set-up."...

The State's reply to Banks's pleading, filed October 6, 1992, "denied each and every allegation of fact made by Banks except those supported by official court records and those specifically admitted." "Nothing was kept secret from the defense," the State represented. In February and July 1993 orders, the state postconviction court rejected Banks's claims....

On March 7, 1996, Banks filed the instant petition for a writ of habeas corpus in the United States District Court for the Eastern District of Texas. He alleged multiple violations of his federal constitutional rights. Relevant here, Banks reasserted that the State had withheld material exculpatory evidence "revealing Robert Farr as a police informant and Mr. Banks' arrest as a set-up."...

Banks renewed his discovery and evidentiary hearing requests in February 1999. This time, he proffered affidavits from both Farr and Cook to back up his claims that, as to each of these two key witnesses, the prosecution had wrongly withheld crucial exculpatory and impeaching evidence. Farr's affidavit affirmed that Farr had "set Delma up" by proposing the drive to Dallas and informing Deputy Sheriff Huff of the trip. Accounting for his unavailability earlier, Farr stated that less than a year after the Banks trial, he had left Texarkana, first for Oklahoma, then for California, because his police-informant work endangered his life. Cook recalled that in preparation for his Banks trial testimony, he had participated in "three or four ... practice sessions" at which prosecutors told him to testify "as they wanted him to, and that he would spend the rest of his life in prison if he did not."...

One item lodged in the District Attorney's files, turned over to Banks pursuant to the Magistrate Judge's disclosure order, was a 74-

page transcript of a Cook interrogation.... The transcript revealed that the State's representatives had closely rehearsed Cook's testimony.... Testifying at the evidentiary hearing, Deputy Sheriff Huff acknowledged, for the first time, that Farr was an informant and that he had been paid $200 for his involvement in the case.

In a May 11, 2000, report and recommendation, the Magistrate Judge recommended a writ of habeas corpus with respect to Banks's death sentence, but not his conviction. The District Court adopted the Magistrate Judge's report.... In an August 20, 2003, unpublished *per curiam* opinion, the Court of Appeals for the Fifth Circuit reversed the judgment of the District Court to the extent that it granted relief.... The Court of Appeals expressed no doubt that the prosecution had suppressed, prior to the federal habeas proceeding, Farr's informant status and his part in the fateful trip to Dallas. But Banks was not appropriately diligent in pursuing his state-court application, the Court of Appeals maintained. In the Fifth Circuit's view, Banks should have at that time attempted to locate Farr and question him; similarly, he should have asked to interview Deputy Sheriff Huff and other officers involved in investigating the crime. If such efforts had proved unavailing, the Court of Appeals suggested, Banks might have applied to the state court for assistance. Banks's lack of diligence in pursuing his 1992 state-court plea, the Court of Appeals concluded, rendered the evidence uncovered in the federal habeas proceeding procedurally barred....

II. A.

... We set out in Strickler v. Greene, 527 U.S. 263 (1999), the three components or essential elements of a *Brady* prosecutorial misconduct claim: "The evidence at issue must be favorable to the accused, either because it is exculpatory, or because it is impeaching; that evidence must have been suppressed by the State, either willfully or inadvertently; and prejudice must have ensued."... As to the first *Brady* component (evidence favorable to the accused), beyond genuine debate, the suppressed evidence relevant here, Farr's paid informant status, qualifies as evidence advantageous to Banks.... Thus, if Banks succeeds in demonstrating [the second and third components, he] succeed in establishing the elements of his Farr *Brady* death penalty due process claim.

B.

Our determination as to "cause" for Banks's failure to develop the facts in state-court proceedings is informed by *Strickler*. In that case, Virginia prosecutors told the petitioner, prior to trial, that "the prosecutor's files were open to the petitioner's counsel," thus "there was no need for a formal *Brady* motion." The prosecution file given to the *Strickler* petitioner, however, did not include several documents prepared by an "important" prosecution witness, recounting the witness' initial difficulty recalling the events to which she testified at the petitioner's trial. Those absent-from-the- file documents could have been used to impeach the witness. In state-court postconviction proceedings, the *Strickler* petitioner had unsuccessfully urged ineffective assistance of trial counsel based on counsel's failure to move, pretrial, for *Brady* material. Answering that plea, the State asserted that a *Brady* motion would have been superfluous, for the prosecution had maintained an open file policy pursuant to which it had disclosed all *Brady* material.

This Court determined that in the federal habeas proceedings, the *Strickler* petitioner had shown cause for his failure to raise a *Brady* claim in state court. Three factors accounted for that determination:

> (a) the prosecution withheld exculpatory evidence; (b) petitioner reasonably relied on the prosecution's open file policy as fulfilling the prosecution's duty to disclose such evidence; and (c) the [State] confirmed petitioner's reliance on the open file policy by asserting during state habeas proceedings that petitioner had already received everything known to the government.

This case is congruent with *Strickler* in all three respects. First, the State knew of, but kept back, Farr's arrangement with Deputy Sheriff Huff. Second, the State asserted, on the eve of trial, that it would disclose all Brady material. As *Strickler* instructs, Banks cannot be faulted for relying on that representation. Third, in his January 1992 state habeas application, Banks asserted that Farr was a police informant and Banks's arrest, "a set-up." In its answer, the State denied Banks's assertion. The State thereby "confirmed" Banks's reliance on the prosecution's representation that it had fully disclosed all relevant information its file contained. In short, because the State persisted in hiding Farr's informant status and misleadingly represented that it had complied in full with its *Brady* disclosure obligations, Banks had cause for failing to investigate, in state postconviction proceedings, Farr's connections to Deputy Sheriff Huff....

Banks's case is stronger than was the petitioner's in *Strickler* in a notable respect. As a prosecution witness in the guilt and penalty phases of Banks's trial, Farr repeatedly misrepresented his dealings with police; each time Farr responded untruthfully, the prosecution allowed his testimony to stand uncorrected. Farr denied taking money from or being promised anything by police officers; he twice denied speaking with police officers, and twice denied informing Deputy Sheriff Huff about Banks's trip to Dallas. It has long been established that the prosecution's "deliberate deception of a court and jurors by the presentation of known false evidence is incompatible with rudimentary demands of justice." Giglio v. United States, 405 U.S. 150 (1972). If it was reasonable for Banks to rely on the prosecution's full disclosure representation, it was also appropriate for Banks to assume that his prosecutors would not stoop to improper litigation conduct to advance prospects for gaining a conviction.

[The State attempts to distinguish *Strickler* by suggesting] that Banks's failure, during state postconviction proceedings, to "attempt to locate Farr and ascertain his true status," or to "interview the investigating officers, such as Deputy Huff, to ascertain Farr's status," undermines a finding of cause.... In the State's view, [the issue here] revolves around Banks's conduct, particularly his lack of appropriate diligence in pursuing the Farr *Brady* claim before resorting to federal court.

We rejected a similar argument in *Strickler*. There, the State contended that examination of a witness' trial testimony, alongside a letter the witness published in a local newspaper, should have alerted the petitioner to the existence of undisclosed interviews of the witness by the police. We found this contention insubstantial. In light of the State's open file policy, we noted, "it is especially unlikely that counsel would have suspected that additional impeaching evidence was being withheld." Our decisions lend no support to the notion that defendants must scavenge for hints of undisclosed *Brady* material when the prosecution represents that all such material has been disclosed. As we observed in *Strickler*, defense counsel has no "procedural obligation to assert constitutional error on the basis of mere suspicion that some prosecutorial misstep may have occurred."

[A rule] declaring "prosecutor may hide, defendant must seek," is not tenable in a system constitutionally bound to accord defendants due process. Ordinarily, we presume that public officials have properly discharged their official duties. We have several times underscored the special role played by the American prosecutor in the search for truth in criminal trials. Courts, litigants, and juries properly anticipate that obligations to refrain from improper methods to secure a conviction "plainly resting upon the prosecuting attorney, will be faithfully observed." Prosecutors' dishonest conduct or unwarranted concealment should attract no judicial approbation....

In summary, Banks's prosecutors represented at trial and in state postconviction proceedings that the State had held nothing back. Moreover, in state postconviction court, the State's pleading denied that Farr was an informant. It was not incumbent on Banks to prove these representations false; rather, Banks was entitled to treat the prosecutor's submissions as truthful. Accordingly, Banks has shown cause for failing to present evidence in state court capable of substantiating his Farr *Brady* claim.

C.

... Kyles v. Whitley, 514 U.S. 419 (1995), instructed that the materiality standard for *Brady* claims is met when "the favorable evidence could reasonably be taken to put the whole case in such a different light as to undermine confidence in the verdict." A defendant need not demonstrate that after discounting the inculpatory evidence in light of the undisclosed evidence, there would not have been enough left to convict. In short, Banks must show a "reasonable probability of a different result."

As the State acknowledged at oral argument, Farr was "paid for a critical role in the scenario that led to the indictment." Farr's declaration, presented to the federal habeas court, asserts that Farr, not Banks, initiated the proposal to obtain a gun to facilitate the commission of robberies. Had Farr not instigated, upon Deputy Sheriff Huff's request, the Dallas excursion to fetch Banks's gun, the prosecution would have had slim, if any, evidence that Banks planned to "continue" committing violent acts. Farr's admission of his instigating role, moreover, would have dampened the prosecution's zeal in urging the jury to bear in mind Banks's "planning and acquisition of a gun to commit robbery," or

Banks's "planned violence."

Because Banks had no criminal record, Farr's testimony about Banks's propensity to commit violent acts was crucial to the prosecution. Without that testimony, the State could not have underscored, as it did three times in the penalty phase, that Banks would use the gun fetched in Dallas to "take care" of trouble arising during the robberies. The stress placed by the prosecution on this part of Farr's testimony, uncorroborated by any other witness, belies the State's suggestion that "Farr's testimony was adequately corroborated." The prosecution's penalty-phase summation, moreover, left no doubt about the importance the State attached to Farr's testimony. What Farr told the jury, the prosecution urged, was "of the utmost significance" to show "[Banks] is a danger to friends and strangers, alike."...

Farr's trial testimony, critical at the penalty phase, was cast in large doubt by the declaration Banks ultimately obtained from Farr and introduced in the federal habeas proceeding. In the guilt phase of Banks's trial, Farr had acknowledged his narcotics use. In the penalty phase, Banks's counsel asked Farr if, "drawn up tight over" previous drug-related activity, he would "testify to anything anybody wanted to hear"; Farr denied this. Farr's declaration supporting Banks's federal habeas petition, however, vividly contradicts that denial: "I assumed that if I did not help [Huff] he would have me arrested for drug charges." Had jurors known of Farr's continuing interest in obtaining Deputy Sheriff Huff's favor, in addition to his receipt of funds to "set Banks up," they might well have distrusted Farr's testimony, and, insofar as it was uncorroborated, disregarded it.

The jury, moreover, did not benefit from customary, truth-promoting precautions that generally accompany the testimony of informants. This Court has long recognized the "serious questions of credibility" informers pose. We have therefore allowed defendants "broad latitude to probe [informants'] credibility by cross-examination" and have counseled submission of the credibility issue to the jury "with careful instructions."

The State argues that "Farr was heavily impeached at trial," rendering his informant status "merely cumulative." The record suggests otherwise. Neither witness called to impeach Farr gave evidence directly relevant to Farr's part in Banks's trial. The impeaching witnesses, Kelley and Owen, moreover, were themselves impeached, as the prosecution stressed on summation. Further, the prosecution turned to its advantage remaining impeachment evidence concerning Farr's drug use. On summation, the prosecution suggested that Farr's admission "that he used dope, that he shot," demonstrated that Farr had been "open and honest with [the jury] in every way."

At least as to the penalty phase, in sum, one can hardly be confident that Banks received a fair trial, given the jury's ignorance of Farr's true role in the investigation and trial of the case. On the record before us, one could not plausibly deny the existence of the requisite "reasonable probability of a different result" had the suppressed information been disclosed to the defense. Accordingly, as to the suppression of Farr's informant status and its bearing on the reliability of the jury's verdict regarding punishment, all three elements of a *Brady* claim are satisfied.

[The Court also held that the State's failure to disclose a transcript showing extensive pre-trial preparation of a prosecution witness (Cook) created another potential ground for habeas corpus relief that the Fifth Circuit improperly refused to consider.]

THOMAS, J., concurring in part and dissenting in part.

… Although I find it to be a very close question, I cannot conclude that the nondisclosure of Farr's informant status was prejudicial under Kyles v. Whitley and *Brady*.

To demonstrate prejudice, Banks must show that the favorable evidence could reasonably be taken to put the whole case in such a different light as to undermine confidence in the verdict. The undisclosed material consisted of evidence that Willie Huff asked Farr to help him find Banks' gun," and that Huff gave Farr about $200 for helping him…. I do not believe that there is a reasonable probability that the jury [after hearing this evidence] would have altered its finding. The jury was presented with … evidence showing that Banks, apparently on a whim, executed Whitehead simply to get his car. The jury was also presented with evidence, in the form of Banks' own testimony, that he was willing to abet another individual in obtaining a gun, with the full knowledge that this gun would aid future armed robberies…. The jury also heard testimony that Banks had violently pistol-whipped and threatened to kill his brother-in-law one week before the murder. Banks now claims that this evidence should be discounted because his trial counsel failed to uncover that the brother-in-law was "responsible for the fight." But ... Banks' response was vastly disproportional to his brother-in-law's actions.

In sum, the jury knew that Banks had murdered a 16-year-old on a whim, had violently attacked and threatened a relative shortly before the murder, and was willing to assist another individual in committing armed robberies by providing the "means and possible death weapon" for these robberies. Even if the jury were to discredit entirely Farr's testimony that Banks was planning more robberies, in all likelihood the jury still would have found "beyond a reasonable doubt" that there was "a probability that Banks would commit criminal acts of violence that would constitute a continuing threat to society." The randomness and wantonness of the murder would perhaps, standing alone, mandate such a finding. Accordingly, I cannot find that the nondisclosure of the evidence was prejudicial.

Because Banks cannot show prejudice, I do not resolve whether he has cause to excuse his failure to present his Farr *Brady* evidence in state court. But there are reasons to doubt the Court's conclusion that Banks can show cause. For instance, the Court concludes that this case is congruent with *Strickler*, relying in part on the State's general denial of all of Banks' factual allegations contained in his January 1992 state habeas application. But, in the relevant state postconviction proceeding in *Strickler*, the State alleged that the petitioner had already received "*everything* known to the government," a statement that federal habeas proceedings established was clearly not true. In the instant case, the particular allegation raised in Banks' state habeas application and denied by the State was that "the prosecution *knowingly* failed to turn over exculpatory evidence *as required by Brady v. Maryland*" (emphasis added). The State, then, could have been denying only that the prosecution *knowingly* failed to turn over the evidence (there is, incidentally, very little evidence in the record tending to show that any prosecutor had actual knowledge of Huff's payment to Farr). Or, the State could have been denying only that it had failed to turn over evidence *in violation of* Brady, *i.e.,* that any evidence the prosecution did not turn over was not material (a position advanced by the State throughout the federal habeas process). Either way, *Strickler* does not clearly control, and the Court's reliance on it is less than compelling.... I therefore conclude that the Court of Appeals did not err when it denied relief to Banks based on his Farr *Brady* claim....

Page 951.   Add this material at the end of note 2.

In Harrington v. State, 659 N.W.2d 509 (Iowa 2003), the court, in a decision twenty years after Harrington's conviction for murder, held that prosecutors had a duty to obtain and disclose police reports focused on a different murder suspect than the defendant, and that those reports were material.

Page 951. Replace note 4 with this material.

4. Brady *and plea bargaining.* While *Brady* information might affect the outcome at trial, it could also affect the negotiating strength of the defendant during plea bargaining. Given the dominance of guilty pleas and plea bargaining in American criminal justice, it is critical to know whether a defendant can challenge the validity of a guilty plea if she discovers later that the prosecutor failed to disclose *Brady* material. A few states have statutes or rules that explicitly link the prosecutor's disclosure obligation to a defendant's not-guilty plea at arraignment. See N.H. Super. Ct. R. 98 (prosecutor to disclose exculpatory material within 30 days from a not-guilty plea). The U.S. Supreme Court addressed one aspect of this question in United States v. Ruiz, 536 U.S. 622 (2002), stating that "the Constitution does not require the Government to disclose material impeachment evidence prior to entering a plea agreement with a criminal defendant." Ruiz was challenging a provision in a proposed plea agreement that required her to waive certain *Brady* rights as part of the arrangement, but the Court's statement appears broad enough to reach guilty pleas reached without any explicit waiver of *Brady* rights in a plea agreement. Note that the ruling extends to impeachment material, but not to exculpatory material.

State courts are split over whether *Brady* violations by the prosecution invalidate a defendant's guilty plea. See Gibson v. State, 514 S.E.2d 320, 324 (S.C. 1999) (*Brady* violation automatically renders plea invalid); State v. Harris, 680 N.W.2d 737, 741 (Wis. 2004) (imposes disclosure at guilty plea stage as matter of state law); State v. Martin, 495 A.2d 1028 (Conn. 1985) (*Brady* claim barred by guilty plea). See generally, Corinna Barrett Lain, Accuracy Where It Matters: Brady v. Maryland in the Plea Bargaining Context, 80 Wash. U. L.Q. 1

(2002); Kevin C. McMunigal, Disclosure and Accuracy in the Guilty Plea Process, 40 Hastings L.J. 957 (1989).

Page 953. Add this material to the end of note 6.

In Illinois v. Fisher, 540 U.S. 544 (2004), the Supreme Court closed a loophole in Arizona v. Youngblood. The state court had ruled that the bad faith requirement does not apply when the evidence was the subject of a defense discovery motion. The Supreme Court, however, distinguished between exculpatory information and information that is merely useful to the defense. Exculpatory information must be turned over the defense, even without any showing of bad faith, but the defense must prove bad faith in the state's failure to preserve evidence when information requested by defense motion is merely useful to the defense.

B. Speedy Trial Preparation

2.   Speedy Trial After Accusation

Page 985. Add this material at the end of note 2.

See also State v. Spivey, 579 S.E.2d 251 (N.C. 2003) (delay of over four years in starting murder trial acceptable under *Barker*; reasons for delay included numerous homicide cases on docket, courthouse renovations).

Page 992. Add this material at the end of note 4.

See also Bulgin v. State, 2005 WL 1176056 (Fla., May 19, 2005) (if state officials do not obtain express waiver of speedy trial rights, days that defendant spend cooperating with investigators must count against statutory limit of 175 days to begin trial).

Chapter 16

Pleas and Bargains

B. Categorical Restrictions on Bargaining

2. Judicial Rules

Page 1014. Insert this material at the end of note 3.

See also State v. Rivera, 109 P.3d 83 (Ariz. 2005) (prosecutor may enter plea agreement that requires defendant to avow accuracy of prior statements to police and to provide truthful testimony in future, but may not enter agreement that requires defendant to testify in future consistently with prior statements).

3. Prosecutorial Guidelines

Page 1025. Insert this material before the notes.

In 2003 Congress enacted the USA PROTECT Act, Public Law 108-21, 117 Stat. 650. The Act changed several features of federal sentencing law, and directed the Attorney General to take steps to discourage "downward departures" from the sentences prescribed by the federal guidelines. The Attorney General promulgated the following policy in response to the PROTECT Act.

Department Policy Concerning Charging Criminal Offenses, Disposition of Charges, and Sentencing
Attorney General John Ashcroft, September 22, 2003

The passage of the Sentencing Reform Act of 1984 was a watershed event in the pursuit of fairness and consistency in the federal criminal justice system.... In contrast to the prior sentencing system—which was characterized by largely unfettered discretion, and by seemingly severe sentences that were often sharply reduced by parole—the Sentencing Reform Act and the Sentencing Guidelines sought to accomplish several important objectives: (1) to ensure honesty and transparency in federal sentencing; (2) to guide sentencing discretion, so as to narrow the disparity between sentences for similar offenses committed by similar offenders; and (3) to provide for the imposition of appropriately different punishments for offenses of differing severity.

The fairness Congress sought to achieve by the Sentencing Reform Act and the PROTECT Act can be attained only if there are fair and reasonably consistent policies with respect to the Department's decisions concerning what charges to bring and how cases should be disposed. Just as the sentence a defendant receives should not depend upon which particular judge presides over the case, so too the charges a defendant faces should not depend upon the particular prosecutor assigned to handle the case....

I. Department Policy Concerning Charging and Prosecution of Criminal Offenses

A. General Duty to Charge and to Pursue the Most Serious, Readily Provable Offense in All Federal Prosecutions

It is the policy of the Department of Justice that, in all federal criminal cases, federal prosecutors must charge and pursue the most serious, readily provable offense or offenses that are supported by the facts of the case, except as authorized by an Assistant Attorney General, United States Attorney, or designated supervisory attorney in the limited circumstances described below. The most serious offense or offenses are those that generate the most substantial sentence under the Sentencing Guidelines, unless a mandatory minimum sentence or count requiring a consecutive sentence would generate a longer sentence. A charge is not "readily provable" if the prosecutor has a good faith doubt, for legal or evidentiary reasons, as to the Government's ability readily to prove a charge at trial. Thus, charges should not be filed simply to exert leverage to induce a plea. Once filed, the most serious readily provable charges may not be dismissed except to the extent permitted in Section B.

B. Limited Exceptions

The basic policy set forth above requires federal prosecutors to charge and to pursue all charges that are determined to be readily provable and that, under the applicable statutes and Sentencing Guidelines, would yield the most substantial sentence. There are, however, certain limited exceptions to this requirement:

1.   *Sentence would not be affected.* First, if the applicable guideline range from which a sentence may be imposed would be unaffected, prosecutors may decline to charge or to pursue readily provable charges. However, if the most serious readily provable charge involves a mandatory minimum sentence that exceeds the applicable guideline range, counts essential to establish a mandatory minimum sentence must be charged and may not be dismissed, except to the extent provided elsewhere below.

2.   *"Fast-track" programs.* With the passage of the PROTECT Act, Congress recognized the importance of early disposition or "fast-track" programs [to handle the high volume of cases (particularly immigration cases) in some districts. As a matter of Department policy, Attorney General authorization is necessary for] any fast-track program that relies on "charge bargaining" — *i.e.*, an expedited disposition program whereby the Government agrees to charge less than the most serious, readily provable offense. Such programs are intended to be exceptional and will be authorized only when clearly warranted by local conditions within a district....

3.   *Post-indictment reassessment.* In cases where post-indictment circumstances cause a prosecutor to determine in good faith that the most serious offense is not readily provable, because of a change in the evidence or some other justifiable reason (*e.g.*, the unavailability of a witness or the need to protect the identity of a witness until he testifies against a more significant defendant), the prosecutor may dismiss the charge(s) with the written or otherwise documented approval of an

Assistant Attorney General, United States Attorney, or designated supervisory attorney.

4. *Substantial assistance.* The preferred means to recognize a defendant's substantial assistance in the investigation or prosecution of another person is to charge the most serious readily provable offense and then to file an appropriate motion or motions under U.S.S.G. §5K1.1, 18 U.S.C. §3553(e), or Federal Rule of Criminal Rule of Procedure 35(b). However, in rare circumstances, where necessary to obtain substantial assistance in an important investigation or prosecution, and with the written or otherwise documented approval of an Assistant Attorney General, United States Attorney, or designated supervisory attorney, a federal prosecutor may decline to charge or to pursue a readily provable charge as part of plea agreement that properly reflects the substantial assistance provided by the defendant in the investigation or prosecution of another person.

5. *Statutory enhancements.* The use of statutory enhancements is strongly encouraged, and federal prosecutors must therefore take affirmative steps to ensure that the increased penalties resulting from specific statutory enhancements [such as use of a weapon] are sought in all appropriate cases. ... In many cases, however, the filing of such enhancements will mean that the statutory sentence exceeds the applicable Sentencing Guidelines range, thereby ensuring that the defendant will not receive any credit for acceptance of responsibility and will have no incentive to plead guilty. Requiring the pursuit of such enhancements to trial in every case could therefore have a significant effect on the allocation of prosecutorial resources within a given district. Accordingly, an Assistant Attorney General, United States Attorney, or designated supervisory attorney may authorize a prosecutor to forego the filing of a statutory enhancement, but *only* in the context of a negotiated plea agreement....

6. *Other Exceptional Circumstances.* Prosecutors may decline to pursue or may dismiss readily provable charges in other exceptional circumstances with the written or otherwise documented approval of an Assistant Attorney General, United States Attorney, or designated supervisory attorney. This exception recognizes that the aims of the Sentencing Reform Act must be sought without ignoring the practical limitations of the federal criminal justice system. For example, a case-specific approval to dismiss charges in a particular case might be given

because the United States Attorney's Office is particularly over-burdened, the duration of the trial would be exceptionally long, and proceeding to trial would significantly reduce the total number of cases disposed of by the office. However, such case-by-case exceptions should be rare; otherwise the goals of fairness and equity will be jeopardized.

II. Department Policy Concerning Plea Agreements

A. Written Plea Agreements

In felony cases, plea agreements should be in writing. If the plea agreement is not in writing, the agreement should be formally stated on the record.... The PROTECT Act specifically requires the court, after sentencing, to provide a copy of the plea agreement to the Sentencing Commission. Written plea agreements also avoid misunderstandings with regard to the terms that the parties have accepted.

B. Honesty in Sentencing

As set forth in my July 28, 2003 Memorandum on "Department Policies and Procedures Concerning Sentencing Recommendations and Sentencing Appeals," Department of Justice policy requires honesty in sentencing, both with respect to the facts and the law....

This policy applies fully to sentencing recommendations that are contained in plea agreements. [F]ederal prosecutors may not "fact bargain," or be party to any plea agreement that results in the sentencing court having less than a full understanding of all readily provable facts relevant to sentencing.

[It] remains Department policy that the sentencing court should be informed if a plea agreement involves a "charge bargain." Accordingly, a negotiated plea that uses any of the options described in Section I(B)(2), (4), (5), or (6) must be made known to the court at the time of the plea hearing and at the time of sentencing, *i.e.*, the court must be informed that a more serious, readily provable offense was not charged or that an applicable statutory enhancement was not filed.

C. Charge Bargaining

Charges may be declined or dismissed pursuant to a plea agreement only to the extent consistent with the principles set forth in Section I of this Memorandum.

D. Sentence Bargaining

There are only two types of permissible sentence bargains.

1.   *Sentences within the Sentencing Guidelines range.* Federal prosecutors may enter into a plea agreement for a sentence that is within the specified guideline range. For example, when the Sentencing Guidelines range is 18-24 months, a prosecutor may agree to recommend a sentence of 18 or 20 months rather than to argue for a sentence at the top of the range. Similarly, a prosecutor may agree to recommend a downward adjustment for acceptance of responsibility under U.S.S.G. §3E1.1 if the prosecutor concludes in good faith that the defendant is entitled to the adjustment.

2.   *Departures.* In passing the PROTECT Act, Congress has made clear its view that there have been too many downward departures from the Sentencing Guidelines, and it has instructed the Commission to take measures "to ensure that the incidence of downward departures [is] substantially reduced." The Department has a duty to ensure that the circumstances in which it will request or accede to downward departures in the future are properly circumscribed.

Accordingly, federal prosecutors must not request or accede to a downward departure except in the limited circumstances specified in this memorandum and with authorization from an Assistant Attorney General, United States Attorney, or designated supervisory attorney....

In sum, plea bargaining must honestly reflect the totality and seriousness of the defendant's conduct, and any departure must be accomplished through the application of appropriate Sentencing Guideline provisions.

Federal criminal law and procedure apply equally throughout the United States. As the sole federal prosecuting entity, the Department of Justice has a unique obligation to ensure that all federal criminal cases are prosecuted according to the same standards. Fundamental fairness requires that all defendants prosecuted in the federal criminal justice system be subject to the same standards and treated in a consistent manner.

C. *Validity of Individual Plea Bargains*

1. Lack of Knowledge

Page 1043. Insert this material before the notes.

Iowa v. Felipe Edgardo Tovar
541 U.S. 77 (2004)

GINSBURG, J.

The Sixth Amendment safeguards to an accused who faces incarceration the right to counsel at all critical stages of the criminal process. The entry of a guilty plea, whether to a misdemeanor or a felony charge, ranks as a "critical stage" at which the right to counsel adheres. Waiver of the right to counsel, as of constitutional rights in the criminal process generally, must be a knowing, intelligent act done with sufficient awareness of the relevant circumstances. This case concerns the extent to which a trial judge, before accepting a guilty plea from an uncounseled defendant, must elaborate on the right to representation....

On November 2, 1996, respondent Felipe Edgardo Tovar, then a 21-year-old college student, was arrested in Ames, Iowa, for operating a motor vehicle while under the influence of alcohol (OWI). An intoxilyzer test administered the night of Tovar's arrest showed he had a blood alcohol level of 0.194. The arresting officer informed Tovar of his rights under Miranda v. Arizona, 384 U.S. 436 (1966). Tovar signed a form stating that he waived those rights and agreed to answer questions.

Some hours after his arrest, Tovar appeared before a judge in the Iowa District Court for Story County. The judge indicated on the Initial Appearance form that Tovar appeared without counsel and waived application for court- appointed counsel. The judge also marked on the form's checklist that Tovar was "informed of the charge and his ... rights and received a copy of the Complaint." ...

At the November 18 arraignment,[2] the court's inquiries of Tovar

---

[2] Tovar appeared in court along with four other individuals charged with misdemeanor offenses. The presiding judge proposed to conduct the plea proceeding for the five cases jointly, and each of the individuals indicated he did not object to that course of action.

began: "Mr. Tovar appears without counsel and I see, Mr. Tovar, that you waived application for a court appointed attorney. Did you want to represent yourself at today's hearing?" Tovar replied: "Yes, sir." The court soon after asked: "How did you wish to plead?" Tovar answered: "Guilty." Tovar affirmed that he had not been promised anything or threatened in any way to induce him to plead guilty.

Conducting the guilty plea colloquy required by the Iowa Rules of Criminal Procedure, the court explained that, if Tovar pleaded not guilty, he would be entitled to a speedy and public trial by jury, and would have the right to be represented at that trial by an attorney, who "could help [Tovar] select a jury, question and cross-examine the State's witnesses, present evidence, if any, in [his] behalf, and make arguments to the judge and jury on [his] behalf." By pleading guilty, the court cautioned, not only would Tovar give up his right to a trial of any kind on the charge against him, he would give up his right to be represented by an attorney at that trial. The court further advised Tovar that, if he entered a guilty plea, he would relinquish the right to remain silent at trial, the right to the presumption of innocence, and the right to subpoena witnesses and compel their testimony.

Turning to the particular offense with which Tovar had been charged, the court informed him that an OWI conviction carried a maximum penalty of a year in jail and a $1,000 fine, and a minimum penalty of two days in jail and a $500 fine. Tovar affirmed that he understood his exposure to those penalties. The court next explained that, before accepting a guilty plea, the court had to assure itself that Tovar was in fact guilty of the charged offense. To that end, the court informed Tovar that the OWI charge had only two elements: first, on the date in question, Tovar was operating a motor vehicle in the State of Iowa; second, when he did so, he was intoxicated. Tovar confirmed that he had been driving in Ames, Iowa, on the night he was apprehended and that he did not dispute the results of the intoxilyzer test administered by the police that night, which showed that his blood alcohol level exceeded the legal limit nearly twice over.

After the plea colloquy, the court asked Tovar if he still wished to plead guilty, and Tovar affirmed that he did. The court then accepted Tovar's plea, observing that there was "a factual basis" for it, and that Tovar had made the plea "voluntarily, with a full understanding of his rights, and ... of the consequences" of pleading guilty.

170

On December 30, 1996, Tovar appeared for sentencing on the OWI charge and, simultaneously, for arraignment on a subsequent charge of driving with a suspended license.[5] Noting that Tovar was again in attendance without counsel, the court inquired: "Mr. Tovar, did you want to represent yourself at today's hearing or did you want to take some time to hire an attorney to represent you?"[6] Tovar replied that he would represent himself. The court then engaged in essentially the same plea colloquy on the suspension charge as it had on the OWI charge the previous month. After accepting Tovar's guilty plea on the suspension charge, the court sentenced him on both counts: For the OWI conviction, the court imposed the minimum sentence of two days in jail and a $500 fine, plus a surcharge and costs; for the suspension conviction, the court imposed a $250 fine, plus a surcharge and costs.

On March 16, 1998, Tovar was convicted of OWI for a second time. He was represented by counsel in that proceeding, in which he pleaded guilty. On December 14, 2000, Tovar was again charged with OWI, this time as a third offense, and additionally with driving while license barred. Iowa law classifies first-offense OWI as a serious misdemeanor and second-offense OWI as an aggravated misdemeanor. Third-offense OWI, and any OWI offenses thereafter, rank as class "D" felonies. Represented by an attorney, Tovar pleaded not guilty to both December 2000 charges.

In March 2001, through counsel, Tovar filed a Motion for Adjudication of Law Points; the motion urged that Tovar's first OWI conviction, in 1996, could not be used to enhance the December 2000 OWI charge from a second-offense aggravated misdemeanor to a third-offense felony. Significantly, Tovar did not allege that he was unaware at the November 1996 arraignment of his right to counsel prior to pleading guilty and at the plea hearing. Instead, he maintained that his 1996 waiver of counsel was invalid—not "full knowing, intelligent, and voluntary"—because he "was never made aware by the court ... of the dangers and disadvantages of self-representation." The court denied Tovar's motion....

---

[5] In order to appear at the OWI arraignment, Tovar drove to the courthouse despite the suspension of his license; he was apprehended en route home.

[6] Prior to asking Tovar whether he wished to hire counsel, the court noted that Tovar had applied for a court-appointed attorney but that his application had been denied because he was financially dependent upon his parents....

Tovar then waived his right to a jury trial and was found guilty by the court of both the OWI third-offense charge and driving while license barred. Four months after that adjudication, Tovar was sentenced. On the OWI third-offense charge, he received a 180-day jail term, with all but 30 days suspended, three years of probation, and a $2,500 fine plus surcharges and costs. For driving while license barred, Tovar received a 30-day jail term, to run concurrently with the OWI sentence, and a suspended $500 fine....

Tovar contends that his waiver of counsel in November 1996, at his first OWI plea hearing, was insufficiently informed, and therefore constitutionally invalid. In particular, he asserts that the trial judge did not elaborate on the value, at that stage of the case, of an attorney's advice and the dangers of self-representation in entering a plea.

We have described a waiver of counsel as intelligent when the defendant "knows what he is doing and his choice is made with eyes open." We have not, however, prescribed any formula or script to be read to a defendant who states that he elects to proceed without counsel. The information a defendant must possess in order to make an intelligent election, our decisions indicate, will depend on a range of case-specific factors, including the defendant's education or sophistication, the complex or easily grasped nature of the charge, and the stage of the proceeding.

As to waiver of trial counsel, we have said that before a defendant may be allowed to proceed *pro se,* he must be warned specifically of the hazards ahead. The defendant in Faretta v. California, 422 U.S. 806 (1975), resisted counsel's aid, preferring to represent himself. The Court held that he had a constitutional right to self-representation. In recognizing that right, however, we cautioned: "Although a defendant need not himself have the skill and experience of a lawyer in order competently and intelligently to choose self-representation, he should be made aware of the dangers and disadvantages of self-representation, so that the record will establish that he knows what he is doing...."

Later, in Patterson v. Illinois, 487 U.S. 285 (1988), we elaborated on "the dangers and disadvantages of self-representation" to which *Faretta* referred. "At trial," we observed, "counsel is required to help even the most gifted layman adhere to the rules of procedure and evidence, comprehend the subtleties of *voir dire,* examine and cross-examine witnesses effectively..., object to improper prosecution questions, and much more." Warnings of the pitfalls of proceeding to trial without counsel, we therefore said, must be "rigorously" conveyed. We clarified, however, that at earlier stages of the criminal process, a less searching or formal colloquy may suffice.

Patterson concerned postindictment questioning by police and prosecutor. At that stage of the case, we held, the warnings required by Miranda v. Arizona adequately informed the defendant not only of his Fifth Amendment rights, but of his Sixth Amendment right to counsel as well. *Miranda* warnings [convey to a defendant] the "ultimate adverse consequence" of making uncounseled admissions, *i.e.,* his statements may be used against him in any ensuing criminal proceeding. The *Miranda* warnings, we added, also [let the defendant] know "what a lawyer could do for him," namely, advise him to refrain from making statements that could prove damaging to his defense.

Patterson describes a "pragmatic approach to the waiver question," one that asks "what purposes a lawyer can serve at the particular stage of the proceedings in question, and what assistance he could provide to an accused at that stage...." We require less rigorous warnings pretrial, *Patterson* explained, not because pretrial proceedings are less important than trial, but because, at that stage, "the full dangers and disadvantages of self-representation ... are less substantial and more obvious to an accused than they are at trial."...

To resolve this case, we need not endorse the State's position that nothing more than the plea colloquy was needed to safeguard Tovar's right to counsel. Preliminarily, we note that there were some things more in this case. Tovar first indicated that he waived counsel at his Initial Appearance, affirmed that he wanted to represent himself at the plea hearing, and declined the court's offer of "time to hire an attorney" at sentencing, when it was still open to him to request withdrawal of his plea. Further, the State does not contest that a defendant must be alerted to his right to the assistance of counsel in entering a plea.... Accordingly, the State presents a narrower question: "Does the Sixth Amendment require a court to give a rigid and detailed admonishment to a *pro se* defendant pleading guilty of the usefulness of an attorney, that an attorney may provide an independent opinion whether it is wise to plead guilty and that without an attorney the defendant risks overlooking a defense?"

Training on that question, we turn to, and reiterate, the particular language the Iowa Supreme Court employed in announcing the warnings it thought the Sixth Amendment required: "The trial judge must advise the defendant generally that there are defenses to criminal charges that may not be known by laypersons and that the danger in waiving the assistance of counsel in deciding whether to plead guilty is the risk that a viable defense will be overlooked"; in addition, "the defendant should be admonished that by waiving his right to an attorney he will lose the opportunity to obtain an independent opinion on whether, under the facts and applicable law, it is wise to plead guilty." Tovar did not receive such advice, and the sole question before us is whether the Sixth Amendment compels the two admonitions here in controversy. We hold it does not.

This Court recently explained, in reversing a lower court determination that a guilty plea was not voluntary: "The law ordinarily considers a waiver knowing, intelligent, and sufficiently aware if the defendant fully understands the nature of the right and how it would likely apply *in general* in the circumstances—even though the defendant may not know the *specific detailed* consequences of invoking it." United States v. Ruiz, 536 U.S. 622, 629 (2002) (emphasis in original).... In prescribing scripted admonitions and holding them necessary in every guilty plea instance, we further note, the Iowa high court overlooked our observations that the information a defendant must have to waive counsel intelligently will "depend, in each case, upon the particular facts and circumstances surrounding that case," Johnson v. Zerbst, 304 U.S. 458, 464 (1938).

Moreover, as Tovar acknowledges, in a collateral attack on an uncounseled conviction, it is the defendant's burden to prove that he did not competently and intelligently waive his right to the assistance of counsel. In that light, we note that Tovar has never claimed that he did not fully understand the charge or the range of punishment for the crime prior to pleading guilty. Further, he has never articulated with precision the additional information counsel could have provided, given the simplicity of the charge. Nor does he assert that he *was* unaware of his right to be counseled prior to and at his arraignment....

Given the particular facts and circumstances surrounding this case, it is far from clear that warnings of the kind required by the Iowa Supreme Court would have enlightened Tovar's decision whether to seek counsel or to represent himself. In a case so straightforward ... the admonitions at issue might confuse or mislead a defendant more than they would inform him: The warnings the Iowa Supreme Court declared mandatory might be misconstrued as a veiled suggestion that a meritorious defense exists or that the defendant could plead to a lesser charge, when neither prospect is a realistic one. If a defendant delays his plea in the vain hope that counsel could uncover a tenable basis for contesting or reducing the criminal charge, the prompt disposition of the case will be impeded, and the resources of either the State (if the defendant is indigent) or the defendant himself (if he is financially ineligible for appointed counsel) will be wasted.

We note, finally, that States are free to adopt by statute, rule, or decision any guides to the acceptance of an uncounseled plea they deem useful. See, *e.g.*, Alaska Rule Crim. Proc. 39(a); Fla. Rule Crim. Proc. 3.111(d); Md. Ct. Rule 4-215; Minn. Rule Crim. Proc. 5.02; Pa. Rule Crim. Proc. 121, comment. We hold only that the two admonitions the Iowa Supreme Court ordered are not required by the Federal Constitution....

Margaret Bradshaw v. John David Stumpf
2005 WL 1383730 (June 13, 2005)

O'CONNOR, J.

[John David Stumpf] and two other men, Clyde Daniel Wesley and Norman Leroy Edmonds, were traveling in Edmonds' car along Interstate 70 through Guernsey County, Ohio. Needing money for gas, the men stopped the car along the highway. While Edmonds waited in the car, Stumpf and Wesley walked to the home of Norman and Mary Jane Stout, about 100 yards away. Stumpf and Wesley, each concealing a gun, talked their way into the home by telling the Stouts they needed to use the phone. Their real object, however, was robbery: Once inside, Stumpf held the Stouts at gunpoint, while Wesley ransacked the house. When Mr. Stout moved toward Stumpf, Stumpf shot him twice in the head, causing Mr. Stout to black out. After he regained consciousness, Mr. Stout heard two male voices coming from another room, and then four gunshots—the shots that killed his wife. Edmonds was arrested shortly afterward, and his statements led the police to issue arrest warrants for Stumpf and Wesley. Stumpf, who surrendered to the police, at first denied any knowledge of the crimes. After he was told that Mr. Stout had survived, however, Stumpf admitted to participating in the robbery and to shooting Mr. Stumpf. But he claimed not to have shot Mrs. Stout, and he has maintained that position ever since....

Stumpf was indicted for aggravated murder, attempted aggravated murder, aggravated robbery, and two counts of grand theft. With respect to the aggravated murder charge, the indictment listed four statutory "specifications"—three of them aggravating circumstances making Stumpf eligible for the death penalty. The case was assigned to a three-judge panel in the Court of Common Pleas.

Rather than proceed to trial, however, Stumpf and the State worked out a plea agreement: Stumpf would plead guilty to aggravated murder and attempted aggravated murder, and the State would drop most of the other charges; with respect to the aggravated murder charge, Stumpf would plead guilty to one of the three capital specifications, with the State dropping the other two. The plea was accepted after a colloquy with the presiding judge, and after a hearing in which the panel satisfied itself as to the factual basis for the plea.

Because the capital specification to which Stumpf pleaded guilty left him eligible for the death penalty, a contested penalty hearing was held before the same three-judge panel. Stumpf's mitigation case was based in part on his difficult childhood, limited education, dependable work history, youth, and lack of prior serious offenses. Stumpf's principal argument, however, was that he had participated in the plot only at the urging and under the influence of Wesley, that it was Wesley who had fired the fatal shots at Mrs. Stout, and that Stumpf's assertedly minor role in the murder counseled against the death sentence. The State, on the other hand, argued that Stumpf had indeed shot Mrs. Stout. Still, while the prosecutor claimed Stumpf's allegedly primary role in the shooting as a special reason to reject Stumpf's mitigation argument, the prosecutor also noted that Ohio law did not restrict the death penalty to those who commit murder by their own hands—an accomplice to murder could also receive the death penalty, so long as he acted with the specific intent to cause death.... The three-judge panel, agreeing with the State's first contention, specifically found that Stumpf "was the principal offender" in the aggravated murder of Mrs. Stout. Determining that the aggravating factors in Stumpf's case outweighed any mitigating factors, the panel sentenced Stumpf to death.

Afterward, Wesley was successfully extradited [from Texas, where he was arrested,] to Ohio to stand trial. His case was tried to a jury, before the same judge who had presided over the panel overseeing Stumpf's proceedings, and with the same prosecutor. This time, however, the prosecutor had new evidence: James Eastman, Wesley's cellmate after his extradition, testified that Wesley had admitted to firing the shots that killed Mrs. Stout. The prosecutor introduced Eastman's testimony in Wesley's trial, and in his closing argument he argued for Wesley's credibility and lack of motive to lie. The prosecutor claimed that Eastman's testimony, combined with certain circumstantial evidence and with the implausibility of Wesley's own account of events, proved that Wesley was the principal offender in Mrs. Stout's murder—and that Wesley therefore deserved to be put to death. One way Wesley countered this argument was by noting that the prosecutor had taken a contrary position in Stumpf's trial, and that Stumpf had already been sentenced to death for the crime. Wesley also took the stand in his own defense, and testified that Stumpf had shot Mrs. Stout. In the end, the jury sentenced Wesley to life imprisonment with the possibility of parole after 20 years.

After the Wesley trial, Stumpf, whose direct appeal was still pending in the Ohio Court of Appeals, returned to the Court of Common Pleas with a motion to withdraw his guilty plea or vacate his death sentence. Stumpf argued that Eastman's testimony, and the prosecution's endorsement of that testimony in Wesley's trial, cast doubt upon Stumpf's conviction and sentence. The State (represented again by the same prosecutor who had tried both Wesley's case and Stumpf's original case) disagreed. According to the prosecutor, the court's first task was to decide whether the Eastman testimony was sufficient to alter the court's prior determination that Stumpf had been the shooter. Contrary to the argument he had presented in the Wesley trial, however, the prosecutor now noted that Eastman's testimony was belied by certain other evidence (ballistics evidence and Wesley's testimony in his own defense) confirming Stumpf to have been the primary shooter. In the alternative, the State noted as it had before that an aider-and-abettor theory might allow the death sentence to be imposed against Stumpf even if he had not shot Mrs. Stout.

[After the state courts rejected Stumpf's claim, he] filed this federal habeas petition in the United States District Court for the Southern District of Ohio in November 1995. [Stumpf argues that his] plea of guilty to aggravated murder was invalid because he was not aware of the specific intent element of the charge—a [contention] we find unsupportable.

Stumpf's guilty plea would indeed be invalid if he had not been aware of the nature of the charges against him, including the elements of the aggravated murder charge to which he pleaded guilty. A guilty plea operates as a waiver of important rights, and is valid only if done voluntarily, knowingly, and intelligently, with sufficient awareness of the relevant circumstances and likely consequences. Where a defendant pleads guilty to a crime without having been informed of the crime's elements, this standard is not met and the plea is invalid.

But [in] Stumpf's plea hearing, his attorneys represented on the record that they had explained to their client the elements of the aggravated murder charge; Stumpf himself then confirmed that this representation was true. While the court taking a defendant's plea is responsible for ensuring a record adequate for any review that may be later sought, we have never held that the judge must himself explain the elements of each charge to the defendant on the record. Rather, the constitutional prerequisites of a valid plea may be satisfied where the record accurately reflects that the nature of the charge and the elements of the crime were explained to the defendant by his own, competent counsel....

Stumpf argues, in essence, that his choice to plead guilty to the aggravated murder charge was so inconsistent with his denial of having shot the victim that he could only have pleaded guilty out of ignorance of the charge's specific intent requirement. But Stumpf's asserted inconsistency is illusory. The aggravated murder charge's intent element did not require any showing that Stumpf had himself shot Mrs. Stout. Rather, Ohio law considers aiders and abettors equally in violation of the aggravated murder statute, so long as the aiding and abetting is done with the specific intent to cause death. As a result, Stumpf's steadfast assertion that he had not shot Mrs. Stout would not necessarily have precluded him from admitting his specific intent under the statute.

That is particularly so given the other evidence in this case. Stumpf and Wesley had gone to the Stouts' home together, carrying guns and intending to commit armed robbery. Stumpf, by his own admission, shot Mr. Stout in the head at close range. Taken together, these facts could show that Wesley and Stumpf had together agreed to kill both of the Stouts in order to leave no witnesses to the crime. And that, in turn, could make both men guilty of aggravated murder regardless of who actually killed Mrs. Stout....

Finally, Stumpf ... relies on the perception that he obtained a bad bargain by his plea—that the State's dropping several non-murder charges and two of the three capital murder specifications was a bad tradeoff for Stumpf's guilty plea. But a plea's validity may not be collaterally attacked merely because the defendant made what turned out, in retrospect, to be a poor deal. Rather, the shortcomings of the deal Stumpf obtained cast doubt on the validity of his plea only if they show either that he made the unfavorable plea on the constitutionally defective advice of counsel, or that he could not have understood the terms of the bargain he and Ohio agreed to. Though Stumpf did bring an independent claim asserting ineffective assistance of counsel, that claim is not before us in this case. And in evaluating the validity of Stumpf's plea, we are reluctant to accord much weight to his post hoc reevaluation of the wisdom of the bargain. Stumpf pleaded guilty knowing that the State had copious evidence against him, including the testimony of Mr. Stout; the plea eliminated two of the three capital specifications the State could rely on in seeking the death penalty; and the plea allowed Stumpf to assert his acceptance of responsibility as an argument in mitigation. Under these circumstances, the plea may well have been a knowing, voluntary, and intelligent reaction to a litigation situation that was difficult, to say the least.

[We also reject Stumpf's argument] that prosecutorial inconsistencies between the Stumpf and Wesley cases required voiding Stumpf's guilty plea. Stumpf's assertions of inconsistency relate entirely to the prosecutor's arguments about which of the two men, Wesley or Stumpf, shot Mrs. Stout. For the reasons given above, the precise identity of the triggerman was immaterial to Stumpf's conviction for aggravated murder. Moreover, Stumpf has never provided an explanation of how the prosecution's postplea use of inconsistent arguments could have affected the knowing, voluntary, and intelligent nature of his plea.

The prosecutor's use of allegedly inconsistent theories may have a more direct effect on Stumpf's sentence, however, for it is at least arguable that the sentencing panel's conclusion about Stumpf's principal role in the offense was material to its sentencing determination. [It] would be premature for this Court to resolve the merits of Stumpf's sentencing claim, and we therefore express no opinion on whether the prosecutor's actions amounted to a due process violation, or whether any such violation would have been prejudicial. The Court of Appeals should have the opportunity to consider, in the first instance, the question of how Eastman's testimony and the prosecutor's conduct in the Stumpf and Wesley cases relate to Stumpf's death sentence in particular....

SOUTER, J., concurring.

... I understand Stumpf to claim that it violates the basic due process standard, barring fundamentally unfair procedure, to allow his death sentence to stand in the aftermath of three positions taken by the State: (1) at Stumpf's sentencing hearing; (2) at the trial of Stumpf's codefendant, Clyde Wesley; and (3) in response to Stumpf's motion to withdraw his guilty plea in light of the State's position at the Wesley trial. At the hearing on Stumpf's sentence, the State argued that he was the triggerman, and it urged consideration of that fact as a reason to impose a death sentence. The trial court found that Stumpf had pulled the trigger and did sentence him to death, though it did not state that finding Stumpf to be the shooter was dispositive in determining the sentence. After the sentencing proceeding was over, the State tried the codefendant, Wesley, and on the basis of testimony from a new witness argued that Wesley was in fact the triggerman, and should be sentenced to death. The new witness was apparently unconvincing to the jury, which in any event was informed that Stumpf had already been sentenced to death for the crime; the jury rejected the specification that named Wesley as the triggerman, and it recommended a sentence of life, not death. Stumpf then challenged his death sentence (along with his conviction) on the basis of the prosecution's position in the Wesley case. In response, the State did not repudiate the position it had taken in the codefendant's case, or explain that it had made a mistake there. Instead, it merely dismissed the testimony of the witness it had vouched for at Wesley's trial, and maintained that Stumpf's death sentence should stand for some or all of the reasons it originally argued for its imposition. At the end of the day, the State was on record as maintaining that Stumpf and Wesley should both be executed on the ground that each was the trigger-man, when it was undisputed that only one of them could have been....

180

As I see it, Stumpf's argument is simply that a death sentence may not be allowed to stand when it was imposed in response to a factual claim that the State necessarily contradicted in subsequently arguing for a death sentence in the case of a codefendant.... If a due process violation is found in the State's maintenance of such inconsistent positions, there will be remedial questions. May the death sentence stand if the State declines to repudiate its inconsistent position in the codefendant's case? Would it be sufficient simply to reexamine the original sentence and if so, which party should have the burden of persuasion? If more would be required, would a de novo sentencing hearing suffice?

THOMAS, J., concurring.

... I agree with the Court that "Stumpf has never provided an explanation of how the prosecution's postplea use of inconsistent arguments could have affected the knowing, voluntary, and intelligent nature of his plea." Similar reasoning applies to Stumpf's sentence. Stumpf equally has never explained how the prosecution's use of postsentence inconsistent arguments—which were based on evidence unavailable until after Stumpf was sentenced—could have affected the reliability or procedural fairness of his death sentence.... The Bill of Rights guarantees vigorous adversarial testing of guilt and innocence and conviction only by proof beyond a reasonable doubt. These guarantees are more than sufficient to deter the State from taking inconsistent positions; a prosecutor who argues inconsistently risks undermining his case, for opposing counsel will bring the conflict to the factfinder's attention.

Page 1044.   Insert this material at the end of note 2.

See also Mitschke v. State, 129 S.W.3d 130 (Tex. Crim. App. 2004) (no advisory from court necessary about sex offender registration; registration is "direct consequence" but also "nonpunitive"); State v. Bellamy, 835 A.2d 1231 (N.J. 2003) (court must advise a guilty-pleading defendant of possible future civil commitment as a sexually violent predator; term could last for life).

Page 1044.   Insert this material at the end of note 3.

See also State v. Paredez, 101 P.3d 799 (N.M. 2004) (when guilty plea makes removal from country virtually certain for a non-citizen, defense counsel has duty to give client immigration advice more specific than an opinion that deportation is "possible").

Page 1045. Insert this material at the end of note 6.

In United States v. Dominguez Benitez, 542 U.S. 74 (2004), the judge failed to warn the defendant, as required by Rule 11(c)(3)(B), that he could not withdraw his plea even if the judge did not accept the recommended sentence. The defendant did not object at the time of sentencing, but later sought to withdraw his guilty plea. Such a failure to warn, the Supreme Court said, is reversible error only if the defendant can show a reasonable probability that he would not have entered the plea after hearing a proper warning. The defendant here could not make such a showing because the government's evidence was strong and the plea agreement, with proper Rule 11 warnings, was read to him in his native Spanish.

2.   Involuntary Pleas

Page 1058. Insert this material at the end of note 3.

See Richard Klein, Due Process Denied: Judicial Coercion in the Plea Bargaining Process, 32 Hofstra L. Rev. 1349 (2004).

D. *Making and Breaking Bargains*

2.   Remedies for Broken Bargains

Page 1070. Insert at the end of note 1.

State v. Mellon, 118 S.W.3d 340 (Tenn. 2003) (defendant could withdraw plea because he was not warned of consequences if he breached agreement; if agreement had been clear, state would be entitled to same remedies available to defendants, including rescission or specific performance).

Chapter 17

Decisionmakers at Trial

B. Selection of Jurors

2. Dismissal for Cause

Page 1114. Add this material after note 4.

5. *Harmless error in denial of challenge for cause.* If the trial court refuses to excuse a juror for cause but the juror does not serve on the panel because the defendant uses a peremptory challenge to remove the juror, has any reversible error happened? What if the defendant had peremptory challenges to spare? Cf. United States v. Martinez-Salazar, 528 U.S. 304 (2000) (when judge fails to remove juror for cause, defendant must allow the juror on the panel to challenge the decision on appeal); Busby v. State, 894 So. 2d 88 (Fla. 2004) (defendant can challenge decision on removal for cause even if juror excluded from panel based on peremptory; no actual harm must be shown).

3. Peremptory Challenges

Page 1129. Add this material before the notes.

Thomas Joe Miller-El v. Doug Dretke
2005 WL 1383365 (June 13, 2005)

SOUTER, J.

... I

In the course of robbing a Holiday Inn in Dallas, Texas in late 1985, Miller-El and his accomplices bound and gagged two hotel employees, whom Miller-El then shot, killing one and severely injuring the other. During jury selection in Miller-El's trial for capital murder, prosecutors used peremptory strikes against 10 qualified black venire members. Miller-El objected that the strikes were based on race and could not be presumed legitimate, given a history of excluding black members from criminal juries by the Dallas County District Attorney's Office.... After reviewing the voir dire record of the explanations given for some of the challenged strikes, and after hearing one of the prosecutors, Paul Macaluso, give his justification for those previously unexplained, the trial court accepted the stated race-neutral reasons for the strikes, which the judge called "completely credible [and] sufficient" as the grounds for a finding of "no purposeful discrimination."

[After his direct appeal, Miller-El] sought habeas relief under 28 U.S.C. § 2254, again pressing his Batson claim, among others not now before us. The District Court denied relief [and the Fifth Circuit refused to reach the merits of the claim, but this Court ruled that] Miller-El was entitled to review on the *Batson* claim. Miller-El v. Cockrell, 534 U.S. 1122 (2002). [The] Fifth Circuit rejected Miller-El's Batson claim on the merits ... and again we reverse.

II

[For] more than a century, this Court consistently and repeatedly has reaffirmed that racial discrimination by the State in jury selection offends the Equal Protection Clause. The rub has been the practical difficulty of ferreting out discrimination in selections discretionary by nature, and choices subject to myriad legitimate influences, whatever the race of the individuals on the panel from which jurors are selected. In

Swain v. Alabama, 380 U.S. 202 (1965), we tackled the problem of "the quantum of proof necessary" to show purposeful discrimination, ... presuming the legitimacy of prosecutors' strikes except in the face of a longstanding pattern of discrimination. In Batson v. Kentucky, 476 U.S. 79 (1986), we recognized that this requirement to show an extended pattern imposed a "crippling burden of proof" that left prosecutors' use of peremptories "largely immune from constitutional scrutiny." [We] accordingly held that a defendant could make out a prima facie case of discriminatory jury selection by "the totality of the relevant facts" about a prosecutor's conduct during the defendant's own trial. Once the defendant makes a prima facie showing, the burden shifts to the State to come forward with a neutral explanation for challenging jurors within an arguably targeted class. [The] prosecutor must give a clear and reasonably specific explanation of his legitimate reasons for exercising the challenge. The trial court then will have the duty to determine if the defendant has established purposeful discrimination....

Although the move from Swain to Batson left a defendant free to challenge the prosecution without having to cast Swain 's wide net, the net was not entirely consigned to history, for Batson 's individualized focus came with a weakness of its own owing to its very emphasis on the particular reasons a prosecutor might give. If any facially neutral reason sufficed to answer a Batson challenge, then Batson would not amount to much more than Swain. Some stated reasons are false, and although some false reasons are shown up within the four corners of a given case, sometimes a court may not be sure unless it looks beyond the case at hand....

Under the Antiterrorism and Effective Death Penalty Act of 1996, Miller-El may obtain relief only by showing the Texas conclusion to be "an unreasonable determination of the facts in light of the evidence presented in the State court proceeding." 28 U.S.C. § 2254(d)(2). Thus we presume the Texas court's factual findings to be sound unless Miller-El rebuts the "presumption of correctness by clear and convincing evidence." § 2254(e)(1)....

III A

The numbers describing the prosecution's use of peremptories are remarkable. Out of 20 black members of the 108-person venire panel for Miller-El's trial, only 1 served. Although 9 were excused for cause or by agreement, 10 were peremptorily struck by the prosecution. The prosecutors used their peremptory strikes to exclude 91% of the eligible African-American venire members. Happenstance is unlikely to produce this disparity.

More powerful than these bare statistics, however, are side-by-side comparisons of some black venire panelists who were struck and white panelists allowed to serve. If a prosecutor's proffered reason for striking a black panelist applies just as well to an otherwise-similar nonblack who is permitted to serve, that is evidence tending to prove purposeful discrimination to be considered at Batson's third step....

The prosecution used its second peremptory strike to exclude Billy Jean Fields, a black man who expressed unwavering support for the death penalty. On the questionnaire filled out by all panel members before individual examination on the stand, Fields said that he believed in capital punishment, and during questioning he disclosed his belief that the State acts on God's behalf when it imposes the death penalty.... He testified that he had no religious or philosophical reservations about the death penalty and that the death penalty deterred crime....

Although at one point in the questioning, Fields indicated that the possibility of rehabilitation might be relevant to the likelihood that a defendant would commit future acts of violence, he responded to ensuing questions by saying that although he believed anyone could be rehabilitated, this belief would not stand in the way of a decision to impose the death penalty:

> ... If for some reason the testimony didn't warrant death, then life imprisonment would give an individual an opportunity to rehabilitate. But, you know, you said that the jurors didn't have the opportunity to make a personal decision in the matter with reference to what I thought or felt, but it was just based on the questions according to the way the law has been handed down.

Fields also noted on his questionnaire that his brother had a criminal history. During questioning, the prosecution [asked whether his brother's conviction for possession of a controlled substance] "would in any way interfere with your service on this jury at all?" [Fields answered "No."]

Fields was struck peremptorily by the prosecution, with prosecutor James Nelson offering a race-neutral reason:

> [We] have concern with reference to some of his statements as to the death penalty in that he said that he could only give death if he thought a person could not be rehabilitated and he later made the comment that any person could be rehabilitated if they find God or are introduced to God and the fact that we have a concern that his religious feelings may affect his jury service in this case.

Thus, Nelson simply mischaracterized Fields's testimony. He represented that Fields said he would not vote for death if rehabilitation was possible, whereas Fields unequivocally stated that he could impose the death penalty regardless of the possibility of rehabilitation....

If, indeed, Fields's thoughts on rehabilitation did make the prosecutor uneasy, he should have worried about a number of white panel members he accepted with no evident reservations. Sandra Hearn said that she believed in the death penalty "if a criminal cannot be rehabilitated and continues to commit the same type of crime."... "People change," she said, making it hard to assess the risk of someone's future dangerousness. "[T]he evidence would have to be awful strong." But the prosecution did not respond to Hearn the way it did to Fields, and without delving into her views about rehabilitation with any further question, it raised no objection to her serving on the jury. White panelist Mary Witt said she would take the possibility of rehabilitation into account in deciding at the penalty phase of the trial about a defendant's probability of future dangerousness, but the prosecutors asked her no further question about her views on reformation, and they accepted her as a juror. Latino venireman Fernando Gutierrez, who served on the jury, said that he would consider the death penalty for someone who could not be rehabilitated, but the prosecutors did not question him further about this view. In sum, nonblack jurors whose remarks on rehabilitation could well have signaled a limit on their willingness to impose a death sentence were not questioned further and drew no objection, but the prosecution expressed apprehension about a black juror's belief in the possibility of reformation even though he repeatedly stated his approval of the death penalty and testified that he could impose it according to state legal standards even when the alternative sentence of life imprisonment would give a defendant (like everyone else in the world) the opportunity to reform.

The unlikelihood that his position on rehabilitation had anything to do with the peremptory strike of Fields is underscored by the prosecution's response after Miller-El's lawyer pointed out that the prosecutor had misrepresented Fields's responses on the subject. A moment earlier the prosecutor had finished his misdescription of Fields's views on potential rehabilitation with the words, "Those are our reasons for exercising our ... strike at this time." When defense counsel called him on his misstatement, he neither defended what he said nor withdrew the strike. Instead, he suddenly came up with Fields's brother's prior conviction as another reason for the strike.

It would be difficult to credit the State's new explanation, which reeks of afterthought. While the Court of Appeals tried to bolster it with the observation that no seated juror was in Fields's position with respect to his brother, the court's readiness to accept the State's substitute reason ignores not only its pretextual timing but the other reasons rendering it implausible. Fields's testimony indicated he was not close to his brother ("I don't really know too much about it"), and the prosecution asked nothing further about the influence his brother's history might have had on Fields, as it probably would have done if the family history had actually mattered....

In sum, when we look for nonblack jurors similarly situated to Fields, we find strong similarities as well as some differences.[6] But the differences seem far from significant, particularly when we read Fields's voir dire testimony in its entirety. Upon that reading, Fields should have been an ideal juror in the eyes of a prosecutor seeking a death sentence, and the prosecutors' explanations for the strike cannot reasonably be accepted.

The prosecution's proffered reasons for striking Joe Warren, another black venireman, are comparably unlikely. Warren gave this answer when he was asked what the death penalty accomplished:

---

[6] The dissent contends that there are no white panelists similarly situated to Fields and to panel member Joe Warren because "'similarly situated' does not mean matching any one of several reasons the prosecution gave for striking a potential juror--it means matching all of them." None of our cases announces a rule that no comparison is probative unless the situation of the individuals compared is identical in all respects, and there is no reason to accept one.... A per se rule that a defendant cannot win a Batson claim unless there is an exactly identical white juror would leave Batson inoperable; potential jurors are not products of a set of cookie cutters.

> I don't know. It's really hard to say because I know sometimes you feel
> that it might help to deter crime and then you feel that the person is not
> really suffering. You're taking the suffering away from him. So it's like
> I said, sometimes you have mixed feelings about whether or not this is
> punishment or, you know, you're relieving personal punishment.

The prosecution said nothing about these remarks when it struck Warren from the panel, but prosecutor Paul Macaluso referred to this answer as the first of his reasons when he testified at the later Batson hearing:

> I thought [Warren's statements on voir dire] were inconsistent
> responses. At one point he says, you know, on a case-by-case basis and
> at another point he said, well, I think—I got the impression, at least,
> that he suggested that the death penalty was an easy way out, that they
> should be made to suffer more.

On the face of it, the explanation is reasonable from the State's point of view, but its plausibility is severely undercut by the prosecution's failure to object to other panel members who expressed views much like Warren's. Kevin Duke, who served on the jury, said, "sometimes death would be better to me than--being in prison would be like dying every day and, if you were in prison for life with no hope of parole, I'd just as soon have it over with than be in prison for the rest of your life." Troy Woods, the one black panelist to serve as juror, said that capital punishment "is too easy. I think that's a quick relief.... I feel like [hard labor is] more of a punishment than putting them to sleep." Sandra Jenkins, whom the State accepted (but who was then struck by the defense) testified that she thought "a harsher treatment is life imprisonment with no parole." Leta Girard, accepted by the State (but also struck by the defense) gave her opinion that "living sometimes is a worse—is worse to me than dying would be." The fact that Macaluso's reason also applied to these other panel members, most of them white, none of them struck, is evidence of pretext.

The suggestion of pretext is not, moreover, mitigated much by Macaluso's explanation that Warren was struck when the State had 10 peremptory challenges left and could afford to be liberal in using them. If that were the explanation for striking Warren and later accepting panel members who thought death would be too easy, the prosecutors should have struck Sandra Jenkins, whom they examined and accepted before Warren....

Macaluso's explanation that the prosecutors grew more sparing with peremptory challenges as the jury selection wore on does, however, weaken any suggestion that the State's acceptance of Woods, the one black juror, shows that race was not in play. Woods was the eighth juror, qualified in the fifth week of jury selection. When the State accepted him, 11 of its 15 peremptory strikes were gone, 7 of them used to strike black panel members. The juror questionnaires show that at least three members of the venire panel yet to be questioned on the stand were opposed to capital punishment. With at least three remaining panel members highly undesirable to the State, the prosecutors had to exercise prudent restraint in using strikes....

The Court of Appeals pretermitted these difficulties by stating that the prosecution's reason for striking Warren was a more general ambivalence about the penalty and his ability to impose it.... But this rationalization was erroneous as a matter of fact and as a matter of law.

As to fact, Macaluso said nothing about any general ambivalence. He simply alluded to the possibility that Warren might think the death penalty too easy on some defendants, saying nothing about Warren's ability to impose the penalty when it appeared to be warranted. On the contrary, though Warren had indeed questioned the extent to which the death penalty served a purpose in society, he explained his position in response to the very next question: it was not any qualm about imposing what society generally deems its harshest punishment, but his concern that the death penalty might not be severe enough. When Warren was asked whether he could impose the death penalty he said he thought he could; when told that answering yes to the special issue questions would be tantamount to voting for death he said he could give yes answers if the evidence supported them.

As for law, the rule in Batson provides an opportunity to the prosecutor to give the reason for striking the juror, and it requires the judge to assess the plausibility of that reason in light of all evidence with a bearing on it. It is true that peremptories are often the subjects of instinct, and it can sometimes be hard to say what the reason is. But when illegitimate grounds like race are in issue, a prosecutor simply has got to state his reasons as best he can and stand or fall on the plausibility of the reasons he gives. A Batson challenge does not call for a mere exercise in thinking up any rational basis. If the stated reason does not hold up, its pretextual significance does not fade because a trial judge, or an appeals court, can imagine a reason that might not have been shown up as false. The Court of Appeals's and the dissent's substitution of a reason for eliminating Warren does nothing to satisfy the prosecutors' burden of stating a racially neutral explanation for their own actions....

B

The case for discrimination goes beyond these comparisons to include broader patterns of practice during the jury selection. The prosecution's shuffling of the venire panel, its enquiry into views on the death penalty, its questioning about minimum acceptable sentences: all indicate decisions probably based on race. Finally, the appearance of discrimination is confirmed by widely known evidence of the general policy of the Dallas County District Attorney's Office to exclude black venire members from juries at the time Miller-El's jury was selected.

The first clue to the prosecutors' intentions, distinct from the peremptory challenges themselves, is their resort during voir dire to a procedure known in Texas as the jury shuffle. In the State's criminal practice, either side may literally reshuffle the cards bearing panel members' names, thus rearranging the order in which members of a venire panel are seated and reached for questioning. Once the order is established, the panel members seated at the back are likely to escape voir dire altogether, for those not questioned by the end of the week are dismissed....

In this case, the prosecution and then the defense shuffled the cards at the beginning of the first week of voir dire; the record does not reflect the changes in order. At the beginning of the second week, when a number of black members were seated at the front of the panel, the prosecution shuffled. At the beginning of the third week, the first four panel members were black. The prosecution shuffled, and these black panel members ended up at the back. Then the defense shuffled, and the black panel members again appeared at the front. The prosecution requested another shuffle, but the trial court refused. Finally, the defense shuffled at the beginning of the fourth and fifth weeks of voir dire; the record does not reflect the panel's racial composition before or after those shuffles.

The State notes in its brief that there might be racially neutral reasons for shuffling the jury, and we suppose there might be. But no racially neutral reason has ever been offered in this case, and nothing stops the suspicion of discriminatory intent from rising to an inference.

The next body of evidence that the State was trying to avoid black jurors is the contrasting voir dire questions posed respectively to black and nonblack panel members, on two different subjects. First, there were the prosecutors' statements preceding questions about a potential juror's thoughts on capital punishment. Some of these prefatory statements were cast in general terms, but some followed the so-called graphic script, describing the method of execution in rhetorical and clinical detail.

[For] 94% of white venire panel members, prosecutors gave a bland description of the death penalty before asking about the individual's feelings on the subject. The abstract account went something like this:

> ... We anticipate that we will be able to present to a jury the quantity and type of evidence necessary to convict him of capital murder and the quantity and type of evidence sufficient to allow a jury to answer these three questions over here in the affirmative. A yes answer to each of those questions results in an automatic death penalty from Judge McDowell.

Only 6% of white venire panelists, but 53% of those who were black, heard a different description of the death penalty before being asked their feelings about it. This is an example of the graphic script:

> [We] are actively seeking the death penalty for Thomas Joe Miller-El.... We do that with the anticipation that, when the death penalty is assessed, at some point Mr. Thomas Joe Miller-El--the man sitting right down there--will be taken to Huntsville and will be put on death row and at some point taken to the death house and placed on a gurney and injected with a lethal substance until he is dead as a result of the proceedings that we have in this court on this case....

The State concedes that this disparate questioning did occur but argues that use of the graphic script turned not on a panelist's race but on expressed ambivalence about the death penalty in the preliminary questionnaire.[15] Prosecutors were trying, the argument goes, to weed out noncommittal or uncertain jurors, not black jurors. And while some white venire members expressed opposition to the death penalty on their questionnaires, they were not read the graphic script because their feelings were already clear. The State says that giving the graphic script to these panel members would only have antagonized them.

This argument, however, first advanced in dissent when the case was last here and later adopted by the State and the Court of Appeals, simply does not fit the facts. Looking at the answers on the questionnaires, and at voir dire testimony expressly discussing answers on the questionnaires, we find that black venire members were more likely than nonblacks to receive the graphic script regardless of their expressions of certainty or ambivalence about the death penalty, and the State's chosen explanation for the graphic script fails in the cases of four out of the eight black panel members who received it. Two of them, Janice Mackey and Anna Keaton, clearly stated opposition to the death penalty but they received the graphic script, while the black panel members Wayman Kennedy and Jeannette Butler were unambiguously in favor but got the graphic description anyway. The State's explanation does even worse in the instances of the five nonblacks who received the graphic script, missing the mark four times out of five: Vivian Sztybel and Filemon Zablan received it, although each was unambiguously in favor of the death penalty, while Dominick Desinise and Clara Evans unambiguously opposed it but were given the graphic version.

The State's purported rationale fails again if we look only to the treatment of ambivalent panel members, ambivalent black individuals having been more likely to receive the graphic description than ambivalent nonblacks. Three nonblack members of the venire indicated ambivalence to the death penalty on their questionnaires; only one of them, Fernando Gutierrez, received the graphic script. But of the four

---

[15] So far as we can tell from the voluminous record before us, many of the juror questionnaires, along with juror information cards, were added to the habeas record after the filing of the petition in the District Court. The State raised no objection to receipt of the supplemental material in the District Court or the Fifth Circuit.... Neither party has referred to the provision that the reasonableness of the state-court determination be judged by the evidence before the state court, 28 U.S.C. § 2254(d)(2), and it is not clear to what extent the lodged material expands upon what the state judge knew; the same judge presided over the voir dire, the Swain hearing, and the Batson hearing, and the jury questionnaires were subjects of reference at the voir dire....

black panel members who expressed ambivalence, all got the graphic treatment.

The State's attempt at a race-neutral rationalization thus simply fails to explain what the prosecutors did. But if we posit instead that the prosecutors' first object was to use the graphic script to make a case for excluding black panel members opposed to or ambivalent about the death penalty, there is a much tighter fit of fact and explanation.[29] Of the 10 nonblacks whose questionnaires expressed ambivalence or opposition, only 30% received the graphic treatment. But of the seven blacks who expressed ambivalence or opposition, 86% heard the graphic script. As between the State's ambivalence explanation and Miller-El's racial one, race is much the better, and the reasonable inference is that race was the major consideration when the prosecution chose to follow the graphic script.

The same is true for another kind of disparate questioning, which might fairly be called trickery. The prosecutors asked members of the panel how low a sentence they would consider imposing for murder. Most potential jurors were first told that Texas law provided for a minimum term of five years, but some members of the panel were not, and if a panel member then insisted on a minimum above five years, the prosecutor would suppress his normal preference for tough jurors and claim cause to strike.... Ninety-four percent of whites were informed of the statutory minimum sentence, compared [with] only twelve and a half percent of African-Americans. No explanation is proffered for the statistical disparity....

The State concedes that the manipulative minimum punishment questioning was used to create cause to strike, but now it offers the extenuation that prosecutors omitted the 5-year information not on the basis of race, but on stated opposition to the death penalty, or ambivalence about it, on the questionnaires and in the voir dire testimony. On the State's identification of black panel members opposed or ambivalent, all were asked the trick question. But the State's rationale

---

[29] The dissent posits that prosecutors did not use the graphic script with panel members opposed to the death penalty because it would only have antagonized them. No answer is offered to the question why a prosecutor would take care with the feelings of a panel member he would excuse for cause or strike yet would antagonize an ambivalent member whose feelings he wanted to smoke out, but who might turn out to be an acceptable juror.

flatly fails to explain why most white panel members who expressed similar opposition or ambivalence were not subjected to it. [Eight] of the 11 nonblack individuals who voiced opposition or ambivalence were asked about the acceptable minimum only after being told what state law required. [FN35] Hence, only 27% of nonblacks questioned on the subject who expressed these views were subjected to the trick question, as against 100% of black members. Once again, the implication of race in the prosecutors' choice of questioning cannot be explained away.[36]

There is a final body of evidence that confirms this conclusion. We know that for decades leading up to the time this case was tried prosecutors in the Dallas County office had followed a specific policy of systematically excluding blacks from juries…. A Dallas County district judge testified that, when he had served in the District Attorney's Office from the late-1950's to early-1960's, his superior warned him that he would be fired if he permitted any African-Americans to serve on a jury. Similarly, another Dallas County district judge and former assistant district attorney from 1976 to 1978 testified that he believed the office had a systematic policy of excluding African-Americans from juries. Of more importance, [a] manual entitled "Jury Selection in a Criminal Case" (sometimes known as the Sparling Manual) was distributed to prosecutors. It contained an article authored by a former prosecutor (and later a judge) under the direction of his superiors in the District Attorney's Office, outlining the reasoning for excluding minorities from jury service. Although the manual was written in 1968, it remained in

---

[36] The dissent reaches a different statistical result that supports the State's explanation. There are two flaws in its calculations. First, it excises from its calculations panel members who were struck for cause or by agreement, on the theory that prosecutors knew they could be rid of those panel members without resorting to the minimum punishment ruse. But the prosecution's calculation about whether to ask these manipulative questions occurred before prosecutors asked the trial court to strike panel members for cause and, frequently, before prosecutors and defense counsel would have reached agreement about removal. It is unlikely that prosecutors were so assured of being able to remove certain panel members for cause or by agreement that they would forgo the chance to create additional grounds for removal by employing the minimum-punishment ruse. Second, as with its analysis of the panelists receiving the graphic script, the dissent characterizes certain panel members in ways that in our judgment are unconvincing. For example, for purposes of the minimum-punishment analysis, the dissent considers Colleen Moses and Noad Vickery to be panelists so favorable to the prosecution that there was no need to resort to the minimum-punishment ruse, yet the dissent acknowledged Moses's and Vickery's ambivalent questionnaire responses in its discussion of the graphic script.

circulation until 1976, if not later, and was available at least to one of the prosecutors in Miller-El's trial. Prosecutors here marked the race of each prospective juror on their juror cards....

It is true, of course, that at some points the significance of Miller-El's evidence is open to judgment calls, but when this evidence on the issues raised is viewed cumulatively its direction is too powerful to conclude anything but discrimination.... The state court's conclusion that the prosecutors' strikes of Fields and Warren were not racially determined is shown up as wrong to a clear and convincing degree; the state court's conclusion was unreasonable as well as erroneous. The judgment of the Court of Appeals is reversed, and the case is remanded for entry of judgment for petitioner together with orders of appropriate relief....

BREYER, J., concurring.

... Miller-El marshaled extensive evidence of racial bias. But despite the strength of his claim, Miller-El's challenge has resulted in 17 years of largely unsuccessful and protracted litigation--including 8 different judicial proceedings and 8 different judicial opinions, and involving 23 judges, of whom 6 found the Batson standard violated and 16 the contrary.

The complexity of this process reflects the difficulty of finding a legal test that will objectively measure the inherently subjective reasons that underlie use of a peremptory challenge.... Batson embodies defects intrinsic to the task.

At Batson's first step, litigants remain free to misuse peremptory challenges as long as the strikes fall below the prima facie threshold level. At Batson's second step, prosecutors need only tender a neutral reason, not a persuasive or even plausible one. And most importantly, at step three, Batson asks judges to engage in the awkward, sometime hopeless, task of second-guessing a prosecutor's instinctive judgment—the underlying basis for which may be invisible even to the prosecutor exercising the challenge. See Batson v. Kentucky, 476 U.S. 79, 106 (1986) (Marshall, J., concurring) (noting that the unconscious internalization of racial stereotypes may lead litigants more easily to conclude "that a prospective black juror is 'sullen,' or 'distant,'" even though that characterization would not have sprung to mind had the prospective juror been white). In such circumstances, it may be impossible for trial courts to discern if a "seat-of-the-pants" peremptory challenge reflects a "seat-of-the-pants" racial stereotype.

Given the inevitably clumsy fit between any objectively measurable standard and the subjective decisionmaking at issue, I am not surprised to find studies and anecdotal reports suggesting that, despite Batson, the discriminatory use of peremptory challenges remains a problem. See, e.g., Baldus, Woodworth, Zuckerman, Weiner, & Broffitt, The Use of Peremptory Challenges in Capital Murder Trials: A Legal and Empirical Analysis, 3 U. Pa. J. Const. L. 3, 52-53, 73, n. 197 (2001) (in 317 capital trials in Philadelphia between 1981 and 1997, prosecutors struck 51% of black jurors and 26% of nonblack jurors; defense counsel struck 26% of black jurors and 54% of nonblack jurors; and race-based uses of prosecutorial peremptories declined by only 2% after Batson); Rose, The Peremptory Challenge Accused of Race or Gender Discrimination? Some Data from One County, 23 Law and Human Behavior 695, 698-699 (1999) (in one North Carolina county, 71% of excused black jurors were removed by the prosecution; 81% of excused white jurors were removed by the defense); Melilli, Batson in Practice: What We Have Learned About Batson and Peremptory Challenges, 71 Notre Dame L. Rev. 447, 462-464 (1996) (finding Batson challenges' success rates lower where peremptories were used to strike black, rather than white, potential jurors).

Practical problems of proof to the side, peremptory challenges seem increasingly anomalous in our judicial system. [The] use of race- and gender-based stereotypes in the jury-selection process seems better organized and more systematized than ever before.... For example, a trial consulting firm advertises a new jury-selection technology: "Whether you are trying a civil case or a criminal case, SmartJURY & trade; has likely determined the exact demographics (age, race, gender, education, occupation, marital status, number of children, religion, and income) of the type of jurors you should select and the type you should strike." SmartJURY Product Information, http://www.cts-america.com/smartjury_ pi.asp.

These examples reflect a professional effort to fulfill the lawyer's obligation to help his or her client. Nevertheless, the outcome in terms of jury selection is the same as it would be were the motive less benign. And as long as that is so, the law's antidiscrimination command and a peremptory jury-selection system that permits or encourages the use of stereotypes work at cross-purposes....

I recognize that peremptory challenges have a long historical pedigree. They may help to reassure a party of the fairness of the jury. But long ago, Blackstone recognized the peremptory challenge as an "arbitrary and capricious species of [a] challenge." 4 W. Blackstone, Commentaries on the Laws of England 346 (1769). If used to express stereotypical judgments about race, gender, religion, or national origin, peremptory challenges betray the jury's democratic origins and undermine its representative function. See 1 A. de Tocqueville, Democracy in America 287 (H. Reeve transl. 1900) ("[T]he institution of the jury raises the people ... to the bench of judicial authority [and] invests [them] with the direction of society"); A. Amar, The Bill of Rights 94-96 (1998) (describing the Founders' vision of juries as venues for democratic participation). The "scientific" use of peremptory challenges may also contribute to public cynicism about the fairness of the jury system and its role in American government. And, of course, the right to a jury free of discriminatory taint is constitutionally protected— the right to use peremptory challenges is not....

In light of the considerations I have mentioned, I believe it necessary to reconsider Batson's test and the peremptory challenge system as a whole. With that qualification, I join the Court's opinion.

THOMAS, J., dissenting.

... Miller-El must show that, based on the evidence before the Texas state courts, the only reasonable conclusion was that prosecutors had racially discriminated against prospective jurors. He has not even come close to such a showing. The state courts held two hearings, but despite ample opportunity, Miller-El presented little evidence that discrimination occurred during jury selection. In view of the evidence actually presented to the Texas courts, their conclusion that the State did not discriminate was eminently reasonable. As a close look at the state-court proceedings reveals, the majority relies almost entirely on evidence that Miller-El has never presented to any Texas state court.

Jury selection in Miller-El's trial took place over five weeks in February and March 1986. During the process, 19 of the 20 blacks on the 108-person venire panel were not seated on the jury: 3 were dismissed for cause, 6 were dismissed by the parties' agreement, and 10 were peremptorily struck by prosecutors. Miller-El objected to 8 of these 10 strikes, asserting that the prosecutors were discriminating against black veniremen. Each time, the prosecutors proffered a race-neutral, case-related reason for exercising the challenge, and the trial court permitted the venireman to be removed. The remaining black venireman, Troy Woods, served on the jury that convicted Miller-El....

At the completion of voir dire, Miller-El moved to strike the jury [and presented juror questionnaires of the 10 black veniremen struck by the State, a manual on jury selection in criminal cases authored by a former Dallas County prosecutor, and nine witnesses]. Their testimony made three things clear. First, the D.A.'s Office had never officially sanctioned or promoted racial discrimination in jury selection.... Second, witnesses testified that, despite the absence of any official policy, individual prosecutors had almost certainly excluded blacks in particular cases. Third and most important, no witness testified that the prosecutors in Miller-El's trial—Norman Kinne, Paul Macaluso, and Jim Nelson—had ever engaged in racially discriminatory jury selection.

[The majority] bases its decision on juror questionnaires and juror cards that Miller-El's new attorneys unearthed during his federal habeas proceedings and that he never presented to the state courts. Worse still, the majority marshals those documents in support of theories that Miller-El never argued to the state courts. AEDPA does not permit habeas petitioners to engage in this sort of sandbagging of state courts.

[The] majority hints that we may ignore AEDPA's limitation on the record under § 2254(d)(2) because the parties have ignored it.... Even if § 2254(d) is not jurisdictional, [it] speaks directly to federal courts when it states that a habeas application by a state prisoner "shall not be granted" except under the specified conditions. The strictures of § 2254(d) are not discretionary or waivable. Through AEDPA, Congress sought to ensure that federal courts would defer to the judgments of state courts, not the wishes of litigants.

Even taken on its own terms, Miller-El's cumulative evidence does not come remotely close to clearly and convincingly establishing that the state court's factual finding was unreasonable. I discuss in turn Miller-El's four types of evidence: (1) the alleged disparate treatment and (2) disparate questioning of black and white veniremen; (3) the prosecution's jury shuffles; and (4) historical discrimination by the D.A.'s Office in the selection of juries....

The majority devotes the bulk of its opinion to a side-by-side comparison of white panelists who were allowed to serve and two black panelists who were struck, Billy Jean Fields and Joe Warren.... But Warren was obviously equivocal about the death penalty. In the end, the majority's case reduces to a single venireman, Fields, and its reading of a 20-year-old voir dire transcript that is ambiguous at best....

From the outset of questioning, Warren did not specify when he would vote to impose the death penalty. When asked by prosecutor Paul Macaluso about his ability to impose the death penalty, Warren stated, "[T]here are some cases where I would agree, you know, and there are others that I don't." Macaluso then explained at length the types of crimes that qualified as capital murder under Texas law, and asked whether Warren would be able to impose the death penalty for those types of heinous crimes. Warren continued to hedge: "I would say it depends on the case and the circumstances involved at the time." He offered no sense of the circumstances that would lead him to conclude that the death penalty was an appropriate punishment....

The majority points to four other panel members—Kevin Duke, Troy Woods, Sandra Jenkins, and Leta Girard—who supposedly expressed views much like Warren's, but who were not struck by the State. According to the majority, this is evidence of pretext. But the majority's premise is faulty. None of these veniremen was as difficult to pin down on the death penalty as Warren. For instance, Duke supported the death penalty ("I've always believed in having the death penalty. I think it serves a purpose")....

Only Sandra Jenkins was questioned early in the voir dire process, and thus only Jenkins was even arguably similarly situated to Warren. However, Jenkins and Warren were different in important respects. Jenkins expressed no doubt whatsoever about the death penalty. She testified that she had researched the death penalty in high school, and she said in response to questioning by both parties that she strongly believed in the death penalty's value as a deterrent to crime....

The majority thinks it can prove pretext by pointing to white veniremen who match only one of the State's proffered reasons for striking Warren. This defies logic. "Similarly situated" does not mean matching any one of several reasons the prosecution gave for striking a potential juror—it means matching all of them. Given limited peremptories, prosecutors often must focus on the potential jurors most likely to disfavor their case.... Of course jurors must not be identical in all respects to gauge pretext, but to isolate race as a variable, the jurors must be comparable in all respects that the prosecutor proffers as important....

The second black venireman on whom the majority relies is Billy Jean Fields. Fields expressed support for the death penalty, but Fields also expressed views that called into question his ability to impose the death penalty. Fields was a deeply religious man, and prosecutors feared that his religious convictions might make him reluctant to impose the death penalty. Those fears were confirmed by Fields' view that all people could be rehabilitated if introduced to God....

As with Warren, the majority attempts to point to similarly situated nonblack veniremen who were not struck by the State, but its efforts again miss their mark for several reasons. First, the majority would do better to begin with white veniremen who were struck by the State. For instance, it skips over Penny Crowson, a white panelist who expressed a firm belief in the death penalty, but who also stated that she probably would not impose the death penalty if she believed there was a chance the defendant could be rehabilitated. The State struck Crowson, which demonstrates that it was concerned about views on rehabilitation when the venireperson was not black.

Second, the nonblack veniremen to whom the majority points— Sandra Hearn, Mary Witt, and Fernando Gutierrez—were more favorable to the State than Fields for various reasons. [For instance], Mary Witt did not even have the same views on rehabilitation as Fields: She testified to the commonplace view that some, but not all, people can be rehabilitated. Moreover, Witt expressed strong support for the death penalty. She testified that the death penalty was appropriate for the crime of murder in the course of a robbery, or for a convict who was released from prison and committed murder (Miller-El previously had twice spent time in prison for armed robberies)....

Miller-El's claims of disparate questioning also do not fit the facts.... The State questioned panelists differently when their questionnaire responses indicated ambivalence about the death penalty. Any racial disparity in questioning resulted from the reality that more nonblack veniremen favored the death penalty and were willing to impose it.

The jury questionnaires asked two questions directly relevant to the death penalty. Question 56 asked, "Do you believe in the death penalty?" It offered panelists the chance to circle "yes" or "no," and then asked them to "please explain your answer" in the provided space. E.g., Joint Lodging 6. Question 58 asked, "Do you have any moral, religious, or personal beliefs that would prevent you from returning a verdict which would ultimately result in the execution of another human being?" and offered panelists only the chance to circle "yes" or "no."

According to the State, those veniremen who took a consistent stand on the death penalty—either for or against it—did not receive the graphic script. These prospective jurors either answered "no" to question 56 and "yes" to question 58 (meaning they did not believe in the death penalty and had qualms about imposing it), or answered "yes" to question 56 and "no" to question 58 (meaning they did believe in the death penalty and had no qualms about imposing it). Only those potential jurors who answered inconsistently, thereby indicating ambivalence about the death penalty, received the graphic script.

The questionnaires bear out this distinction. Fifteen blacks were questioned during voir dire. Only eight of them—or 53%—received the graphic script. All eight had given ambivalent questionnaire answers regarding their ability to impose the death penalty. The majority claims that Keaton, Kennedy, and Mackey were not ambivalent, but their questionnaire answers show otherwise. For instance, Keaton circled "no" for question 56, indicating she did not believe in the death penalty, and wrote, "It's not for me to punished [sic] anyone." However, she then circled "no" for question 58, indicating that she had no qualms about imposing the death penalty.

[The majority] hypothesizes that the script was used to remove only those black veniremen ambivalent about or opposed to the death penalty. But that explanation accounts for only 12 out of 15 veniremen, or 80%. The majority cannot explain why prosecutors did not use the script on Mosley and Smith, who were opposed to the death penalty, or Carter, who was ambivalent. Because the majority does not account for veniremen like Carter, and also mischaracterizes veniremen like Keaton, Kennedy, and Mackey, it arrives at different percentages. This is not clear and convincing evidence of racial bias.

The State's explanation also accounts for its treatment of the 12 nonblack veniremen (10 whites, 1 Hispanic, and 1 Filipino) on whom the majority relies. [Of] the five nonblacks who received the graphic script—Desinise, Evans, Gutierrez, Sztybel, and Zablan—four were ambivalent. On his questionnaire, Gutierrez answered both that he believed in the death penalty and that he had qualms about imposing it. Sztybel and Zablan averred that they believed in the death penalty and could impose it, but their written answers to question 56 made it unclear under what circumstances they could vote to impose the death penalty. Desinise is a closer call, but he was genuinely undecided about his ability to impose the death penalty, and the parties struck him by agreement. Of the five nonblacks who received the graphic script, Evans was the only one steadfastly opposed to the death penalty.

Of the seven nonblacks who allegedly did not receive the graphic script, four were strongly opposed to the death penalty…. Administering the graphic script to these potential jurors would have been useless. No trial lawyer would willingly antagonize a potential juror ardently opposed to the death penalty with an extreme portrait of its implementation. Of the remaining three nonblacks, [Girard] confirms the State's explanation. It was not clear from Girard's questionnaire whether she was ambivalent. On the stand, prosecutor Nelson started off with the abstract script. But it quickly became apparent that Girard was "just not real sure" about her ability to impose the death penalty, and she testified that she had not decided its value as a form of punishment. At that point, Nelson gave her the graphic script….

In any event, again the State's explanation fares well. The State's explanation accounts for prosecutors' choice between the abstract and graphic scripts for 9 of 12 nonblack veniremen, or 75%. Moses and Vickery were likely ambivalent but did not receive the graphic script, while Evans was opposed to the death penalty but did receive it. However, the majority's theory accounts for the State's treatment of only 6 of 12 nonblacks, or 50%. The majority can explain why jurors like Moses and Vickery did not receive the graphic script, because it believes the State was using the graphic script primarily with blacks opposed to or ambivalent about the death penalty. But the majority cannot explain the State's use of the script with an opposed nonblack like Evans, or ambivalent nonblacks like Desinise, Girard, Gutierrez, Sztybel, and Zablan….

Miller-El's argument that prosecutors shuffled the jury to remove blacks is pure speculation. At the Batson hearing, Miller-El did not raise, nor was there any discussion of, the topic of jury shuffling as a racial tactic. The record shows only that the State shuffled the jury during the first three weeks of jury selection, while Miller-El shuffled the jury during each of the five weeks. This evidence no more proves that prosecutors sought to eliminate blacks from the jury, than it proves that Miller-El sought to eliminate whites even more often.

Miller-El notes that the State twice shuffled the jury (in the second and third weeks) when a number of blacks were seated at the front of the panel. According to the majority, this gives rise to an "inference" that prosecutors were discriminating. But Miller-El should not be asking this Court to draw "inferences"; he should be asking it to examine clear and convincing proof....

The majority then tars prosecutors with a manual ... authored by John Sparling, a former Dallas County prosecutor. There is no evidence, however, that Kinne, Macaluso, or Nelson had ever read the Manual—which was written in 1968, almost two decades before Miller-El's trial. The reason there is no evidence on the question is that Miller-El never asked....

Thomas Joe Miller-El's charges of racism have swayed the Court, and AEDPA's restrictions will not stand in its way. But Miller-El has not established, much less established by clear and convincing evidence, that prosecutors racially discriminated in the selection of his jury—and he certainly has not done so on the basis of the evidence presented to the Texas courts. On the basis of facts and law, rather than sentiments, Miller-El does not merit the writ. I respectfully dissent.

Page 1131. Add this material at the end of note 3.

See also Johnson v. California, 2005 WL 1383731 (June 13, 2005) (party trying to establish prima facie case under *Batson* need not show by preponderance of evidence that peremptory challenge was based on improper bias).

Page 1132. Add this material at the end of note 4.

The Supreme Court said in Purkett v. Elem, 514 U.S. 765, 768 (1995), that a "silly" or "superstitious" reason for excluding a jury can overcome a prima facie case of discrimination, so long as the silliness is race neutral. But see Commonwealth v. Maldonado, 788 N.E.2d 968

(Mass. 2003) (reasons based on subjective data such as juror's looks or gestures, or attorney's "gut" feeling should "rarely be accepted as adequate because such explanations can easily be used as pretexts for discrimination").

C. Jury Deliberations and Verdicts

1. Instructions to Deadlocked Juries

Page 1141. Add this material at the end of note 6.

For a more complete version of the Hannaford, et al., study mentioned in the text (sponsored by the National Center for State Courts), see http://www.ncsconline.org/WC/Publications/Res_Juries_HungJuriesPub. pdf.

Page 1145. Add this material at the end of note 5.

See also State v. Dilliner, 569 S.E.2d 211 (W. Va. 2002) (use of special interrogatories in criminal case in absence of statutory authorization is reversible error).

Page 1147. Add this material before the notes.

Must the identity of the jurors be shared with the defendant and the public? The use of so-called "anonymous juries" is becoming increasingly common. In what situations, if any, is the use of an anonymous jury appropriate? Why not make all juries anonymous?

State v. Sherrie Tucker
657 N.W.2d 374 (Wis. 2003)

BABLITCH, J.
We are asked to decide under what circumstances a circuit court may restrict the disclosure of juror information in a criminal trial, and, if juror information is restricted, what precautions must be taken to avoid prejudice to the criminal defendant....

In March 1998, law enforcement officers executed a search warrant at an apartment shared by Tucker and her boyfriend, Damien McCray (McCray). In the apartment, officers found cocaine in a bag marked "Shiree Tucker," a .38 caliber revolver, and bullets. Tucker made a statement to police after a *Miranda* warning was given, in which she admitted that the cocaine belonged to her and that she had been selling cocaine for about a month. Tucker was tried and convicted of possession of cocaine with intent to deliver within 1,000 feet of a school while armed with a dangerous weapon, which resulted in a seven-year prison sentence. The circuit court judge stayed the prison sentence and instead ordered seven years of probation for Tucker.

Prior to jury selection for Tucker's trial, the circuit court judge told counsel off the record that "it has been my practice to use numbers and not names in this court.... What I'm prohibiting is the names of jurors being stated in the courtroom and for the record when other people may be sitting in the audience and using those names for any other reason." When defense counsel objected, the judge explained that the use of numbers is appropriate because this was a case "involving drugs and an allegation of drug dealing which I think raises the bar to some extent in terms of any danger to jurors."... During the trial, the judge corrected defense counsel when he referred to a juror by name, stating "it's my practice to refer to the jurors by number, so please follow the practice." There was no other statement made in front of the jury regarding the use of numbers instead of their names....

Both parties had access to all the juror information, including the jurors' names. Furthermore, the public presumably could have obtained the jurors' names by inquiring at the clerk of courts' office. A jury is typically deemed "anonymous" when juror information is withheld from the public and the *parties themselves.* Therefore, the jury in this case was not a classic "anonymous" jury. Notwithstanding whether the jury in this case is characterized as an "anonymous" or a "numbers" jury, if restrictions are placed on juror identification or information, due process concerns are raised regarding a defendant's rights to an impartial jury and a presumption of innocence. Accordingly, although this case does not deal with the classic "anonymous" jury, the reasoning in cases involving anonymous juries is beneficial to our analysis.

The empanelling of an anonymous jury is a relatively recent phenomenon that was rarely utilized before the Second Circuit's opinion in United States v. Barnes, 604 F.2d 121 (2d Cir. 1979). The court in *Barnes* addressed juror anonymity with respect to its effect on the practice of voir dire. In *Barnes,* the district court ordered that the jurors' identities, addresses, religious affiliations, and ethnic backgrounds remain anonymous, even from the parties themselves. The court ... examined each of the restrictions placed on juror information and concluded that the jurors' demeanors and responses to questions regarding their family, education and other matters would provide substantially the same information as the juror information that was restricted. Consequently, the court rejected the argument that the defendant was denied the ability to intelligently exercise peremptory challenges.... Although not explicit, the court essentially weighed the need to protect the jury, which was prompted by the defendant's ties to the mafia, against the rights of the defendant to an impartial jury.

A few years later, the Second Circuit addressed a different concern with the use of an anonymous jury in United States v. Thomas, 757 F.2d 1359 (2d Cir. 1985). In *Thomas,* the defendants argued that an anonymous jury is an unconstitutional infringement on a defendant's presumption of innocence because it gives jurors the impression that the defendant is dangerous and a threat to the jurors' safety. The court in *Thomas* acknowledged the fundamental tenet that a defendant is presumed innocent until proven guilty, but nevertheless determined that an anonymous jury might be permissible if jurors are in need of protection. Therefore, the court rejected a per se rule against empanelling an anonymous jury, but concluded that an anonymous jury is warranted *only if* there is a "strong reason" to believe that the jury needs protection and if the court takes "reasonable precautions" to minimize the impact of anonymity on the jurors' views of the defendant. The court noted that reasonable precautions were taken in that case, in part, because the judge gave the jury an "intelligent, reasonable and believable explanation for his actions that did not cast the defendants in an unfavorable light." In other words, the curative or precautionary instruction served to rebut any notion that the use of an anonymous jury was somehow a negative reflection on the defendant's guilt or character. The Second Circuit's approach in *Thomas* has been widely adopted by both federal and state courts....

[We also find the reasoning in *Thomas* persuasive.] Therefore, before a circuit court restricts any juror information in an individual case, it should determine that the jurors are in need of protection and take reasonable precautions to avoid prejudice to the defendant. In this case, Tucker concedes that her opportunity for voir dire was not impeded since both parties had access to all the juror information. However, Tucker claims that her presumption of innocence was eroded by the circuit court's use of numbers without an individualized determination that the jury needed protection nor a precautionary statement made to the jury regarding the use of numbers instead of names.

Serious concerns regarding a defendant's presumption of innocence are raised when juror information is restricted, as in this case. [The] empanelment of an anonymous jury triggers due process scrutiny because this practice is likely to taint the jurors' opinion of the defendant, thereby burdening the presumption of innocence. Therefore, courts must attempt to ensure that juror anonymity should not cast any adverse reflection upon the defendant.

[Accordingly, we] conclude that if a court withholds any juror information, it must both: (1) find that a jury needs protection; and (2) take reasonable precautions to avoid prejudicing the defendant. We now examine whether the circuit court in this case satisfied this two-prong test. [W]e hold that the circuit court erroneously exercised its discretion by failing to apply the correct standard of law....

First, the circuit court did not make an individualized determination that the jurors needed protection based on the specific circumstances present in Tucker's case. Rather, the court informed counsel that "it has been my *practice* to use numbers and not names" in drug cases. The circuit court repeatedly referred to its "practice" of using numbers without specifically noting any particular factors that warranted the use of numbers in Tucker's case.

There are various factors that may be taken into account in making an individualized determination that a jury needs protection. Such factors may include, but are not limited to: (1) the defendant's involvement in organized crime; (2) the defendant's participation in a group with the capacity to harm jurors; (3) the defendant's past attempts to interfere with the judicial process; and (4) extensive publicity that could enhance the possibility that jurors' names would become public and expose them to intimidation or harassment.

Second, the circuit court did not take necessary precautions to minimize any prejudicial effect to Tucker. Although the circuit court explained the use of numbers instead of jurors' names to counsel off the record, the court did not make any statement to the jurors regarding its use of numbers. Rather, the jurors were just referred to by number instead of name. The only statement heard by the jurors regarding the use of numbers was when the circuit court corrected defense counsel by stating, "it's my practice to refer to the jurors by number, so please follow the practice." The circuit court did instruct the jury on Tucker's presumption of innocence and on the State's burden of proving guilt beyond a reasonable doubt. However, we conclude that this instruction, by itself, was insufficient. When jurors' names are withheld, as in this case, the circuit court, at a minimum, must make a precautionary statement to the jury that the use of numbers instead of names should in no way be interpreted as a reflection of the defendant's guilt or innocence....

Any additional precautionary statements that are made to a jury when juror information is restricted should be based on factors and influences that may be present in a case, which could warrant withholding juror information. A precautionary statement must not mislead a jury, but must be based on factors and influences that are relevant in a particular case....

Although the circuit court erred [in its use of numbered jurors in this case], the error in this case was harmless. An error is harmless if it is clear beyond a reasonable doubt that a rational jury would have found the defendant guilty absent the error.... In this case, Tucker admitted to police after she was given a *Miranda* warning that the cocaine belonged to her and that she had been selling cocaine for about a month.... In addition, the cocaine found in Tucker and McCray's apartment was in a plastic bag marked "Shiree Tucker."...

BRADLEY, J., concurring.

... If this were an anonymous jury, then I agree with the majority that the circuit court was required to make an individualized determination of the need for such a jury. I part ways with the majority because it fails to draw a distinction between a numbers jury, as here, and an anonymous jury. The result of this failure is that in concluding that harmless error applies in this "numbers only" situation, it incorrectly extends harmless error as a remedy in all truly anonymous jury cases. Such a widespread extension is contrary to precedent....

Ultimately, I concur in the mandate of the majority because I conclude that there was no error. The defendant had access to all juror information, including their names. Given that the only limitation here was how the jurors were addressed and that the judge advised the jury that it was her practice to use numbers rather than names, I do not find that the defendant's rights were violated.

Measures to shield juror information not only implicate the defendant's rights, but also contradict the presumption of openness that defines the American judicial system. The selection of jurors has always presumptively been a public process.

Since the sixteenth century jurors have been selected in public. It is not surprising that trials in colonial America adopted the presumptive openness of the jury selection process that developed in England. This openness enhances both the basic fairness of the criminal trial and the appearance of fairness so essential to public confidence in the system....

A few years ago this court unanimously rejected a petition for an administrative rule governing juror confidentiality. The petition provided that jurors be referred to only by number and that no personal juror identifying information could be elicited during voir dire. It allowed that a party may, after the trial, petition the court for access to personal juror identifying information for purposes of developing a motion for a new trial.

The breadth of such a proposal and its effect on our tradition of public trials were apparent to many who appeared in opposition to the proposal at the public hearing. The State Bar of Wisconsin was one of the groups that appeared in opposition to the petition. It cautioned that an anonymous jury should be used only in "an extremely rare circumstance."

A trial is a public event and a public trial lies at the foundation of our legal tradition. The public trial is rooted in the "principle that justice cannot survive behind walls of silence." Sheppard v. Maxwell, 384 U.S. 333 (1966).

The majority's failure to distinguish between a numbers jury and an anonymous jury serves to dilute the jurisprudence on anonymous juries. It compounds this problem by applying an across-the-board "no harm, no foul" analysis of the harmless error rule thus serving to make the use of anonymous juries more commonplace. [Instead, the use of an anonymous jury should be] the "last resort" and "a drastic measure."...

The most common rationale for an anonymous jury is the protection of the jurors. A jury that sits in fear may not fill the expectation of impartiality. Yet, the use of an anonymous jury is a double-edged sword—it can give a sense of security or it can breed and feed fear. When fear is the result, then jury anonymity is a solution that exacerbates the problem it was intended to solve.

SYKES, J., concurring.
… The parties and the public had unrestricted access to all juror identifying information. As such, the anonymous jury case law does not apply. The majority opinion nevertheless applies the anonymous jury case law, assumes that the presumption of innocence has been violated, and imposes the procedural requirements prescribed by the inapplicable anonymous jury cases…. I cannot agree with this approach.

Voir dire by number does not implicate the presumption of innocence in the same way that the cases have assumed the use of an anonymous jury does. It has not been demonstrated—in this case or in the case law—that mere voir dire by number, without any restriction on access to juror information, has any serious adverse impact on the presumption of innocence. Any suggestion that it does is pure speculation. Indeed, the majority engages in no evaluation of this point at all, but merely extrapolates a presumption of innocence/due process violation from cases that involved true anonymous juries rather than the far more innocuous practice of voir dire by number.

Our courthouses today are equipped with various security precautions—metal detectors at courthouse entrances, security glass in individual courtrooms, armed deputy sheriffs in the courtroom and in the courthouse hallways—all of which suggest at least some level of risk to the people who work and visit there, including the jurors. It cannot seriously be suggested that the presumption of innocence has necessarily been compromised by the use of any of these sorts of generalized protections. Certain special security precautions are sometimes taken in individual cases, such as posting extra deputies in the courtroom, without encumbering the presumption of innocence or requiring particularized due process justifications. Voir dire by number (if a circuit court chooses to use this technique) falls within this category of routine security measures, whether used as a general practice, in a certain class of cases, or case-by-case.

In my view, voir dire by number, without any other restriction on the scope of voir dire or the parties' or the public's access to juror identifying information, does not rise to the level of an encumbrance on the presumption of innocence so as to implicate the defendant's right to due process....

Notes

1. *Anonymous juries.* The use of anonymous juries appears to be on the rise. Should the use of numbered jurors be treated the same as anonymous jurors? See Adam Liptak, Nameless Juries Are on the Rise in Crime Cases, N.Y. Times, Nov. 18, 2002:

> Anonymous juries have since been used in the trials of the Branch Davidians, of the police officers accused of assaulting Rodney King and Abner Louima, and of John Gotti, O. J. Simpson and Oliver North.... Increasingly, they are being used in more mundane cases.... Statistics on anonymous juries are hard to come by, but there is little doubt that their use is increasing....

2. Jury Nullification

Page 1150. Add this material at the end of note 1.

See also People v. Engelman, 49 P.3d 209 (Cal. 2002) (pattern instruction stated that jurors were required to conduct themselves as required by instructions and other jurors had obligation to advise court if juror refused to deliberate or expressed intention to decide case on improper basis; instruction did not violate constitution, but created unnecessary and inadvisable risk to proper functioning of jury deliberations and should not be given in future trials).

Page 1153. Add this material at the end of note 5.

See People v. Harlan, 109 P.3d 116 (Colo. 2005) (vacating death sentence due to jurors' use of Bible during deliberations, because "the judicial system works very hard to emphasize the rarified, solemn and sequestered nature of jury deliberations").

Chapter 18

Witnesses and Proof

A. *Burden of Proof*

1. Reasonable Doubt

Page 1184.   Add this material at the end of note 3.

For a careful review of the history of the reasonable doubt standard in the United States, see Steve Sheppard, The Metamorphoses of Reasonable Doubt: How Changes in the Burden of Proof Have Weakened the Presumption of Innocence, 78 Notre Dame L. Rev. 1165 (2003) (tracking twentieth-century shift to interpretation that emphasizes assignment of reasons as operational meaning of reasonableness).

2. Presumptions

Page 1189.   Add this material before the notes.

Virginia v. Barry Elton Black
538 U.S. 343 (2003)

O'CONNOR, J.

In this case we consider whether the Commonwealth of Virginia's statute banning cross burning with "an intent to intimidate a person or group of persons" violates the First Amendment. Va. Code Ann. §18.2-423. We conclude that while a State, consistent with the First

Amendment, may ban cross burning carried out with the intent to intimidate, the provision in the Virginia statute treating any cross burning as prima facie evidence of intent to intimidate renders the statute unconstitutional in its current form.

I.

Respondents Barry Black, Richard Elliott, and Jonathan O'Mara were convicted separately of violating Virginia's cross-burning statute. That statute provides:

> It shall be unlawful for any person or persons, with the intent of intimidating any person or group of persons, to burn, or cause to be burned, a cross on the property of another, a highway or other public place. . . . Any such burning of a cross shall be prima facie evidence of an intent to intimidate a person or group of persons.

On August 22, 1998, Barry Black led a Ku Klux Klan rally in Carroll County, Virginia. Twenty-five to thirty people attended this gathering, which occurred on private property with the permission of the owner, who was in attendance. . . . When the sheriff of Carroll County learned that a Klan rally was occurring in his county, he went to observe it from the side of the road. During the approximately one hour that the sheriff was present, about 40 to 50 cars passed the site, a "few" of which stopped to ask the sheriff what was happening on the property. Eight to ten houses were located in the vicinity of the rally. Rebecca Sechrist, who was related to the owner of the property where the rally took place, "sat and watched to see what was going on" from the lawn of her in-laws' house. She ... heard Klan members speak about "what they were" and "what they believed in." The speakers "talked real bad about the blacks and the Mexicans." One speaker told the assembled gathering that "he would love to take a .30/.30 and just randomly shoot the blacks." The speakers also talked about "President Clinton and Hillary Clinton," and about how their tax money "goes to the black people." Sechrist testified that this language made her "very scared." At the conclusion of the rally, the crowd circled around a 25- to 30-foot cross. The cross was between 300 and 350 yards away from the road. According to the sheriff, the cross "then all of a sudden ... went up in a flame." ... The sheriff then went down the driveway, entered the rally, and asked "who was responsible for burning the cross." Black responded, "I guess I am because I'm the head of the rally." The sheriff then told Black, "There's a law in the State of Virginia that you cannot burn a cross and I'll have to place you under arrest for this." . . .

At his trial, the jury was instructed that "intent to intimidate means the motivation to intentionally put a person or a group of persons in fear of bodily harm. Such fear must arise from the willful conduct of the accused rather than from some mere temperamental timidity of the victim." The trial court also instructed the jury that "the burning of a cross by itself is sufficient evidence from which you may infer the required intent."... The jury found Black guilty, and fined him $2,500....

On May 2, 1998, respondents Richard Elliott and Jonathan O'Mara, as well as a third individual, attempted to burn a cross on the yard of James Jubilee. Jubilee, an African-American, was Elliott's next-door neighbor in Virginia Beach, Virginia. Four months prior to the incident, Jubilee and his family had moved from California to Virginia Beach. Before the cross burning, Jubilee spoke to Elliott's mother to inquire about shots being fired from behind the Elliott home. Elliott's mother explained to Jubilee that her son shot firearms as a hobby, and that he used the backyard as a firing range.

On the night of May 2, respondents drove a truck onto Jubilee's property, planted a cross, and set it on fire. Their apparent motive was to "get back" at Jubilee for complaining about the shooting in the backyard. Respondents were not affiliated with the Klan. The next morning, as Jubilee was pulling his car out of the driveway, he noticed the partially burned cross approximately 20 feet from his house. After seeing the cross, Jubilee was "very nervous" because he "didn't know what would be the next phase," and because "a cross burned in your yard ... tells you that it's just the first round."

Elliott and O'Mara were charged with attempted cross burning and conspiracy to commit cross burning. [At trial], the court instructed the jury that the Commonwealth must prove that "the defendant intended to commit cross burning," that "the defendant did a direct act toward the commission of the cross burning," and that "the defendant had the intent of intimidating any person or group of persons." The court did not instruct the jury on the meaning of the word "intimidate," nor on the prima facie evidence provision of §18.2-423. The jury found Elliott guilty of attempted cross burning and acquitted him of conspiracy to commit cross burning. It sentenced Elliott to 90 days in jail and a $2,500 fine....

II.

... Burning a cross in the United States is inextricably intertwined with the history of the Ku Klux Klan. The first Ku Klux Klan began in Pulaski, Tennessee, in the spring of 1866.... The Klan fought Reconstruction and the corresponding drive to allow freed blacks to participate in the political process.... The Klan employed tactics such as whipping, threatening to burn people at the stake, and murder....

The genesis of the second Klan began in 1905, with the publication of Thomas Dixon's The Clansmen: An Historical Romance of the Ku Klux Klan. Dixon's book was a sympathetic portrait of the first Klan, depicting the Klan as a group of heroes "saving" the South from blacks and the "horrors" of Reconstruction.... When D.W. Griffith turned Dixon's book into the movie "The Birth of a Nation" in 1915, the association between cross burning and the Klan became indelible....

From the inception of the second Klan, cross burnings have been used to communicate both threats of violence and messages of shared ideology. The first initiation ceremony occurred on Stone Mountain near Atlanta, Georgia. While a 40-foot cross burned on the mountain, the Klan members took their oaths of loyalty.... Often, the Klan used cross burnings as a tool of intimidation and a threat of impending violence. For example, in 1939 and 1940, the Klan burned crosses in front of synagogues and churches. After one cross burning at a synagogue, a Klan member noted that if the cross burning did not "shut the Jews up, we'll cut a few throats and see what happens."...

To this day, regardless of whether the message is a political one or whether the message is also meant to intimidate, the burning of a cross is a symbol of hate. [While] a burning cross does not inevitably convey a message of intimidation, often the cross burner intends that the recipients of the message fear for their lives. And when a cross burning is used to intimidate, few if any messages are more powerful.

III.

The First Amendment, applicable to the States through the Fourteenth Amendment, provides that "Congress shall make no law ... abridging the freedom of speech." The hallmark of the protection of free speech is to allow "free trade in ideas"—even ideas that the overwhelming majority of people might find distasteful or discomforting....

The protections afforded by the First Amendment, however, are not absolute, and we have long recognized that the government may regulate certain categories of expression consistent with the Constitution. The First Amendment permits restrictions upon the content of speech in a few limited areas, which are of such slight social value as a step to truth that any benefit that may be derived from them is clearly outweighed by the social interest in order and morality.

We have consequently held that fighting words—"those personally abusive epithets which, when addressed to the ordinary citizen, are, as a matter of common knowledge, inherently likely to provoke violent reaction"—are generally proscribable under the First Amendment. Cohen v. California, 403 U.S. 15, 20 (1971).... And the First Amendment also permits a State to ban a "true threat." Watts v. United States, 394 U.S. 705, 708 (1969). "True threats" encompass those statements where the speaker means to communicate a serious expression of an intent to commit an act of unlawful violence to a particular individual or group of individuals.... Intimidation in the constitutionally proscribable sense of the word is a type of true threat, where a speaker directs a threat to a person or group of persons with the intent of placing the victim in fear of bodily harm or death. Respondents do not contest that some cross burnings fit within this meaning of intimidating speech, and rightly so.

[The] Virginia statute does not single out for opprobrium only that speech directed toward ... specified disfavored topics. It does not matter whether an individual burns a cross with intent to intimidate because of the victim's race, gender, or religion, or because of the victim's political affiliation, union membership, or homosexuality....

The First Amendment permits Virginia to outlaw cross burnings done with the intent to intimidate because burning a cross is a particularly virulent form of intimidation. Instead of prohibiting all intimidating messages, Virginia may choose to regulate this subset of intimidating messages in light of cross burning's long and pernicious history as a signal of impending violence....

IV.

The Supreme Court of Virginia ruled ... that Virginia's cross-burning statute was unconstitutionally overbroad due to its provision stating that "any such burning of a cross shall be prima facie evidence of an intent to intimidate a person or group of persons." [The Court] stated that "the act of burning a cross alone, with no evidence of intent to intimidate, will nonetheless suffice for arrest and prosecution and will insulate the Commonwealth from a motion to strike the evidence at the end of its case-in-chief." [The judge in Barry Black's case] instructed the jury that the provision means: "The burning of a cross, by itself, is sufficient evidence from which you may infer the required intent." This jury instruction is the same as the Model Jury Instruction in the Commonwealth of Virginia.

The prima facie evidence provision, as interpreted by the jury instruction, renders the statute unconstitutional.... As construed by the jury instruction, the prima facie provision strips away the very reason why a State may ban cross burning with the intent to intimidate. The prima facie evidence provision permits a jury to convict in every cross-burning case in which defendants exercise their constitutional right not to put on a defense. And even where a defendant like Black presents a defense, the prima facie evidence provision makes it more likely that the jury will find an intent to intimidate regardless of the particular facts of the case. The provision permits the Commonwealth to arrest, prosecute, and convict a person based solely on the fact of cross burning itself.

It is apparent that the provision as so interpreted would create an unacceptable risk of the suppression of ideas. The act of burning a cross may mean that a person is engaging in constitutionally proscribable intimidation. But that same act may mean only that the person is engaged in core political speech. The prima facie evidence provision in this statute blurs the line between these two meanings of a burning cross....

As the history of cross burning indicates, a burning cross is not always intended to intimidate. Rather, sometimes the cross burning is a statement of ideology, a symbol of group solidarity. It is a ritual used at Klan gatherings, and it is used to represent the Klan itself.... Indeed, occasionally a person who burns a cross does not intend to express either a statement of ideology or intimidation. Cross burnings have appeared in movies such as "Mississippi Burning," and in plays such as the stage adaptation of Sir Walter Scott's "The Lady of the Lake."

The prima facie provision makes no effort to distinguish among these different types of cross burnings. It does not distinguish between a cross burning done with the purpose of creating anger or resentment and a cross burning done with the purpose of threatening or intimidating a victim. It does not distinguish between a cross burning at a public rally or a cross burning on a neighbor's lawn. It does not treat the cross burning directed at an individual differently from the cross burning directed at a group of like-minded believers. It allows a jury to treat a cross burning on the property of another with the owner's acquiescence in the same manner as a cross burning on the property of another without the owner's permission.... The prima facie evidence provision in this case ignores all of the contextual factors that are necessary to decide whether a particular cross burning is intended to intimidate. The First Amendment does not permit such a shortcut....

SCALIA, J., concurring in part and dissenting in part.

The established meaning in Virginia ... of the term "prima facie evidence" appears to be perfectly orthodox: It is evidence that suffices, on its own, to establish a particular fact. But it is hornbook law that this is true only to the extent that the evidence goes unrebutted. [Where] the Commonwealth has demonstrated through its case in chief that the defendant burned a cross in public view, this is sufficient, at least until the defendant has come forward with rebuttal evidence, to create a jury issue with respect to the intent element of the offense.

It is important to note that the Virginia Supreme Court did not suggest (as did the trial court's jury instructions in respondent Black's case) that a jury may, in light of the prima-facie-evidence provision, ignore any rebuttal evidence that has been presented and, solely on the basis of a showing that the defendant burned a cross, find that he intended to intimidate. Nor, crucially, did that court say that the presentation of prima facie evidence is always sufficient to get a case to a jury, *i.e.*, that a court may never direct a verdict for a defendant who has been shown to have burned a cross in public view, even if, by the end of trial, the defendant has presented rebuttal evidence....

The question presented, then, is whether, given this understanding of the term "prima facie evidence," the cross-burning statute is constitutional. [Some] individuals who engage in protected speech may, because of the prima-facie-evidence provision, be subject to conviction. Such convictions, assuming they are unconstitutional, could be challenged on a case-by-case basis. The plurality, however, with little in the way of explanation, leaps to the conclusion that the *possibility* of such convictions justifies facial invalidation of the statute.... As the plurality concedes, the only persons who might impermissibly be convicted by reason of that provision are those who adopt a particular trial strategy, to wit, abstaining from the presentation of a defense....

The potential improper convictions of which the plurality complains are more appropriately classified as the sort of marginal applications of a statute in light of which facial invalidation is inappropriate. [What] appears to have happened is that the plurality has facially invalidated not §18.2-423, but its own hypothetical interpretation of §18.2-423, and has then remanded to the Virginia Supreme Court to learn the *actual* interpretation of §18.2-423. Words cannot express my wonderment at this virtuoso performance.

[Because] the Virginia Supreme Court has not yet offered an authoritative construction of §18.2-423, I concur in the Court's decision to vacate and remand the judgment with respect to respondents Elliott and O'Mara. I also agree that respondent Black's conviction cannot stand.... Because I believe the constitutional defect in Black's conviction is rooted in a jury instruction and not in the statute itself, I would not dismiss the indictment and would permit the Commonwealth to retry Black if it wishes to do so....

THOMAS, J., dissenting.

In every culture, certain things acquire meaning well beyond what outsiders can comprehend. That goes for both the sacred and the profane. I believe that cross burning is the paradigmatic example of the latter. Although I agree with the majority's conclusion that it is constitutionally permissible to ban cross burning carried out with intent to intimidate, I believe that the majority errs in imputing an expressive component to the activity in question. In my view, whatever expressive value cross burning has, the legislature simply wrote it out by banning only intimidating conduct undertaken by a particular means....

Even assuming that the statute implicates the First Amendment, in my view, the fact that the statute permits a jury to draw an inference of intent to intimidate from the cross burning itself presents no constitutional problems.... We have categorized the presumptions as either permissive inferences or mandatory presumptions. To the extent we do have a construction of this statute by the Virginia Supreme Court, we know that both the majority and the dissent agreed that the presumption was "a statutorily supplied *inference*." Under Virginia law, the term "inference" has a well-defined meaning and is distinct from the term "presumption." See Martin v. Phillips, 369 S.E.2d 397 (Va. 1988):

> A presumption is a rule of law that compels the fact finder to draw a certain conclusion or a certain inference from a given set of facts. [FN1: In contrast, *an inference,* sometimes loosely referred to as a presumption of fact, *does not compel a specific conclusion. An inference merely applies to the rational potency or probative value of an evidentiary fact to which the fact finder may attach whatever force or weight it deems best.* 9 J. Wigmore, Evidence in Trials at Common Law §2491(1), at 304 (Chad. rev. 1981).] The primary significance of a presumption is that it operates to shift to the opposing party the burden of producing evidence tending to rebut the presumption. [FN2: *An inference, on the other hand, does not invoke this procedural consequence of shifting the burden of production.*] No presumption, however, can operate to shift the ultimate burden of persuasion from the party upon whom it was originally cast....

[Inferences] raise no constitutional flags unless no rational trier could make a connection permitted by the inference....

But even with respect to statutes containing a mandatory irrebuttable presumption as to intent, the Court has not shown much concern. For instance, there is no scienter requirement for statutory rape. That is, a person can be arrested, prosecuted, and convicted for having sex with a minor, without the government ever producing any evidence, let alone proving beyond a reasonable doubt, that a minor did not consent.... The legislature finds the behavior so reprehensible that the intent is satisfied by the mere act committed by a perpetrator. Considering the horrific effect cross burning has on its victims, it is also reasonable to presume intent to intimidate from the act itself.... Because I would uphold the validity of this statute, I respectfully dissent.

B. *Confrontation of Witnesses*

2. Unavailable Prosecution Witnesses

Page 1211.   Add this material before the notes.

The following decision reconstructing the federal Confrontation Clause may have immense implications for police work and prosecution. As you read the case, consider what kinds of cases typically rely on the evidence that will now be barred or severely limited, and what you might do to respond to these new legal obligations as a police administrator or prosecutor.

Michael Crawford v. Washington
541 U.S. 36 (2004)

SCALIA, J.

Petitioner Michael Crawford stabbed a man who allegedly tried to rape his wife, Sylvia. At his trial, the State played for the jury Sylvia's tape-recorded statement to the police describing the stabbing, even though he had no opportunity for cross-examination. The Washington Supreme Court upheld petitioner's conviction after determining that Sylvia's statement was reliable. The question presented is whether this procedure complied with the Sixth Amendment's guarantee that, "[i]n all criminal prosecutions, the accused shall enjoy the right ... to be confronted with the witnesses against him."

I.

On August 5, 1999, Kenneth Lee was stabbed at his apartment. Police arrested petitioner later that night. After giving petitioner and his wife *Miranda* warnings, detectives interrogated each of them twice. Petitioner eventually confessed that he and Sylvia had gone in search of Lee because he was upset over an earlier incident in which Lee had tried to rape her. The two had found Lee at his apartment, and a fight ensued in which Lee was stabbed in the torso and petitioner's hand was cut. Petitioner gave the following account of the fight:

> Q. Okay. Did you ever see anything in [Lee's] hands?
> A. I think so, but I'm not positive.
> Q. Okay, when you think so, what do you mean by that?
> A. I coulda swore I seen him goin' for somethin' before, right before everything happened. He was like reachin', fiddlin' around down here and stuff ... and I just ... I don't know, I think, this is just a possibility, but I think, I think that he pulled somethin' out and I grabbed for it and that's how I got cut ... but I'm not positive....

Sylvia generally corroborated petitioner's story about the events leading up to the fight, but her account of the fight itself was arguably different—particularly with respect to whether Lee had drawn a weapon before petitioner assaulted him:

> Q. Did Kenny do anything to fight back from this assault?
> A. (pausing) I know he reached into his pocket ... or somethin' ... I don't know what.
> Q. After he was stabbed?
> A. He saw Michael coming up. He lifted his hand ... his chest open, he might [have] went to go strike his hand out or something and then (inaudible).
> Q. Okay, you, you gotta speak up.
> A. Okay, he lifted his hand over his head maybe to strike Michael's hand down or something and then he put his hands in his ... put his right hand in his right pocket ... took a step back ... Michael proceeded to stab him ... then his hands were like ... how do you explain this ... open arms ... with his hands open and he fell down ... and we ran (describing subject holding hands open, palms toward assailant).
> Q. Okay, when he's standing there with his open hands, you're talking about Kenny, correct?
> A. Yeah, after, after the fact, yes.
> Q. Did you see anything in his hands at that point?
> A. (pausing) um um (no).

The State charged petitioner with assault and attempted murder. At trial, he claimed self-defense. Sylvia did not testify because of the state marital privilege, which generally bars a spouse from testifying without the other spouse's consent. In Washington, this privilege does not extend to a spouse's out-of-court statements admissible under a hearsay exception, so the State sought to introduce Sylvia's tape-recorded statements to the police as evidence that the stabbing was not in self-defense. Noting that Sylvia had admitted she led petitioner to Lee's apartment and thus had facilitated the assault, the State invoked the hearsay exception for statements against penal interest, Wash. Rule Evid. 804(b)(3).

Petitioner countered that, state law notwithstanding, admitting the evidence would violate his federal constitutional right to be "confronted with the witnesses against him." Amdt. 6. According to our description of that right in Ohio v. Roberts, 448 U.S. 56 (1980), it does not bar admission of an unavailable witness's statement against a criminal defendant if the statement bears "adequate indicia of reliability." To meet that test, evidence must either fall within a "firmly rooted hearsay exception" or bear "particularized guarantees of trustworthiness." The trial court here admitted the statement on the latter ground, offering several reasons why it was trustworthy: Sylvia was not shifting blame but rather corroborating her husband's story that he acted in self-defense or "justified reprisal"; she had direct knowledge as an eyewitness; she was describing recent events; and she was being questioned by a "neutral" law enforcement officer. The prosecution played the tape for the jury and relied on it in closing, arguing that it was "damning evidence" that "completely refutes [petitioner's] claim of self-defense." The jury convicted petitioner of assault.

The Washington Court of Appeals reversed. It applied a nine-factor test to determine whether Sylvia's statement bore particularized guarantees of trustworthiness, and noted several reasons why it did not: The statement contradicted one she had previously given; it was made in response to specific questions; and at one point she admitted she had shut her eyes during the stabbing.... The Washington Supreme Court reinstated the conviction [and we] granted certiorari to determine whether the State's use of Sylvia's statement violated the Confrontation Clause.

II.

The Sixth Amendment's Confrontation Clause provides that, "[i]n all criminal prosecutions, the accused shall enjoy the right ... to be confronted with the witnesses against him." We have held that this bedrock procedural guarantee applies to both federal and state prosecutions.... Petitioner argues that [the *Roberts*] test strays from the original meaning of the Confrontation Clause and urges us to reconsider it.

The Constitution's text does not alone resolve this case. One could plausibly read "witnesses against" a defendant to mean those who actually testify at trial, those whose statements are offered at trial, or something in-between. We must therefore turn to the historical background of the Clause to understand its meaning.

The right to confront one's accusers is a concept that dates back to Roman times. The founding generation's immediate source of the concept, however, was the common law. English common law has long differed from continental civil law in regard to the manner in which witnesses give testimony in criminal trials. The common-law tradition is one of live testimony in court subject to adversarial testing, while the civil law condones examination in private by judicial officers. See 3 W. Blackstone, Commentaries on the Laws of England 373-374 (1768).

Nonetheless, England at times adopted elements of the civil-law practice. Justices of the peace or other officials examined suspects and witnesses before trial. These examinations were sometimes read in court in lieu of live testimony.... Pretrial examinations became routine under two statutes passed during the reign of Queen Mary in the 16th century, 1 & 2 Phil. & M., c. 13 (1554), and 2 & 3 *id.*, c. 10 (1555). These Marian bail and committal statutes required justices of the peace to examine suspects and witnesses in felony cases and to certify the results to the court....

The most notorious instances of civil-law examination occurred in the great political trials of the 16th and 17th centuries. One such was the 1603 trial of Sir Walter Raleigh for treason. Lord Cobham, Raleigh's alleged accomplice, had implicated him in an examination before the Privy Council and in a letter. At Raleigh's trial, these were read to the jury. Raleigh argued that Cobham had lied to save himself: "Cobham is absolutely in the King's mercy; to excuse me cannot avail him; by accusing me he may hope for favour." 1 D. Jardine, Criminal Trials 435 (1832). Suspecting that Cobham would recant, Raleigh demanded that the judges call him to appear, arguing that "[t]he Proof of the Common Law is by witness and jury: let Cobham be here, let him speak it. Call my accuser before my face...." The judges refused, and, despite Raleigh's protestations that he was being tried "by the Spanish Inquisition," the jury convicted, and Raleigh was sentenced to death.

One of Raleigh's trial judges later lamented that "the justice of England has never been so degraded and injured as by the condemnation of Sir Walter Raleigh." Through a series of statutory and judicial reforms, English law developed a right of confrontation that limited these abuses. For example, treason statutes required witnesses to confront the accused "face to face" at his arraignment. Courts, meanwhile, developed relatively strict rules of unavailability, admitting examinations only if the witness was demonstrably unable to testify in person. Several authorities also stated that a suspect's confession could be admitted only against himself, and not against others he implicated.

One recurring question was whether the admissibility of an unavailable witness's pretrial examination depended on whether the defendant had had an opportunity to cross-examine him. In 1696, the Court of King's Bench answered this question in the affirmative, in the widely reported misdemeanor libel case of King v. Paine, 87 Eng. Rep. 584. The court ruled that, even though a witness was dead, his examination was not admissible where "the defendant not being present when [it was] taken before the mayor ... had lost the benefit of a cross-examination."...

Controversial examination practices were also used in the Colonies. Early in the 18th century, for example, the Virginia Council protested against the Governor for having "privately issued several commissions to examine witnesses against particular men *ex parte,*" complaining that "the person accused is not admitted to be confronted with, or defend himself against his defamers." A Memorial Concerning the Maladministrations of His Excellency Francis Nicholson, reprinted in 9 English Historical Documents 253, 257 (D. Douglas ed. 1955). A decade before the Revolution, England gave jurisdiction over Stamp Act offenses to the admiralty courts, which followed civil-law rather than common-law procedures and thus routinely took testimony by deposition or private judicial examination. Colonial representatives protested that the Act subverted their rights "by extending the jurisdiction of the courts of admiralty beyond its ancient limits." John Adams, defending a merchant in a high-profile admiralty case, argued: "Examinations of witnesses upon Interrogatories, are only by the Civil Law. Interrogatories are unknown at common Law, and Englishmen and common Lawyers have an aversion to them if not an Abhorrence of them."

Many declarations of rights adopted around the time of the Revolution guaranteed a right of confrontation. The proposed Federal Constitution, however, did not. At the Massachusetts ratifying convention, Abraham Holmes objected to this omission precisely on the ground that it would lead to civil-law practices: "The mode of trial is altogether indetermined; ... whether [the defendant] is to be allowed to confront the witnesses, and have the advantage of cross-examination, we are not yet told.... [W]e shall find Congress possessed of powers enabling them to institute judicatories little less inauspicious than a certain tribunal in Spain, ... the *Inquisition.*" 2 Debates on the Federal Constitution 110-111 (J. Elliot 2d ed. 1863).... The First Congress responded by including the Confrontation Clause in the proposal that became the Sixth Amendment.

Early state decisions shed light upon the original understanding of the common-law right. *State v. Webb,* 2 N.C. 103 (1794) *(per curiam),* decided a mere three years after the adoption of the Sixth Amendment, held that depositions could be read against an accused only if they were taken in his presence. Rejecting a broader reading of the English authorities, the court held: "[I]t is a rule of the common law, founded on natural justice, that no man shall be prejudiced by evidence which he had not the liberty to cross examine."...

III.

This history supports two inferences about the meaning of the Sixth Amendment.... First, the principal evil at which the Confrontation Clause was directed was the civil-law mode of criminal procedure, and particularly its use of *ex parte* examinations as evidence against the accused. It was these practices that the Crown deployed in notorious treason cases like Raleigh's; that the Marian statutes invited; that English law's assertion of a right to confrontation was meant to prohibit; and that the founding-era rhetoric decried. The Sixth Amendment must be interpreted with this focus in mind.

Accordingly, we once again reject the view that the Confrontation Clause applies of its own force only to in-court testimony, and that its application to out-of-court statements introduced at trial depends upon "the law of Evidence for the time being." Leaving the regulation of out-of-court statements to the law of evidence would render the Confrontation Clause powerless to prevent even the most flagrant inquisitorial practices. Raleigh was, after all, perfectly free to confront those who read Cobham's confession in court.

This focus also suggests that not all hearsay implicates the Sixth Amendment's core concerns. An off-hand, overheard remark might be unreliable evidence and thus a good candidate for exclusion under hearsay rules, but it bears little resemblance to the civil-law abuses the Confrontation Clause targeted. On the other hand, *ex parte* examinations might sometimes be admissible under modern hearsay rules, but the Framers certainly would not have condoned them.

The text of the Confrontation Clause reflects this focus. It applies to "witnesses" against the accused—in other words, those who "bear testimony." 1 N. Webster, An American Dictionary of the English Language (1828). "Testimony," in turn, is typically "[a] solemn declaration or affirmation made for the purpose of establishing or proving some fact." An accuser who makes a formal statement to government officers bears testimony in a sense that a person who makes a casual remark to an acquaintance does not. The constitutional text, like the history underlying the common-law right of confrontation, thus reflects an especially acute concern with a specific type of out-of-court statement....

Regardless of the precise [definition of "testimonial" statements], some statements qualify under any definition—for example, *ex parte* testimony at a preliminary hearing. Statements taken by police officers in the course of interrogations are also testimonial under even a narrow standard. Police interrogations bear a striking resemblance to examinations by justices of the peace in England. The statements are not *sworn* testimony, but the absence of oath was not dispositive. Cobham's examination was unsworn, yet Raleigh's trial has long been thought a paradigmatic confrontation violation.

That interrogators are police officers rather than magistrates does not change the picture either. Justices of the peace conducting examinations under the Marian statutes were not magistrates as we understand that office today, but had an essentially investigative and prosecutorial function.... In sum, even if the Sixth Amendment is not solely concerned with testimonial hearsay, that is its primary object, and interrogations by law enforcement officers fall squarely within that class.[4] ...

The historical record also supports a second proposition: that the Framers would not have allowed admission of testimonial statements of a witness who did not appear at trial unless he was unavailable to testify, and the defendant had had a prior opportunity for cross-examination. The text of the Sixth Amendment does not suggest any open-ended exceptions from the confrontation requirement to be developed by the courts. Rather, the "right ... to be confronted with the witnesses against him," Amdt. 6, is most naturally read as a reference to the right of confrontation at common law, admitting only those exceptions established at the time of the founding. As the English authorities above reveal, the common law in 1791 conditioned admissibility of an absent witness's examination on unavailability and a prior opportunity to cross-examine. The Sixth Amendment therefore incorporates those limitations....

We do not read the historical sources to say that a prior opportunity to cross-examine was merely a sufficient, rather than a necessary, condition for admissibility of testimonial statements. They suggest that this requirement was dispositive, and not merely one of several ways to establish reliability. This is not to deny ... that "[t]here were always exceptions to the general rule of exclusion" of hearsay evidence. Several had become well established by 1791. But there is scant evidence that exceptions were invoked to admit *testimonial* statements against the accused in a *criminal* case.[6] Most of the hearsay exceptions covered

---

[4] We use the term "interrogation" in its colloquial, rather than any technical legal, sense. Cf. Rhode Island v. Innis, 446 U.S. 291 (1980). Just as various definitions of "testimonial" exist, one can imagine various definitions of "interrogation," and we need not select among them in this case. Sylvia's recorded statement, knowingly given in response to structured police questioning, qualifies under any conceivable definition.

[6] The one deviation we have found involves dying declarations. The existence of that exception as a general rule of criminal hearsay law cannot be disputed. Although many dying declarations may not be testimonial, there is authority for admitting even those that clearly are. We need not decide in this case whether the Sixth Amendment incorporates an exception for testimonial dying declarations. If this exception must be accepted on historical grounds, it is *sui generis*.

statements that by their nature were not testimonial—for example, business records or statements in furtherance of a conspiracy. We do not infer from these that the Framers thought exceptions would apply even to prior testimony....

Our case law has been largely consistent with these two principles. Our leading early decision, for example, involved a deceased witness's prior trial testimony. Mattox v. United States, 156 U.S. 237 (1895). In allowing the statement to be admitted, we relied on the fact that the defendant had had, at the first trial, an adequate opportunity to confront the witness....

V.

Although the results of our decisions have generally been faithful to the original meaning of the Confrontation Clause, the same cannot be said of our rationales. *Roberts* conditions the admissibility of all hearsay evidence on whether it falls under a "firmly rooted hearsay exception" or bears "particularized guarantees of trustworthiness." This test departs from the historical principles identified above in two respects. First, it is too broad: It applies the same mode of analysis whether or not the hearsay consists of *ex parte* testimony. This often results in close constitutional scrutiny in cases that are far removed from the core concerns of the Clause. At the same time, however, the test is too narrow: It admits statements that *do* consist of *ex parte* testimony upon a mere finding of reliability. This malleable standard often fails to protect against paradigmatic confrontation violations....

Where testimonial statements are involved, we do not think the Framers meant to leave the Sixth Amendment's protection to the vagaries of the rules of evidence, much less to amorphous notions of "reliability." ... Admitting statements deemed reliable by a judge is fundamentally at odds with the right of confrontation. To be sure, the Clause's ultimate goal is to ensure reliability of evidence, but it is a procedural rather than a substantive guarantee. It commands, not that evidence be reliable, but that reliability be assessed in a particular manner: by testing in the crucible of cross-examination. The Clause thus reflects a judgment, not only about the desirability of reliable evidence (a point on which there could be little dissent), but about how reliability can best be determined.

The *Roberts* test allows a jury to hear evidence, untested by the adversary process, based on a mere judicial determination of reliability. It thus replaces the constitutionally prescribed method of assessing reliability with a wholly foreign one....

The Raleigh trial itself involved the very sorts of reliability determinations that *Roberts* authorizes. In the face of Raleigh's repeated demands for confrontation, the prosecution responded with many of the arguments a court applying *Roberts* might invoke today: that Cobham's statements were self-inculpatory, that they were not made in the heat of passion, and that they were not "extracted from [him] upon any hopes or promise of Pardon." It is not plausible that the Framers' only objection to the trial was that Raleigh's judges did not properly weigh these factors before sentencing him to death. Rather, the problem was that the judges refused to allow Raleigh to confront Cobham in court, where he could cross-examine him and try to expose his accusation as a lie.

Dispensing with confrontation because testimony is obviously reliable is akin to dispensing with jury trial because a defendant is obviously guilty. This is not what the Sixth Amendment prescribes....

The legacy of *Roberts* in other courts vindicates the Framers' wisdom in rejecting a general reliability exception. The framework is so unpredictable that it fails to provide meaningful protection from even core confrontation violations.

Reliability is an amorphous, if not entirely subjective, concept. There are countless factors bearing on whether a statement is reliable; the nine-factor balancing test applied by the Court of Appeals below is representative. See, e.g., People v. Farrell, 34 P.3d 401 (Colo. 2001) (eight-factor test). Whether a statement is deemed reliable depends heavily on which factors the judge considers and how much weight he accords each of them. Some courts wind up attaching the same significance to opposite facts....

Roberts' failings were on full display in the proceedings below. Sylvia Crawford made her statement while in police custody, herself a potential suspect in the case. Indeed, she had been told that whether she would be released "depend[ed] on how the investigation continues." In response to often leading questions from police detectives, she implicated her husband in Lee's stabbing and at least arguably undermined his self-defense claim. Despite all this, the trial court admitted her statement, listing several reasons why it was reliable. In its opinion reversing, the Court of Appeals listed several *other* reasons why the statement was *not* reliable. Finally, the State Supreme Court relied exclusively on the interlocking character of the statement and disregarded every other factor the lower courts had considered. The case is thus a self-contained demonstration of *Roberts'* unpredictable and inconsistent application....

We readily concede that we could resolve this case by simply reweighing the "reliability factors" under *Roberts* and finding that Sylvia Crawford's statement falls short. But we view this as one of those rare cases in which the result below is so improbable that it reveals a fundamental failure on our part to interpret the Constitution in a way that secures its intended constraint on judicial discretion....

We have no doubt that the courts below were acting in utmost good faith when they found reliability. The Framers, however, would not have been content to indulge this assumption. They knew that judges, like other government officers, could not always be trusted to safeguard the rights of the people; the likes of the dread Lord Jeffreys were not yet too distant a memory. They were loath to leave too much discretion in judicial hands. By replacing categorical constitutional guarantees with open-ended balancing tests, we do violence to their design. Vague standards are manipulable, and, while that might be a small concern in run-of-the-mill assault prosecutions like this one, the Framers had an eye toward politically charged cases like Raleigh's—great state trials where the impartiality of even those at the highest levels of the judiciary might not be so clear. It is difficult to imagine *Roberts'* providing any meaningful protection in those circumstances....

Where nontestimonial hearsay is at issue, it is wholly consistent with the Framers' design to afford the States flexibility in their development of hearsay law—as does *Roberts,* and as would an approach that exempted such statements from Confrontation Clause scrutiny altogether. Where testimonial evidence is at issue, however, the Sixth Amendment demands what the common law required: unavailability and a prior opportunity for cross-examination. We leave for another day any effort to spell out a comprehensive definition of "testimonial." Whatever else the term covers, it applies at a minimum to prior testimony at a preliminary hearing, before a grand jury, or at a former trial; and to police interrogations. These are the modern practices with closest kinship to the abuses at which the Confrontation Clause was directed....

REHNQUIST, C.J., concurring in the judgment.

I dissent from the Court's decision to overrule Ohio v. Roberts, 448 U.S. 56 (1980). I believe that the Court's adoption of a new interpretation of the Confrontation Clause is not backed by sufficiently persuasive reasoning to overrule long-established precedent. Its decision casts a mantle of uncertainty over future criminal trials in both federal and state courts, and is by no means necessary to decide the present case.

The Court's distinction between testimonial and nontestimonial statements, contrary to its claim, is no better rooted in history than our current doctrine. Under the common law, although the courts were far from consistent, out-of-court statements made by someone other than the accused and not taken under oath, unlike *ex parte* depositions or affidavits, were generally not considered substantive evidence upon which a conviction could be based. Testimonial statements such as accusatory statements to police officers likely would have been disapproved of in the 18th century, not necessarily because they resembled *ex parte* affidavits or depositions as the Court reasons, but more likely than not because they were not made under oath. Without an oath, one usually did not get to the second step of whether confrontation was required. Thus, while I agree that the Framers were mainly concerned about sworn affidavits and depositions, it does not follow that they were similarly concerned about the Court's broader category of testimonial statements....

I therefore see no reason why the distinction the Court draws is preferable to our precedent. Starting with Chief Justice Marshall's interpretation as a Circuit Justice in 1807, 16 years after the ratification of the Sixth Amendment, United States v. Burr, 25 F. Cas. 187, 193 (No. 14,694) (CC Va. 1807), continuing with our cases in the late 19th century, and through today, we have never drawn a distinction between testimonial and nontestimonial statements. And for that matter, neither has any other court of which I am aware. I see little value in trading our precedent for an imprecise approximation at this late date....

Nor was the English law at the time of the framing entirely consistent in its treatment of testimonial evidence. Generally *ex parte* affidavits and depositions were excluded as the Court notes, but even that proposition was not universal.... With respect to unsworn testimonial statements, there is no indication that once the hearsay rule was developed courts ever excluded these statements if they otherwise fell within a firmly rooted exception. Dying declarations are one example....

Between 1700 and 1800 the rules regarding the admissibility of out-of-court statements were still being developed.... It is one thing to trace the right of confrontation back to the Roman Empire; it is quite another to conclude that such a right absolutely excludes a large category of evidence. It is an odd conclusion indeed to think that the Framers created a cut-and-dried rule with respect to the admissibility of testimonial statements when the law during their own time was not fully settled....

Exceptions to confrontation have always been derived from the experience that some out-of-court statements are just as reliable as cross-examined in-court testimony due to the circumstances under which they were made.... That a statement might be testimonial does nothing to undermine the wisdom of one of these exceptions. [C]ross-examination is a tool used to flesh out the truth, not an empty procedure. [In] a given instance [cross-examination may] be superfluous....

The Court grandly declares that "we leave for another day any effort to spell out a comprehensive definition of 'testimonial.'" But the thousands of federal prosecutors and the tens of thousands of state prosecutors need answers as to what beyond the specific kinds of "testimony" the Court lists is covered by the new rule. They need them now, not months or years from now. Rules of criminal evidence are applied every day in courts throughout the country, and parties should not be left in the dark in this manner....

Page 1212.   Add this material at the end of note 2.

See Jefferson v. State, 2005 WL 2609803 (Ark., Nov. 18, 2004) (in a case involving a small cast of characters, replacing defendant's name in co-defendant's confession did not solve *Bruton* problem).

Page 1213.   Add this material at the end of note 4.

See State v. Davis, (Wash. 2005) (application of *Crawford* to 911 call should be assessed on case-by-case basis; a single call may contain some portions that are testimonial and some that are not; victim of domestic violence called 911 but hung up before speaking, operator called back and asked what was happening, victim replied "He's here jumpin' on me again," in response to operator questions she identified the assailant as her husband).

C. *Self-Incrimination Privilege at Trial*

Page 1234.   Add this material at the end of note 4.

See Weitzel v. State, 863 A.2d 999 (Md. 2004) (pre-arrest silence despite allegations from other witnesses is not probative enough to qualify as substantive evidence of guilt; right to silence is widely known even without *Miranda* warnings); State v. Leach, 807 N.E.2d 335 (Ohio 2004) (allows pre-arrest silence for impeachment, but not as substantive evidence of guilt).

D. *Ethics and Lies at Trial*

Page 1244.   Add this material at the end of note 1.

See also Mitchell v. Commonwealth, 781 N.E.2d 1237 (Mass. 2003) (attorney's "firm basis in objective fact" creates proper basis for attorney to reveal to court that client plans to commit perjury; defense attorney may allow defendant to testify in narrative form and may argue to jury only truthful portions of defendant's testimony); People v. Andrades, 4 N.Y.3d 355 (N.Y. 2005) (defense attorney who asked at suppression hearing to be relieved of case based on ethical conflict, hinted to judge that his client intended to commit perjury, allowed defendant to testify in narrative form, and declined to give closing argument, did not deny defendant right to effective assistance or violate any ethical obligation).

Chapter 19

Sentencing

A. Who Sentences?

2. Legislative Sentencing

Page 1262.   Add this material before the notes.

Gary Ewing v. California
538 U.S. 11 (2003)

O'CONNOR, J.

In this case, we decide whether the Eighth Amendment prohibits the State of California from sentencing a repeat felon to a prison term of 25 years to life under the State's "Three Strikes and You're Out" law.

I.

California's three strikes law reflects a shift in the State's sentencing policies toward incapacitating and deterring repeat offenders who threaten the public safety. The law was designed "to ensure longer prison sentences and greater punishment for those who commit a felony and have been previously convicted of serious and/or violent felony offenses." Cal. Penal Code §667(b). . . .

California's current three strikes law consists of two virtually identical statutory schemes designed to increase the prison terms of repeat felons. When a defendant is convicted of a felony, and he has previously been convicted of one or more prior felonies defined as "serious" or "violent" in Cal. Penal Code Ann. §§667.5 and 1192.7, sentencing is conducted pursuant to the three strikes law.... If the defendant has one prior "serious" or "violent" felony conviction, he must be sentenced to twice the term otherwise provided as punishment for the current felony conviction. If the defendant has two or more prior "serious" or "violent" felony convictions, he must receive an indeterminate term of life imprisonment. Defendants sentenced to life under the three strikes law become eligible for parole on a date calculated by reference to a "minimum term," which is the greater of (a) three times the term otherwise provided for the current conviction, (b) 25 years, or (c) the term determined by the court pursuant to §1170 for the underlying conviction, including any enhancements.

Under California law, certain offenses may be classified as either felonies or misdemeanors. These crimes are known as "wobblers." Some crimes that would otherwise be misdemeanors become "wobblers" because of the defendant's prior record. For example, petty theft, a misdemeanor, becomes a "wobbler" when the defendant has previously served a prison term for committing specified theft-related crimes. Other crimes, such as grand theft, are "wobblers" regardless of the defendant's prior record. Both types of "wobblers" are triggering offenses under the three strikes law only when they are treated as felonies. Under California law, a "wobbler" is presumptively a felony and remains a felony except when the discretion is actually exercised to make the crime a misdemeanor.

In California, prosecutors may exercise their discretion to charge a "wobbler" as either a felony or a misdemeanor. [Trial] courts may avoid imposing a three strikes sentence in two ways: first, by reducing "wobblers" to misdemeanors (which do not qualify as triggering offenses), and second, by vacating allegations of prior "serious" or "violent" felony convictions.

On parole from a 9-year prison term, petitioner Gary Ewing walked into the pro shop of the El Segundo Golf Course in Los Angeles County on March 12, 2000. He walked out with three golf clubs, priced at $399 apiece, concealed in his pants leg. A shop employee, whose suspicions were aroused when he observed Ewing limp out of the pro shop, telephoned the police. The police apprehended Ewing in the parking lot.

Ewing is no stranger to the criminal justice system. In 1984, at the age of 22, he pleaded guilty to theft. The court sentenced him to six months in jail (suspended), three years' probation, and a $300 fine. In 1988, he was convicted of felony grand theft auto and sentenced to one year in jail and three years' probation. After Ewing completed probation, however, the sentencing court reduced the crime to a misdemeanor, permitted Ewing to withdraw his guilty plea, and dismissed the case. In 1990, he was convicted of petty theft with a prior and sentenced to 60 days in the county jail and three years' probation. In 1992, Ewing was convicted of battery and sentenced to 30 days in the county jail and two years' summary probation. One month later, he was convicted of theft and sentenced to 10 days in the county jail and 12 months' probation. In January 1993, Ewing was convicted of burglary and sentenced to 60 days in the county jail and one year's summary probation. In February 1993, he was convicted of possessing drug paraphernalia and sentenced to six months in the county jail and three years' probation. In July 1993, he was convicted of appropriating lost property and sentenced to 10 days in the county jail and two years' summary probation. In September 1993, he was convicted of unlawfully possessing a firearm and trespassing and sentenced to 30 days in the county jail and one year's probation.

In October and November 1993, Ewing committed three burglaries and one robbery at a Long Beach, California, apartment complex over a 5-week period. [During the robbery], Ewing accosted a victim in the mailroom of the apartment complex. Ewing claimed to have a gun and ordered the victim to hand over his wallet. When the victim resisted, Ewing produced a knife and forced the victim back to the apartment itself. While Ewing rifled through the bedroom, the victim fled the apartment screaming for help. Ewing absconded with the victim's money and credit cards.... A jury convicted Ewing of first-degree robbery and three counts of residential burglary. Sentenced to nine years and eight months in prison, Ewing was paroled in 1999.

Only 10 months later, Ewing stole the golf clubs at issue in this case. He was charged with, and ultimately convicted of, one count of felony grand theft of personal property in excess of $400. As required by the three strikes law, the prosecutor formally alleged, and the trial court later found, that Ewing had been convicted previously of four serious or violent felonies for the three burglaries and the robbery in the Long Beach apartment complex....

Before sentencing Ewing, the trial court took note of his entire criminal history, including the fact that he was on parole when he committed his latest offense.... In the end, the trial judge determined that the grand theft should remain a felony. The court also ruled that the four prior strikes for the three burglaries and the robbery in Long Beach should stand. As a newly convicted felon with two or more "serious" or "violent" felony convictions in his past, Ewing was sentenced under the three strikes law to 25 years to life. . . .

II.

The Eighth Amendment, which forbids cruel and unusual punishments, contains a narrow proportionality principle that applies to noncapital sentences. We have most recently addressed the proportionality principle as applied to terms of years in a series of cases beginning with Rummel v. Estelle, 445 U.S. 263 (1980).

In *Rummel*, we held that it did not violate the Eighth Amendment for a State to sentence a three-time offender to life in prison with the possibility of parole. Like Ewing, Rummel was sentenced to a lengthy prison term under a recidivism statute. Rummel's two prior offenses were a 1964 felony for "fraudulent use of a credit card to obtain $80 worth of goods or services," and a 1969 felony conviction for "passing a forged check in the amount of $28.36." His triggering offense was a conviction for felony theft—"obtaining $120.75 by false pretenses."

This Court ruled that having twice imprisoned him for felonies, Texas was entitled to place upon Rummel the onus of one who is simply unable to bring his conduct within the social norms prescribed by the criminal law of the State. The recidivism statute is nothing more than a societal decision that when such a person commits yet another felony, he should be subjected to the admittedly serious penalty of incarceration for life, subject only to the State's judgment as to whether to grant him parole. We noted that this Court has on occasion stated that the Eighth Amendment prohibits imposition of a sentence that is grossly disproportionate to the severity of the crime. But outside the context of capital punishment, successful challenges to the proportionality of particular sentences have been exceedingly rare. Although we stated that the proportionality principle would "come into play in the extreme example ... if a legislature made overtime parking a felony punishable by life imprisonment," we held that the mandatory life sentence imposed upon this petitioner does not constitute cruel and unusual punishment under the Eighth and Fourteenth Amendments....

Three years after *Rummel*, in Solem v. Helm, 463 U.S. 277, 279 (1983), we held that the Eighth Amendment prohibited "a life sentence without possibility of parole for a seventh nonviolent felony." The triggering offense in *Solem* was uttering a "no account" check for $100. We ... explained that three factors may be relevant to a determination of whether a sentence is so disproportionate that it violates the Eighth Amendment: "(i) the gravity of the offense and the harshness of the penalty; (ii) the sentences imposed on other criminals in the same jurisdiction; and (iii) the sentences imposed for commission of the same crime in other jurisdictions."

Applying these factors in *Solem*, we struck down the defendant's sentence of life without parole. We specifically noted the contrast between that sentence and the sentence in *Rummel*, pursuant to which the defendant was eligible for parole. Indeed, we explicitly declined to overrule *Rummel*....

Eight years after *Solem*, we grappled with the proportionality issue again in Harmelin v. Michigan, 501 U.S. 957 (1991). *Harmelin* was not a recidivism case, but rather involved a first-time offender convicted of possessing 672 grams of cocaine. He was sentenced to life in prison without possibility of parole. A majority of the Court rejected Harmelin's claim that his sentence was so grossly disproportionate that it violated the Eighth Amendment. The Court, however, could not agree on why his proportionality argument failed. Justice Scalia, joined by the Chief Justice, wrote that the proportionality principle was "an aspect of our death penalty jurisprudence, rather than a generalizable aspect of Eighth Amendment law." He would thus have declined to apply gross disproportionality principles except in reviewing capital sentences.

Justice Kennedy, joined by two other Members of the Court, concurred in part and concurred in the judgment. Justice Kennedy specifically recognized that "the Eighth Amendment proportionality principle also applies to noncapital sentences." He then identified four principles of proportionality review—"the primacy of the legislature, the variety of legitimate penological schemes, the nature of our federal system, and the requirement that proportionality review be guided by objective factors"—that inform the final one: "The Eighth Amendment does not require strict proportionality between crime and sentence. Rather, it forbids only extreme sentences that are 'grossly disproportionate' to the crime." ...

Throughout the States, legislatures enacting three strikes laws made a deliberate policy choice that individuals who have repeatedly engaged in serious or violent criminal behavior, and whose conduct has not been deterred by more conventional approaches to punishment, must be isolated from society in order to protect the public safety. Though three strikes laws may be relatively new, our tradition of deferring to state legislatures in making and implementing such important policy decisions is longstanding.

Our traditional deference to legislative policy choices finds a corollary in the principle that the Constitution does not mandate adoption of any one penological theory. A sentence can have a variety of justifications, such as incapacitation, deterrence, retribution, or rehabilitation. Some or all of these justifications may play a role in a State's sentencing scheme. Selecting the sentencing rationales is generally a policy choice to be made by state legislatures, not federal courts.

When the California Legislature enacted the three strikes law, it made a judgment that protecting the public safety requires incapacitating criminals who have already been convicted of at least one serious or violent crime. Nothing in the Eighth Amendment prohibits California from making that choice. To the contrary, our cases establish that States have a valid interest in deterring and segregating habitual criminals. Recidivism has long been recognized as a legitimate basis for increased punishment....

California's justification is no pretext.... In 1996, when the Sacramento Bee studied 233 three strikes offenders in California, it found that they had an aggregate of 1,165 prior felony convictions, an average of 5 apiece. The prior convictions included 322 robberies and 262 burglaries. About 84 percent of the 233 three strikes offenders had been convicted of at least one violent crime. In all, they were responsible for 17 homicides, 7 attempted slayings, and 91 sexual assaults and child molestations....

The State's interest in deterring crime also lends some support to the three strikes law.... Four years after the passage of California's three strikes law, the recidivism rate of parolees returned to prison for the commission of a new crime dropped by nearly 25 percent. California Dept. of Justice, Office of the Attorney General, "Three Strikes and

You're Out"—Its Impact on the California Criminal Justice System After Four Years 10 (1998)....

To be sure, California's three strikes law has sparked controversy. Critics have doubted the law's wisdom, cost-efficiency, and effectiveness in reaching its goals. This criticism is appropriately directed at the legislature, which has primary responsibility for making the difficult policy choices that underlie any criminal sentencing scheme. We do not sit as a "superlegislature" to second-guess these policy choices. It is enough that the State of California has a reasonable basis for believing that dramatically enhanced sentences for habitual felons advances the goals of its criminal justice system in any substantial way.

III.

Against this backdrop, we consider Ewing's claim that his three strikes sentence of 25 years to life is unconstitutionally disproportionate to his offense of "shoplifting three golf clubs." We first address the gravity of the offense compared to the harshness of the penalty. At the threshold, we note that Ewing incorrectly frames the issue. The gravity of his offense was not merely "shoplifting three golf clubs." Rather, Ewing was convicted of felony grand theft for stealing nearly $1,200 worth of merchandise after previously having been convicted of at least two "violent" or "serious" felonies. Even standing alone, Ewing's theft should not be taken lightly.... Theft of $1,200 in property is a felony under federal law, 18 U.S.C. §641, and in the vast majority of States.

That grand theft is a "wobbler" under California law is of no moment. Though California courts have discretion to reduce a felony grand theft charge to a misdemeanor, it remains a felony for all purposes unless and until the trial court imposes a misdemeanor sentence. The purpose of the trial judge's sentencing discretion to downgrade certain felonies is to "impose a misdemeanor sentence in those cases in which the rehabilitation of the convicted defendant either does not require or would be adversely affected by, incarceration in a state prison as a felon." In re Anderson, 447 P.2d 117 (Cal. 1968) (Tobriner, J., concurring)....

In weighing the gravity of Ewing's offense, we must place on the scales not only his current felony, but also his long history of felony recidivism. Any other approach would fail to accord proper deference to the policy judgments that find expression in the legislature's choice of sanctions. . . . To give full effect to the State's choice of this legitimate penological goal, our proportionality review of Ewing's sentence must take that goal into account....

To be sure, Ewing's sentence is a long one. But it reflects a rational legislative judgment, entitled to deference, that offenders who have committed serious or violent felonies and who continue to commit felonies must be incapacitated.... Ewing's is not the rare case in which a threshold comparison of the crime committed and the sentence imposed leads to an inference of gross disproportionality. We hold that Ewing's sentence of 25 years to life in prison, imposed for the offense of felony grand theft under the three strikes law, is not grossly disproportionate and therefore does not violate the Eighth Amendment's prohibition on cruel and unusual punishments....

SCALIA, J., concurring.

[The] Eighth Amendment's prohibition of "cruel and unusual punishments" was aimed at excluding only certain *modes* of punishment, and was not a guarantee against disproportionate sentences.... Proportionality—the notion that the punishment should fit the crime—is inherently a concept tied to the penological goal of retribution. It becomes difficult even to speak intelligently of "proportionality," once deterrence and rehabilitation are given significant weight—not to mention giving weight to the purpose of California's three strikes law: incapacitation. In the present case, the game is up once the plurality has acknowledged that "the Constitution does not mandate adoption of any one penological theory."... That acknowledgment having been made, it no longer suffices merely to assess the gravity of the offense compared to the harshness of the penalty...; that classic description of the proportionality principle (alone and in itself quite resistant to policy-free, legal analysis) now becomes merely the "first" step of the inquiry. [After comparing the gravity of the offense to the harshness of the penalty], the plurality must then *add* an analysis to show that "Ewing's sentence is justified by the State's public-safety interest in incapacitating and deterring recidivist felons."...

Which indeed it is—though why that has anything to do with the principle of proportionality is a mystery. Perhaps the plurality should revise its terminology, so that what it reads into the Eighth Amendment is not the unstated proposition that all punishment should be reasonably proportionate to the gravity of the offense, but rather the unstated proposition that all punishment should reasonably pursue the multiple purposes of the criminal law. That formulation would make it clearer than ever, of course, that the plurality is not applying law but evaluating policy....

STEVENS, J., dissenting....

The Eighth Amendment succinctly prohibits "excessive" sanctions. See U.S. Const., Amdt. 8 ("Excessive bail shall not be required, nor excessive fines imposed, nor cruel and unusual punishments inflicted"). Faithful to the Amendment's text, this Court has held that the Constitution directs judges to apply their best judgment in determining the proportionality of fines, bail, and other forms of punishment, including the imposition of a death sentence, see, *e.g.*, Coker v. Georgia, 433 U.S. 584 (1977). It would be anomalous indeed to suggest that the Eighth Amendment makes proportionality review applicable in the context of bail and fines but not in the context of other forms of punishment, such as imprisonment. . . .

Throughout most of the Nation's history—before guideline sentencing became so prevalent—federal and state trial judges imposed specific sentences pursuant to grants of authority that gave them uncabined discretion within broad ranges.... In exercising their discretion, sentencing judges wisely employed a proportionality principle that took into account all of the justifications for punishment— namely, deterrence, incapacitation, retribution and rehabilitation.... Likewise, I think it clear that the Eighth Amendment's prohibition of "cruel and unusual punishments" expresses a broad and basic proportionality principle that takes into account all of the justifications for penal sanctions. It is this broad proportionality principle that would preclude reliance on any of the justifications for punishment to support, for example, a life sentence for overtime parking. Accordingly, I respectfully dissent.

BREYER, J., dissenting.

[Courts] faced with a "gross disproportionality" claim must first make "a threshold comparison of the crime committed and the sentence imposed." *Harmelin*, at 1005 (Kennedy, J., concurring). If a claim crosses that threshold—itself a *rare* occurrence—then the court should compare the sentence at issue to other sentences imposed on other criminals in the same, or in other, jurisdictions. The comparative analysis will validate or invalidate an initial judgment that a sentence is grossly disproportionate to a crime…. I believe that the case before us is a "rare" case—one in which a court can say with reasonable confidence that the punishment is "grossly disproportionate" to the crime.

Ewing's claim crosses the gross disproportionality "threshold." [Precedent] makes clear that Ewing's sentence raises a serious disproportionality question. Ewing is a recidivist. Hence the two cases most directly in point are those in which the Court considered the constitutionality of recidivist sentencing: *Rummel* and *Solem.* Ewing's claim falls between these two cases. It is stronger than the claim presented in *Rummel,* where the Court upheld a recidivist's sentence as constitutional. It is weaker than the claim presented in *Solem,* where the Court struck down a recidivist sentence as unconstitutional.

Three kinds of sentence-related characteristics define the relevant comparative spectrum: (a) the length of the prison term in real time, *i.e.,* the time that the offender is likely actually to spend in prison; (b) the sentence-triggering criminal conduct, *i.e.,* the offender's actual behavior or other offense-related circumstances; and (c) the offender's criminal history….

In *Rummel,* the Court held constitutional (a) a sentence of life imprisonment *with parole available within 10 to 12 years,* (b) for the offense of obtaining $120 by false pretenses, (c) committed by an offender with two prior felony convictions (involving small amounts of money)…. In *Solem,* the Court held unconstitutional (a) a sentence of life imprisonment *without parole,* (b) for the crime of writing a $100 check on a nonexistent bank account, (c) committed by an offender with six prior felony convictions (including three for burglary)…. Which of the three pertinent comparative factors made the constitutional difference?…

The one critical factor that explains the difference in the outcome is the length of the likely prison term measured in real time. In *Rummel,* where the Court upheld the sentence, the state sentencing statute authorized parole for the offender, Rummel, after 10 or 12 years. In *Solem,* where the Court struck down the sentence, the sentence required the offender, Helm, to spend the rest of his life in prison.

Now consider the present case. The third factor, *offender characteristics*—*i.e.*, prior record—does not differ significantly here from that in *Solem*. Ewing's prior record consists of four prior felony convictions (involving three burglaries, one with a knife) contrasted with Helm's six prior felony convictions (including three burglaries, though none with weapons). The second factor, *offense behavior*, is worse than that in *Solem*, but only to a degree. It would be difficult to say that the actual behavior itself here (shoplifting) differs significantly from that at issue in *Solem* (passing a bad check) or in *Rummel* (obtaining money through false pretenses). Rather the difference lies in the *value* of the goods obtained. That difference, measured in terms of the most relevant feature (loss to the victim, *i.e.*, wholesale value) and adjusted for the irrelevant feature of inflation, comes down (in 1979 values) to about $379 here compared with $100 in *Solem*, or (in 1973 values) to $232 here compared with $120.75 in *Rummel*....

The difference in *length* of the real prison term—the first, and critical, factor in *Solem* and *Rummel*—is considerably more important. Ewing's sentence here amounts, in real terms, to at least 25 years without parole or good-time credits. That sentence is considerably shorter than Helm's sentence in *Solem*, which amounted, in real terms, to life in prison. Nonetheless Ewing's real prison term is more than twice as long as the term at issue in *Rummel*, which amounted, in real terms, to at least 10 or 12 years. And, Ewing's sentence, unlike Rummel's (but like Helm's sentence in *Solem*), is long enough to consume the productive remainder of almost any offender's life. (It means that Ewing himself, seriously ill when sentenced at age 38, will likely die in prison.) The upshot is that the length of the real prison term—the factor that explains the *Solem/Rummel* difference in outcome—places Ewing closer to *Solem* than to *Rummel*....

Believing Ewing's argument a strong one, sufficient to pass the threshold, I turn to the comparative analysis. A comparison of Ewing's sentence with other sentences requires answers to two questions. First, how would other jurisdictions (or California at other times, *i.e.*, without the three strikes penalty) punish the *same offense conduct?* Second, upon what other conduct would other jurisdictions (or California) impose the *same prison term?* Moreover, since hypothetical punishment is beside the point, the relevant prison time, for comparative purposes, is *real* prison time, *i.e.*, the time that an offender must *actually serve*. . . .

As to California itself, we know the following: First, between the end of World War II and 1994 (when California enacted the three strikes law, ...), *no one* like Ewing could have served more than *10* years in prison. ... Second, statistics suggest that recidivists *of all sorts* convicted during that same time period in California served a small fraction of Ewing's real-time sentence. On average, recidivists served three to four additional (recidivist-related) years in prison, with 90 percent serving less than an additional real seven to eight years. Third, we know that California has reserved, and still reserves, Ewing-type prison time, *i.e.*, at least 25 real years in prison, for criminals convicted of crimes far worse than was Ewing's. Statistics for the years 1945 to 1981, for example, indicate that typical (nonrecidivist) male first-degree murderers served between 10 and 15 real years in prison, with 90 percent of all such murderers serving less than 20 real years....

As to other jurisdictions, we know the following: The United States, bound by the federal Sentencing Guidelines, would impose upon a recidivist, such as Ewing, a sentence that, in any ordinary case, would not exceed 18 months in prison. USSG §2B1.1(a) (assuming a base offense level of 6, a criminal history of VI, and no mitigating or aggravating adjustments). The Guidelines, based in part upon a study of some 40,000 actual federal sentences ... reserve a Ewing-type sentence for Ewing-type *recidivists* who currently commit such crimes as murder, §2A1.2; air piracy, §2A5.1; robbery (involving the discharge of a firearm, serious bodily injury, and about $1 million), §2B3.1; drug offenses involving more than, for example, 20 pounds of heroin, §2D1.1; aggravated theft of more than $100 million, §2B1.1; and other similar offenses.

[We] do not have before us information about actual time served by Ewing-type offenders in other States. We do know, however, that the law would make it legally impossible for a Ewing-type offender to serve more than 10 years in prison in 33 jurisdictions, as well as the federal courts, ... more than 15 years in 4 other States, ... and more than 20 years in 4 additional States.... In nine other States, the law *might* make it legally possible to impose a sentence of 25 years or more, [but that] does not mean that judges have actually done so....

The upshot is that comparison of other sentencing practices, both in other jurisdictions and in California at other times (or in respect to other crimes), validates what an initial threshold examination suggested....

Outside the California three strikes context, Ewing's recidivist sentence is virtually unique in its harshness for his offense of conviction, and by a considerable degree.

This is not the end of the matter. [It] is important to consider whether special criminal justice concerns related to California's three strikes policy might justify including Ewing's theft within the class of triggering criminal conduct (thereby imposing a severe punishment), even if Ewing's sentence would otherwise seem disproportionately harsh.

I can find no such special criminal justice concerns that might justify this sentence. The most obvious potential justification for bringing Ewing's theft within the ambit of the statute is administrative. California must draw some kind of workable line between conduct that will trigger, and conduct that will not trigger, a "three strikes" sentence.... The administrative line that the statute draws separates "felonies" from "misdemeanors." [However], California uses those words in a way unrelated to the seriousness of offense conduct in a set of criminal statutes called "wobblers," ..., one of which is at issue in this case. ...

"Wobbler" statutes cover a wide variety of criminal behavior, ranging from assault with a deadly weapon, §245, vehicular manslaughter, §193(c)(1), and money laundering, §186.10(a), to the defacement of property with graffiti, §594(b)(2)(A), or stealing more than \$100 worth of chickens, nuts, or avocados, §487(b)(1)(A); §489. Some of this behavior is obviously less serious, even if engaged in twice, than other criminal conduct that California statutes classify as pure misdemeanors....

There is no obvious reason why the statute could not enumerate, consistent with its purposes, the relevant triggering crimes. Given that possibility and given the anomalies that result from California's chosen approach, I do not see how California can justify on *administrative* grounds a sentence as seriously disproportionate as Ewing's....

Given the omission of vast categories of property crimes— including grand theft (unarmed)—from the "strike" definition, one cannot argue, on *property-crime-related incapacitation grounds*, for inclusion of Ewing's crime among the triggers.... No one argues for Ewing's inclusion within the ambit of the three strikes statute on grounds of retribution. [In] terms of "deterrence," Ewing's 25-year term amounts to overkill.... And "rehabilitation" is obviously beside the point. The upshot is that, in my view, the State cannot find in its three strikes law a special criminal justice need sufficient to rescue a sentence that other relevant considerations indicate is unconstitutional....

C. Revisiting Pleas and Trials

1.   Revisiting Proof at Trial

Page 1298.   Add this material before the notes.

Ralph Blakely v. Washington
124 S. Ct. 2531 (2004)

SCALIA, J.

Petitioner Ralph Howard Blakely, Jr., pleaded guilty to the kidnaping of his estranged wife. The facts admitted in his plea, standing alone, supported a maximum sentence of 53 months. Pursuant to state law, the court imposed an "exceptional" sentence of 90 months after making a judicial determination that he had acted with "deliberate cruelty." We consider whether this violated petitioner's Sixth Amendment right to trial by jury.

I.

Petitioner married his wife Yolanda in 1973. He was evidently a difficult man to live with, having been diagnosed at various times with psychological and personality disorders including paranoid schizophrenia. His wife ultimately filed for divorce. In 1998, he abducted her from their orchard home in Grant County, Washington, binding her with duct tape and forcing her at knifepoint into a wooden box in the bed of his pickup truck. In the process, he implored her to dismiss the divorce suit and related trust proceedings.

When the couple's 13-year-old son Ralphy returned home from school, petitioner ordered him to follow in another car, threatening to harm Yolanda with a shotgun if he did not do so. Ralphy escaped and sought help when they stopped at a gas station, but petitioner continued on with Yolanda to a friend's house in Montana. He was finally arrested after the friend called the police.

The State charged petitioner with first-degree kidnaping. Upon reaching a plea agreement, however, it reduced the charge to second-degree kidnaping involving domestic violence and use of a firearm. Petitioner entered a guilty plea admitting the elements of second-degree kidnaping and the domestic-violence and firearm allegations, but no other relevant facts.

The case then proceeded to sentencing. In Washington, second-degree kidnaping is a class B felony. State law provides that "no person convicted of a [class B] felony shall be punished by confinement ... exceeding ... a term of ten years." §9A.20.021(1)(b). Other provisions of state law, however, further limit the range of sentences a judge may impose. Washington's Sentencing Reform Act specifies, for petitioner's offense of second-degree kidnaping with a firearm, a "standard range" of 49 to 53 months. See §9.94A.320 (seriousness level V for second-degree kidnaping); App. 27 (offender score 2 based on §9.94A.360); §9.94A.310(1), box 2-V (standard range of 13-17 months); §9.94A.310(3)(b) (36-month firearm enhancement). A judge may impose a sentence above the standard range if he finds "substantial and compelling reasons justifying an exceptional sentence." §9.94A.120(2). The Act lists aggravating factors that justify such a departure, which it recites to be illustrative rather than exhaustive. Nevertheless, "a reason offered to justify an exceptional sentence can be considered only if it takes into account factors other than those which are used in computing the standard range sentence for the offense." State v. Gore, 21 P.3d 262 277 (Wash. 2001). When a judge imposes an exceptional sentence, he must set forth findings of fact and conclusions of law supporting it. A reviewing court will reverse the sentence if it finds that "under a clearly erroneous standard there is insufficient evidence in the record to support the reasons for imposing an exceptional sentence." *Gore*, 21 P.3d, at 277.

Pursuant to the plea agreement, the State recommended a sentence within the standard range of 49 to 53 months. After hearing Yolanda's description of the kidnaping, however, the judge rejected the State's recommendation and imposed an exceptional sentence of 90 months—37 months beyond the standard maximum. He justified the sentence on the ground that petitioner had acted with "deliberate cruelty," a statutorily enumerated ground for departure in domestic-violence cases. §9.94A.390(2)(h)(iii).

Faced with an unexpected increase of more than three years in his sentence, petitioner objected. The judge accordingly conducted a 3-day bench hearing featuring testimony from petitioner, Yolanda, Ralphy, a police officer, and medical experts. After the hearing, he issued 32 findings of fact, [reaffirming] his initial determination of deliberate cruelty. Petitioner appealed, arguing that this sentencing procedure deprived him of his federal constitutional right to have a jury determine beyond a reasonable doubt all facts legally essential to his sentence....

II.

This case requires us to apply the rule we expressed in Apprendi v. New Jersey, 530 U.S. 466, 490 (2000): "Other than the fact of a prior conviction, any fact that increases the penalty for a crime beyond the prescribed statutory maximum must be submitted to a jury, and proved beyond a reasonable doubt." This rule reflects two longstanding tenets of common-law criminal jurisprudence: that the "truth of every accusation" against a defendant "should afterwards be confirmed by the unanimous suffrage of twelve of his equals and neighbours," 4 W. Blackstone, Commentaries on the Laws of England 343 (1769), and that "an accusation which lacks any particular fact which the law makes essential to the punishment is ... no accusation within the requirements of the common law, and it is no accusation in reason," 1 J. Bishop, Criminal Procedure §87, p. 55 (2d ed. 1872).[5] These principles have been acknowledged by courts and treatises since the earliest days of graduated sentencing....

In this case, petitioner was sentenced to more than three years above the 53-month statutory maximum of the standard range because he had acted with "deliberate cruelty." The facts supporting that finding were neither admitted by petitioner nor found by a jury. The State nevertheless contends that there was no *Apprendi* violation because the

---

[5] ... Bishop was not addressing the problem of statutes that aggravate common-law offenses. Rather, the entire chapter of his treatise is devoted to the point that "every fact which is legally essential to the punishment" must be charged in the indictment and proved to a jury. 1 J. Bishop, Criminal Procedure, ch. 6, pp. 50-56 (2d ed. 1872). As one example of this principle (appearing several pages before the language we quote in text above), he notes a statute aggravating common-law assault. But nowhere is there the slightest indication that his general principle was *limited* to that example....

relevant "statutory maximum" is not 53 months, but the 10-year maximum for class B felonies in §9A.20.021(1)(b). It observes that no exceptional sentence may exceed that limit. Our precedents make clear, however, that the "statutory maximum" for *Apprendi* purposes is the maximum sentence a judge may impose *solely on the basis of the facts reflected in the jury verdict or admitted by the defendant.* See Ring v. Arizona, 536 U.S. 584, 602 (2002) ("the maximum he would receive if punished according to the facts reflected in the jury verdict alone"); Harris v. United States, 536 U.S. 545, 563 (2002) (plurality opinion) (same); cf. *Apprendi,* 530 U.S. at 488 (facts admitted by the defendant). In other words, the relevant "statutory maximum" is not the maximum sentence a judge may impose after finding additional facts, but the maximum he may impose *without* any additional findings. When a judge inflicts punishment that the jury's verdict alone does not allow, the jury has not found all the facts "which the law makes essential to the punishment," Bishop, §87, at 55, and the judge exceeds his proper authority.

The judge in this case could not have imposed the exceptional 90-month sentence solely on the basis of the facts admitted in the guilty plea. Those facts alone were insufficient because, as the Washington Supreme Court has explained, "a reason offered to justify an exceptional sentence can be considered only if it takes into account factors other than those which are used in computing the standard range sentence for the offense," *Gore,* 21 P.3d at 277, which in this case included the elements of second-degree kidnaping and the use of a firearm, see §§9.94A.320, 9.94A.310(3)(b). Had the judge imposed the 90-month sentence solely on the basis of the plea, he would have been reversed.

[The] State tries to distinguish *Apprendi* ... by pointing out that the enumerated grounds for departure in its regime are illustrative rather than exhaustive. This distinction is immaterial. Whether the judge's authority to impose an enhanced sentence depends on finding a specified fact (as in *Apprendi*), one of several specified facts ... or *any* aggravating fact (as here), it remains the case that the jury's verdict alone does not authorize the sentence. The judge acquires that authority only upon finding some additional fact.[8] Because the State's sentencing

---

[8] Nor does it matter that the judge must, after finding aggravating facts, make a judgment that they present a compelling ground for departure. He cannot make that judgment without finding some facts to support it beyond the bare elements

procedure did not comply with the Sixth Amendment, petitioner's sentence is invalid.[9]

III.

Our commitment to *Apprendi* in this context reflects not just respect for longstanding precedent, but the need to give intelligible content to the right of jury trial. That right is no mere procedural formality, but a fundamental reservation of power in our constitutional structure. Just as suffrage ensures the people's ultimate control in the legislative and executive branches, jury trial is meant to ensure their control in the judiciary. See John Adams, Diary Entry (Feb. 12, 1771) ("The common people, should have as complete a control . . . in every judgment of a court of judicature" as in the legislature); Letter from Thomas Jefferson to the Abbe Arnoux (July 19, 1789) ("Were I called upon to decide whether the people had best be omitted in the Legislative or Judiciary department, I would say it is better to leave them out of the Legislative"). *Apprendi* carries out this design by ensuring that the judge's authority to sentence derives wholly from the jury's verdict. Without that restriction, the jury would not exercise the control that the Framers intended.

Those who would reject *Apprendi* are resigned to one of two alternatives. The first is that the jury need only find whatever facts the legislature chooses to label elements of the crime, and that those it labels sentencing factors—no matter how much they may increase the punishment—may be found by the judge. This would mean, for example, that a judge could sentence a man for committing murder even if the jury convicted him only of illegally possessing the firearm used to commit it—or of making an illegal lane change while fleeing the death scene. Not even *Apprendi*'s critics would advocate this absurd result. The jury could not function as circuitbreaker in the State's machinery of justice if it were relegated to making a determination that the defendant at some point did something wrong, a mere preliminary to a judicial inquisition into the facts of the crime the State *actually* seeks to punish.

---

of the offense. Whether the judicially determined facts *require* a sentence enhancement or merely *allow* it, the verdict alone does not authorize the sentence.

[9] ... The Federal Guidelines are not before us, and we express no opinion on them.

The second alternative is that legislatures may establish legally essential sentencing factors *within limits*—limits crossed when, perhaps, the sentencing factor is a "tail which wags the dog of the substantive offense." *McMillan*, 477 U.S. at 88. What this means in operation is that the law must not go *too far*—it must not exceed the judicial estimation of the proper role of the judge.

The subjectivity of this standard is obvious. Petitioner argued below that second-degree kidnaping with deliberate cruelty was essentially the same as first-degree kidnaping, the very charge he had avoided by pleading to a lesser offense.... Petitioner's 90-month sentence exceeded the 53-month standard maximum by almost 70%; the Washington Supreme Court in other cases has upheld exceptional sentences 15 times the standard maximum. See State v. Oxborrow, 723 P.2d 1123 (Wash. 1986) (15-year exceptional sentence; 1-year standard maximum sentence). Did the court go *too far* in any of these cases? There is no answer that legal analysis can provide. With *too far* as the yardstick, it is always possible to disagree with such judgments and never to refute them.

Whether the Sixth Amendment incorporates this manipulable standard rather than *Apprendi*'s bright-line rule depends on the plausibility of the claim that the Framers would have left definition of the scope of jury power up to judges' intuitive sense of how far is *too far*. We think that claim not plausible at all, because the very reason the Framers put a jury-trial guarantee in the Constitution is that they were unwilling to trust government to mark out the role of the jury.

IV.

... This case is not about whether determinate sentencing is constitutional, only about how it can be implemented in a way that respects the Sixth Amendment. Several policies prompted Washington's adoption of determinate sentencing, including proportionality to the gravity of the offense and parity among defendants. Nothing we have said impugns those salutary objectives.

Justice O'Connor argues that, because determinate sentencing schemes involving judicial factfinding entail less judicial discretion than indeterminate schemes, the constitutionality of the latter implies the constitutionality of the former. This argument is flawed on a number of levels. First, the Sixth Amendment by its terms is not a limitation on judicial power, but a reservation of jury power. It limits judicial power only to the extent that the claimed judicial power infringes on the province of the jury. Indeterminate sentencing does not do so. It increases judicial discretion, to be sure, but not at the expense of the jury's traditional function of finding the facts essential to lawful imposition of the penalty. Of course indeterminate schemes involve judicial factfinding, in that a judge (like a parole board) may implicitly rule on those facts he deems important to the exercise of his sentencing discretion. But the facts do not pertain to whether the defendant has a legal *right* to a lesser sentence—and that makes all the difference insofar as judicial impingement upon the traditional role of the jury is concerned. In a system that says the judge may punish burglary with 10 to 40 years, every burglar knows he is risking 40 years in jail. In a system that punishes burglary with a 10-year sentence, with another 30 added for use of a gun, the burglar who enters a home unarmed is *entitled* to no more than a 10-year sentence—and by reason of the Sixth Amendment the facts bearing upon that entitlement must be found by a jury.

... Determinate judicial-factfinding schemes entail less judicial power than indeterminate schemes, but more judicial power than determinate *jury*-factfinding schemes. Whether *Apprendi* increases judicial power overall depends on what States with determinate judicial-factfinding schemes would do, given the choice between the two alternatives.... When the Kansas Supreme Court found *Apprendi* infirmities in that State's determinate-sentencing regime in State v. Gould, 23 P.3d 801, 809-814 (Kan. 2001), the legislature responded not by reestablishing indeterminate sentencing but by applying *Apprendi*'s requirements to its current regime. The result was less, not more, judicial power.

Justice Breyer argues that *Apprendi* works to the detriment of criminal defendants who plead guilty by depriving them of the opportunity to argue sentencing factors to a judge. But nothing prevents a defendant from waiving his *Apprendi* rights. When a defendant pleads guilty, the State is free to seek judicial sentence enhancements so long as the defendant either stipulates to the relevant facts or consents to judicial factfinding. If appropriate waivers are procured, States may continue to offer judicial factfinding as a matter of course to all defendants who plead guilty. Even a defendant who stands trial may consent to judicial factfinding as to sentence enhancements, which may well be in his interest if relevant evidence would prejudice him at trial. We do not understand how *Apprendi* can possibly work to the detriment of those who are free, if they think its costs outweigh its benefits, to render it inapplicable.

Nor do we see any merit to Justice Breyer's contention that *Apprendi* is unfair to criminal defendants because, if States respond by enacting "17-element robbery crimes," prosecutors will have more elements with which to bargain (citing Stephanos Bibas, Judicial Fact-Finding and Sentence Enhancements in a World of Guilty Pleas, 110 Yale L.J. 1097 (2001)). Bargaining already exists with regard to sentencing factors because defendants can either stipulate or contest the facts that make them applicable. If there is any difference between bargaining over sentencing factors and bargaining over elements, the latter probably favors the defendant. Every new element that a prosecutor can threaten to charge is also an element that a defendant can threaten to contest at trial and make the prosecutor prove beyond a reasonable doubt. Moreover, given the sprawling scope of most criminal codes, and the power to affect sentences by making (even nonbinding) sentencing recommendations, there is already no shortage of *in terrorem* tools at prosecutors' disposal. See Nancy King & Susan Klein, *Apprendi* and Plea Bargaining, 54 Stan. L. Rev. 295, 296 (2001) ("Every prosecutorial bargaining chip mentioned by Professor Bibas existed pre-*Apprendi* exactly as it does post-*Apprendi*").

Any evaluation of *Apprendi*'s "fairness" to criminal defendants must compare it with the regime it replaced, in which a defendant, with no warning in either his indictment or plea, would routinely see his maximum potential sentence balloon from as little as five years to as much as life imprisonment,[13] based not on facts proved to his peers beyond a reasonable doubt, but on facts extracted after trial from a report compiled by a probation officer who the judge thinks more likely got it

---

[13] To be sure, Justice Breyer and the other dissenters would forbid those increases of sentence that violate the constitutional principle that tail shall not wag dog. The source of this principle is entirely unclear. Its precise effect, if precise effect it has, is presumably to require that the ratio of sentencing-factor add-on to basic criminal sentence be no greater than the ratio of caudal vertebrae to body in the breed of canine with the longest tail. Or perhaps no greater than the average such ratio for all breeds. Or perhaps the median. Regrettably, *Apprendi* has prevented full development of this line of jurisprudence.

right than got it wrong.... The implausibility of Justice Breyer's contention that *Apprendi* is unfair to criminal defendants is exposed by the lineup of *amici* in this case. It is hard to believe that the National Association of Criminal Defense Lawyers was somehow duped into arguing for the wrong side....

Justice Breyer also claims that *Apprendi* will attenuate the connection between "real criminal conduct and real punishment" by encouraging plea bargaining and by restricting alternatives to adversarial factfinding. [Our decision, however,] cannot turn on whether or to what degree trial by jury impairs the efficiency or fairness of criminal justice. One can certainly argue that both these values would be better served by leaving justice entirely in the hands of professionals; many nations of the world, particularly those following civil-law traditions, take just that course. There is not one shred of doubt, however, about the Framers' paradigm for criminal justice: not the civil-law ideal of administrative perfection, but the common-law ideal of limited state power accomplished by strict division of authority between judge and jury....

Petitioner was sentenced to prison for more than three years beyond what the law allowed for the crime to which he confessed, on the basis of a disputed finding that he had acted with "deliberate cruelty." The Framers would not have thought it too much to demand that, before depriving a man of three more years of his liberty, the State should suffer the modest inconvenience of submitting its accusation to "the unanimous suffrage of twelve of his equals and neighbours," 4 Blackstone, Commentaries, at 343, rather than a lone employee of the State....

O'CONNOR, J., dissenting.

The legacy of today's opinion, whether intended or not, will be the consolidation of sentencing power in the State and Federal Judiciaries. The Court says to Congress and state legislatures: If you want to constrain the sentencing discretion of judges and bring some uniformity to sentencing, it will cost you—dearly. Congress and States, faced with the burdens imposed by the extension of *Apprendi* to the present context, will either trim or eliminate altogether their sentencing guidelines schemes and, with them, 20 years of sentencing reform. It is thus of little moment that the majority does not expressly declare guidelines schemes unconstitutional, for as residents of "*Apprendi*-land" are fond of saying, "the relevant inquiry is one not of form, but of effect." Apprendi v. New Jersey, 530 U.S. 466, 494 (2000). The "effect" of today's decision will be greater judicial discretion and less uniformity in sentencing. Because I find it implausible that the Framers would have considered such a result to be required by the Due Process Clause or the Sixth Amendment, and because the practical consequences of today's decision may be disastrous, I respectfully dissent....

II.

Far from disregarding principles of due process and the jury trial right, as the majority today suggests, Washington's reform has served them. Before passage of the Act, a defendant charged with second degree kidnaping, like petitioner, had no idea whether he would receive a 10-year sentence or probation. The ultimate sentencing determination could turn as much on the idiosyncracies of a particular judge as on the specifics of the defendant's crime or background. A defendant did not know what facts, if any, about his offense or his history would be considered relevant by the sentencing judge or by the parole board. After passage of the Act, a defendant charged with second degree kidnaping knows what his presumptive sentence will be; he has a good idea of the types of factors that a sentencing judge can and will consider when deciding whether to sentence him outside that range; he is guaranteed meaningful appellate review to protect against an arbitrary sentence. Criminal defendants still face the same statutory maximum sentences, but they now at least know, much more than before, the real consequences of their actions.

Washington's move to a system of guided discretion has served equal protection principles as well. Over the past 20 years, there has been a substantial reduction in racial disparity in sentencing across the State. The reduction is directly traceable to the constraining effects of the guidelines—namely, its presumptive ranges and limits on the imposition of exceptional sentences outside of those ranges.

[Extension] of *Apprendi* to the present context will impose significant costs on a legislature's determination that a particular fact, not historically an element, warrants a higher sentence. While not a constitutional prohibition on guidelines schemes, the majority's decision today exacts a substantial constitutional tax.

The costs are substantial and real. Under the majority's approach, any fact that increases the upper bound on a judge's sentencing discretion is an element of the offense. Thus, facts that historically have been taken into account by sentencing judges to assess a sentence within a broad range—such as drug quantity, role in the offense, risk of bodily harm—all must now be charged in an indictment and submitted to a jury simply because it is the legislature, rather than the judge, that constrains the extent to which such facts may be used to impose a sentence within a pre-existing statutory range.

While that alone is enough to threaten the continued use of sentencing guidelines schemes, there are additional costs. For example, a legislature might rightly think that some factors bearing on sentencing, such as prior bad acts or criminal history, should not be considered in a jury's determination of a defendant's guilt—such "character evidence" has traditionally been off limits during the guilt phase of criminal proceedings because of its tendency to inflame the passions of the jury. See, *e.g.*, Fed. Rule Evid. 404. If a legislature desires uniform consideration of such factors at sentencing, but does not want them to impact a jury's initial determination of guilt, the State may have to bear the additional expense of a separate, full-blown jury trial during the penalty phase proceeding.

Some facts that bear on sentencing either will not be discovered, or are not discoverable, prior to trial. For instance, a legislature might desire that defendants who act in an obstructive manner during trial or post-trial proceedings receive a greater sentence than defendants who do not. [Trial] or sentencing proceedings of a drug distribution defendant might reveal that he sold primarily to children. Under the majority's approach, a State wishing such a revelation to result in a higher sentence within a pre-existing statutory range either must vest judges with sufficient discretion to account for it (and trust that they exercise that discretion) *or* bring a separate criminal prosecution. Indeed, the latter choice might not be available—a separate prosecution, if it is for an aggravated offense, likely would be barred altogether by the Double Jeopardy Clause. Blockburger v. United States, 284 U.S. 299 (1932) (cannot prosecute for separate offense unless the two offenses both have at least one element that the other does not).

The majority may be correct that States and the Federal Government will be willing to bear some of these costs. But simple economics dictate that they will not, and cannot, bear them all. To the extent that they do not, there will be an inevitable increase in judicial discretion with all of its attendant failings.

III.

Washington's Sentencing Reform Act did not alter the statutory maximum sentence to which petitioner was exposed. Petitioner was informed in the charging document, his plea agreement, and during his plea hearing that he faced a potential statutory maximum of 10 years in prison. [The] guidelines served due process by providing notice to petitioner of the consequences of his acts; they vindicated his jury trial right by informing him of the stakes of risking trial; they served equal protection by ensuring petitioner that invidious characteristics such as race would not impact his sentence.

Given these observations, it is difficult for me to discern what principle besides doctrinaire formalism actually motivates today's decision. The majority chides the *Apprendi* dissenters for preferring a nuanced interpretation of the Due Process Clause and Sixth Amendment jury trial guarantee that would generally defer to legislative labels while acknowledging the existence of constitutional constraints—what the majority calls the "the law must not go too far" approach. If indeed the choice is between adopting a balanced case-by-case approach that takes into consideration the values underlying the Bill of Rights, as well as the history of a particular sentencing reform law, and adopting a rigid rule that destroys everything in its path, I will choose the former....

The majority is correct that rigid adherence to such an approach *could conceivably* produce absurd results, but as today's decision demonstrates, rigid adherence to the majority's approach *does and will continue* to produce results that disserve the very principles the majority purports to vindicate. The pre-*Apprendi* rule of deference to the legislature retains a built-in political check to prevent lawmakers from shifting the prosecution for crimes to the penalty phase proceedings of lesser included and easier-to-prove offenses—*e.g.*, the majority's hypothesized prosecution of murder in the guise of a traffic offense sentencing proceeding. There is no similar check, however, on application of the majority's "any fact that increases the upper bound of judicial discretion" by courts.

The majority claims the mantle of history and original intent. But as I have explained elsewhere, a handful of state decisions in the mid-19th century and a criminal procedure treatise have little if any persuasive value as evidence of what the Framers of the Federal Constitution intended in the late 18th century. See *Apprendi*, 530 U.S., at 525-528. Because broad judicial sentencing discretion was foreign to the Framers, they were never faced with the constitutional choice between submitting every fact that increases a sentence to the jury or vesting the sentencing judge with broad discretionary authority to account for differences in offenses and offenders.

IV.

The consequences of today's decision will be as far reaching as they are disturbing. Washington's sentencing system is by no means unique. Numerous other States have enacted guidelines systems, as has the Federal Government. [The opinion cites statutes from ten jurisdictions.] Today's decision casts constitutional doubt over them all and, in so doing, threatens an untold number of criminal judgments....

The structure of the Federal Guidelines [does not] provide any grounds for distinction. Washington's scheme is almost identical to the upward departure regime established by 18 U.S.C. §3553(b) and implemented in USSG §5K2.0. If anything, the structural differences that do exist make the Federal Guidelines more vulnerable to attack. The provision struck down here provides for an increase in the upper bound of the presumptive sentencing range if the sentencing court finds, "considering the purpose of [the Act], that there are substantial and compelling reasons justifying an exceptional sentence." Wash. Rev. Code Ann. §9.94A.120. The Act elsewhere provides a nonexhaustive list of aggravating factors that satisfy the definition. §9.94A.390. The Court flatly rejects respondent's argument that such soft constraints, which still allow Washington judges to exercise a substantial amount of discretion, survive *Apprendi*. This suggests that the hard constraints found throughout chapters 2 and 3 of the Federal Sentencing Guidelines, which require an increase in the sentencing range upon specified factual findings, will meet the same fate. See, *e.g.*, USSG §2K2.1 (increases in offense level for firearms offenses based on number of firearms involved, whether possession was in connection with another offense, whether the firearm was stolen)....

What I have feared most has now come to pass: Over 20 years of sentencing reform are all but lost, and tens of thousands of criminal judgments are in jeopardy. I respectfully dissent.

KENNEDY, J., dissenting.

... The Court, in my respectful submission, disregards the fundamental principle under our constitutional system that different branches of government "converse with each other on matters of vital common interest." Mistretta v. United States, 488 U.S. 361, 408 (1989). As the Court in *Mistretta* explained, the Constitution establishes a system of government that presupposes, not just "autonomy" and "separateness," but also "interdependence" and "reciprocity." Constant, constructive discourse between our courts and our legislatures is an integral and admirable part of the constitutional design. Case-by-case judicial determinations often yield intelligible patterns that can be refined by legislatures and codified into statutes or rules as general standards. As these legislative enactments are followed by incremental judicial interpretation, the legislatures may respond again, and the cycle repeats. This recurring dialogue, an essential source for the elaboration and the evolution of the law, is basic constitutional theory in action.

Sentencing guidelines are a prime example of this collaborative process. Dissatisfied with the wide disparity in sentencing, participants in the criminal justice system, including judges, pressed for legislative reforms. In response, legislators drew from these participants' shared experiences and enacted measures to correct the problems....

Numerous States that have enacted sentencing guidelines similar to the one in Washington State are now commanded to scrap everything and start over. [Because] the Constitution does not prohibit the dynamic and fruitful dialogue between the judicial and legislative branches of government that has marked sentencing reform on both the state and the federal levels for more than 20 years, I dissent.

BREYER, J., dissenting.

... I agree that, classically speaking, the difference between a traditional sentencing factor and an element of a greater offense often comes down to a legislative choice about which label to affix. But I cannot jump from there to the conclusion that the Sixth Amendment always requires identical treatment of the two scenarios. That jump is fraught with consequences that threaten the fairness of our traditional criminal justice system; it distorts historical sentencing or criminal trial practices; and it upsets settled law on which legislatures have relied in designing punishment systems....

I.

The majority ignores the adverse consequences inherent in its conclusion. As a result of the majority's rule, sentencing must now take one of three forms, each of which risks either impracticality, unfairness, or harm to the jury trial right the majority purports to strengthen. This circumstance shows that the majority's Sixth Amendment interpretation cannot be right.

A first option for legislators is to create a simple, pure or nearly pure "charge offense" or "determinate" sentencing system. In such a system, an indictment would charge a few facts which, taken together, constitute a crime, such as robbery. Robbery would carry a single sentence, say, five years' imprisonment. And every person convicted of robbery would receive that sentence—just as, centuries ago, everyone convicted of almost any serious crime was sentenced to death.

Such a system assures uniformity, but at intolerable costs. First, simple determinate sentencing systems impose identical punishments on people who committed their crimes in very different ways....

Second, in a world of statutorily fixed mandatory sentences for many crimes, determinate sentencing gives tremendous power to prosecutors to manipulate sentences through their choice of charges. Prosecutors can simply charge, or threaten to charge, defendants with crimes bearing higher mandatory sentences. Defendants, knowing that they will not have a chance to argue for a lower sentence in front of a judge, may plead to charges that they might otherwise contest. Considering that most criminal cases do not go to trial and resolution by plea bargaining is the norm, the rule of *Apprendi*, to the extent it results in a return to determinate sentencing, threatens serious unfairness. See

Stephanos Bibas, Judicial Fact-Finding and Sentence Enhancements in a World of Guilty Pleas, 110 Yale L.J. 1097, 1100-1101 (2001) (explaining that the rule of *Apprendi* hurts defendants by depriving them of sentencing hearings, "the only hearings they were likely to have"; forcing defendants to surrender sentencing issues like drug quantity when they agree to the plea; and transferring power to prosecutors).

A second option for legislators is to return to a system of indeterminate sentencing, such as California had before the recent sentencing reform movement. Under indeterminate systems, the length of the sentence is entirely or almost entirely within the discretion of the judge or of the parole board, which typically has broad power to decide when to release a prisoner. When such systems were in vogue, they were criticized, and rightly so, for producing unfair disparities, including race-based disparities, in the punishment of similarly situated defendants....

Returning to such a system would diminish the "reason" the majority claims it is trying to uphold. It also would do little to ensure the control of what the majority calls "the people," *i.e.*, the jury, "in the judiciary," since "the people" would only decide the defendant's guilt, a finding with no effect on the duration of the sentence. While "the judge's authority to sentence" would formally derive from the jury's verdict, the jury would exercise little or no control over the sentence itself. It is difficult to see how such an outcome protects the structural safeguards the majority claims to be defending.

A third option is that which the Court seems to believe legislators will in fact take. That is the option of retaining structured schemes that attempt to punish similar conduct similarly and different conduct differently, but modifying them to conform to *Apprendi*'s dictates. Judges would be able to depart *downward* from presumptive sentences upon finding that mitigating factors were present, but would not be able to depart *upward* unless the prosecutor charged the aggravating fact to a jury and proved it beyond a reasonable doubt. The majority argues, based on the single example of Kansas, that most legislatures will enact amendments along these lines in the face of the oncoming *Apprendi* train. It is therefore worth exploring how this option could work in practice, as well as the assumptions on which it depends.

This option can be implemented in one of two ways. The first way would be for legislatures to subdivide each crime into a list of complex crimes, each of which would be defined to include commonly found sentencing factors such as drug quantity, type of victim, presence of violence, degree of injury, use of gun, and so on. A legislature, for example, might enact a robbery statute, modeled on robbery sentencing guidelines, that increases punishment depending upon (1) the nature of the institution robbed, (2) the (a) presence of, (b) brandishing of, (c) other use of, a firearm, (3) making of a death threat, (4) presence of (a) ordinary, (b) serious, (c) permanent or life threatening, bodily injury, (5) abduction, (6) physical restraint, (7) taking of a firearm, (8) taking of drugs, (9) value of property loss, etc. Cf. United States Sentencing Commission, Guidelines Manual §2B3.1 (Nov. 2003).

This possibility is, of course, merely a highly calibrated form of the "pure charge" system discussed [above]. And it suffers from some of the same defects. The prosecutor, through control of the precise charge, controls the punishment, thereby marching the sentencing system directly away from, not toward, one important guideline goal: rough uniformity of punishment for those who engage in roughly the same *real* criminal conduct....

This "complex charge offense" system also prejudices defendants who seek trial, for it can put them in the untenable position of contesting material aggravating facts in the guilt phases of their trials. Consider a defendant who is charged, not with mere possession of cocaine, but with the specific offense of possession of more than 500 grams of cocaine. Or consider a defendant charged, not with murder, but with the new crime of murder using a machete. Or consider a defendant whom the prosecution wants to claim was a "supervisor," rather than an ordinary gang member. How can a Constitution that guarantees due process put these defendants, as a matter of course, in the position of arguing, "I did not sell drugs, and if I did, I did not sell more than 500 grams" or, "I did not kill him, and if I did, I did not use a machete," or "I did not engage in gang activity, and certainly not as a supervisor" to a single jury? The system can tolerate this kind of problem up to a point (consider the defendant who wants to argue innocence, and, in the alternative, second-degree, not first-degree, murder). But a rereading of the many distinctions made in a typical robbery guideline suggests that an effort to incorporate any real set of guidelines in a complex statute would reach well beyond that point.

The majority announces that there really is no problem here because "States may continue to offer judicial factfinding as a matter of course to all defendants who plead guilty" and defendants may "stipulate to the relevant facts or consent to judicial factfinding." The problem, of course, concerns defendants who do not want to plead guilty to those elements that, until recently, were commonly thought of as sentencing factors. As to those defendants, the fairness problem arises because States may very well decide that they will *not* permit defendants to carve subsets of facts out of the new, *Apprendi*-required 17-element robbery crime, seeking a judicial determination as to some of those facts and a jury determination as to others. Instead, States may simply require defendants to plead guilty to all 17 elements or proceed with a (likely prejudicial) trial on all 17 elements....

The second way to make sentencing guidelines *Apprendi*-compliant would be to require at least two juries for each defendant whenever aggravating facts are present: one jury to determine guilt of the crime charged, and an additional jury to try the disputed facts that, if found, would aggravate the sentence. Our experience with bifurcated trials in the capital punishment context suggests that requiring them for run-of-the-mill sentences would be costly, both in money and in judicial time and resources. In the context of noncapital crimes, the potential need for a second indictment alleging aggravating facts, the likely need for formal evidentiary rules to prevent prejudice, and the increased difficulty of obtaining relevant sentencing information, all will mean greater complexity, added cost, and further delay.

[An] *amicus curiae* brief filed by the Kansas Appellate Defender Office ... suggests that a two-jury system has proved workable in Kansas. And that may be so. But in all likelihood, any such workability reflects an uncomfortable fact, a fact at which the majority hints, but whose constitutional implications it does not seem to grasp. The uncomfortable fact that could make the system seem workable—even desirable in the minds of some, including defense attorneys—is called "plea bargaining." The Court can announce that the Constitution requires at least two jury trials for each criminal defendant—one for guilt, another for sentencing—but only because it knows full well that more than 90% of defendants will not go to trial even once, much less insist on two or more trials.

What will be the consequences of the Court's holding for the 90% of defendants who do not go to trial? The truthful answer is that we do not know. Some defendants may receive bargaining advantages if the increased cost of the "double jury trial" guarantee makes prosecutors more willing to cede certain sentencing issues to the defense. Other defendants may be hurt if a "single-jury-decides-all" approach makes them more reluctant to risk a trial—perhaps because they want to argue that they did not know what was in the cocaine bag, that it was a small amount regardless, that they were unaware a confederate had a gun, etc.

At the least, the greater expense attached to trials and their greater complexity, taken together in the context of an overworked criminal justice system, will likely mean, other things being equal, fewer trials and a greater reliance upon plea bargaining—a system in which punishment is set not by judges or juries but by advocates acting under bargaining constraints. At the same time, the greater power of the prosecutor to control the punishment through the charge would likely weaken the relation between real conduct and real punishment as well....

Efforts to tie real punishment to real conduct are not new. They are embodied in well-established pre-guidelines sentencing practices— practices under which a judge, looking at a presentence report, would seek to tailor the sentence in significant part to fit the criminal conduct in which the offender actually engaged. For more than a century, questions of *punishment* (not those of guilt or innocence) have reflected determinations made, not only by juries, but also by judges, probation officers, and executive parole boards. Such truth-seeking determinations have rested upon both adversarial and non-adversarial processes. The Court's holding undermines efforts to reform these processes, for it means that legislatures cannot *both* permit judges to base sentencing upon real conduct *and* seek, through guidelines, to make the results more uniform....

Is there a fourth option? Perhaps. Congress and state legislatures might, for example, rewrite their criminal codes, attaching astronomically high sentences to each crime, followed by long lists of mitigating facts, which, for the most part, would consist of the absence of aggravating facts. But political impediments to legislative action make such rewrites difficult to achieve; and it is difficult to see why the Sixth Amendment would require legislatures to undertake them.

It may also prove possible to find combinations of, or variations upon, my first three options. But I am unaware of any variation that does not involve (a) the shift of power to the prosecutor (weakening the connection between real conduct and real punishment) inherent in any charge offense system, (b) the lack of uniformity inherent in any system of pure judicial discretion, or (c) the complexity, expense, and increased reliance on plea bargains involved in a "two-jury" system. The simple fact is that the design of any fair sentencing system must involve efforts to make practical compromises among competing goals. The majority's reading of the Sixth Amendment makes the effort to find those compromises—already difficult—virtually impossible.

II.

The majority rests its conclusion in significant part upon a claimed historical (and therefore constitutional) imperative. According to the majority, the rule it applies in this case is rooted in "longstanding tenets of common-law criminal jurisprudence" that every accusation against a defendant must be proved to a jury and that "an accusation which lacks any particular fact which the law makes essential to the punishment is … no accusation within the requirements of the common law, and it is no accusation in reason." The historical sources upon which the majority relies, however, do not compel the result it reaches. The quotation from Bishop, to which the majority attributes great weight, stands for nothing more than the unremarkable proposition that where a legislature passes a statute setting forth heavier penalties than were available for committing a common-law offense and specifying those facts that triggered the statutory penalty, "a defendant could receive the greater statutory punishment only if the indictment expressly charged and the prosecutor proved the facts that made up the statutory offense, as opposed to simply those facts that made up the common-law offense."

This is obvious when one considers the problem that Bishop was addressing. He provides as an example "statutes whereby, when [a common-law crime] is committed with a particular intent, or with a particular weapon, or the like, it is subjected to a particular corresponding punishment, heavier than that for" the simple common-law offense (though, of course, his concerns were not limited to that example). Bishop, §82 at 51-52 (discussing the example of common assault and enhanced-assault statutes, *e.g.,* "assaults committed with the intent to rob"). That indictments historically had to charge all of the statutorily labeled elements of the offense is a proposition on which all can agree.

Neither Bishop nor any other historical treatise writer, however, disputes the proposition that judges historically had discretion to vary the sentence, within the range provided by the statute, based on facts not proved at the trial. See Bishop, *supra,* §85, at 54 ("Within the limits of any discretion as to the punishment which the law may have allowed, the judge, when he pronounces sentence, may suffer his discretion to be influenced by matter shown in aggravation or mitigation, not covered by the allegations of the indictment")....

Modern structured sentencing schemes like Washington's do not change the statutorily fixed maximum penalty, nor do they purport to establish new elements for the crime. Instead, they undertake to structure the previously unfettered discretion of the sentencing judge, channeling and limiting his or her discretion even *within* the statutory range....

Historical treatises do not speak to such a practice because it was not done in the 19th century. This makes sense when one considers that, prior to the 19th century, the prescribed penalty for felonies was often death, which the judge had limited, and sometimes no, power to vary. The 19th century saw a movement to a rehabilitative mode of punishment in which prison terms became a norm, shifting power to the judge to impose a longer or shorter term within the statutory maximum. The ability of legislatures to guide the judge's discretion by designating presumptive ranges, while allowing the judge to impose a more or less severe penalty in unusual cases, was therefore never considered....

Given history's silence on the question of laws that structure a judge's discretion within the range provided by the legislatively labeled maximum term, it is not surprising that our modern, pre-*Apprendi* cases made clear that legislatures could, within broad limits, distinguish between "sentencing facts" and "elements of crimes." By their choice of label, legislatures could indicate whether a judge or a jury must make the relevant factual determination. History does not preclude legislatures from making this decision....

Is there a risk of unfairness involved in permitting Congress to make this labeling decision? Of course. As we have recognized, the "tail" of the sentencing fact might "wag the dog of the substantive offense." McMillan v. Pennsylvania, 477 U.S. 79, 88 (1986). Congress might permit a judge to sentence an individual for murder though convicted only of making an illegal lane change. But that is the kind of problem that the Due Process Clause is well suited to cure. *McMillan* foresaw the possibility that judges would have to use their own judgment in dealing with such a problem; but that is what judges are there for....

IV.

... Why does the Sixth Amendment permit a jury trial right (in respect to a particular fact) to depend upon a legislative labeling decision, namely, the legislative decision to label the fact a *sentencing fact*, instead of an *element of the crime?* The answer is that the fairness and effectiveness of a sentencing system, and the related fairness and effectiveness of the criminal justice system itself, depends upon the legislature's possessing the constitutional authority (within due process limits) to make that labeling decision. To restrict radically the legislature's power in this respect, as the majority interprets the Sixth Amendment to do, prevents the legislature from seeking sentencing systems that are consistent with, and indeed may help to advance, the Constitution's greater fairness goals.

To say this is not simply to express concerns about fairness to defendants. It is also to express concerns about the serious practical (or impractical) changes that the Court's decision seems likely to impose upon the criminal process; about the tendency of the Court's decision to embed further plea bargaining processes that lack transparency and too often mean nonuniform, sometimes arbitrary, sentencing practices; about the obstacles the Court's decision poses to legislative efforts to bring about greater uniformity between real criminal conduct and real punishment; and ultimately about the limitations that the Court imposes upon legislatures' ability to make democratic legislative decisions. Whatever the faults of guidelines systems—and there are many—they are more likely to find their cure in legislation emerging from the experience of, and discussion among, all elements of the criminal justice community, than in a virtually unchangeable constitutional decision of this Court....

Page 1298.   Add this material in place of note 2.

2.   *Juries and determinate sentencing laws.* The decisions in *Apprendi* and *Blakely* created a great deal of upheaval for state and federal sentencing systems. Defendants can now insist that juries rather than judges must find any facts that authorize an increase in the legally available range of sentences. The key appears to be appellate review: if a judge could be overturned on appeal for selecting a given sentence without establishing the existence of a given fact, the jury trial right attaches to that fact. This dynamic applies to at least some sentences in most states.

In the federal system, the implications of Blakely are slowly sorting themselves out. In United States v. Booker, 125 S. Ct. 738 (2005), the Court held that *Blakely* invalidated the use of the federal sentencing guidelines as a binding set of rules governing the maximum available sentence. Under that system, judges find facts that influence the maximum guideline sentence available and the possibility of any departure from the guidelines. Such a system violated the jury trial rights of federal criminal defendants. However, the Court also crafted a surprising remedy by holding that appellate courts could continue to review sentences imposed after conviction, and could use the guidelines to determine the "reasonableness" of the sentence (the relevant language from the appellate review statute).

The *Apprendi* ruling also has implications for capital sentencing, where findings about "aggravating factors" are a precondition to the court imposing the death penalty. See Ring v. Arizona, 536 U.S. 584 (2002) (jury rather than judge must find an aggravating circumstance necessary for imposing death penalty). However, the *Apprendi* jury trial right is limited to facts that change the *maximum* authorized sentence. In Harris v. United States, 536 U.S. 545 (2002), the Court reaffirmed *McMillan* and held that a judge rather than a jury could find the facts necessary to increase the *minimum* sentence.

Suppose you are advising a sentencing commission in a jurisdiction with sentencing guidelines affected by *Apprendi* and *Blakely*. What changes would you advise the commission to make to comply with these cases?

Chapter 20

Appeals

A. Who Appeals?

2. Appeals by Indigent Defendants

Page 1353.   Add this material at the end of note 1.

See also State v. Arabie, 663 N.W.2d 250 (S.D. 2003) (describes alternative method for filing brief containing apparently non-meritorious claims at insistence of client).

B. Appellate Review of Factual Findings

Page 1371.   Add this material at the end of note 2.

See Smith v. Massachusetts, 125 S. Ct. 1129 (2005) (after motion for finding of not guilty on one of several charges, trial judge evaluated government's evidence and decided it was not sufficient to sustain conviction; after this "mid-trial judgment of acquittal" and defense completed presentation of evidence on other counts, double jeopardy barred any reconsideration by judge on this count).

C. Retroactivity

Page 1378.   Add this material in place of Problem 20-2.

In recent years several states have enacted statutes extending the statute of limitations for various crimes, and especially for sex offenses against children, which often do not surface for years or decades after the acts occur. Sometimes these statutes have "revivified" offenses for which the prior time bar had run. The few state courts that had considered the issue divided on the federal and state constitutionality of revivification statutes. The United States Supreme Court addressed the federal constitutionality of revivification statutes in the following case.

Marion Reynolds Stogner v. California
539 U.S. 607 (2003)

BREYER, J.

California has brought a criminal prosecution after expiration of the time periods set forth in previously applicable statutes of limitations. California has done so under the authority of a new law that (1) permits resurrection of otherwise time-barred criminal prosecutions, and (2) was itself enacted *after* pre-existing limitations periods had expired. We conclude that the Constitution's *Ex Post Facto* Clause, Art. I, §10, cl. 1, bars application of this new law to the present case.

In 1993, California enacted a new criminal statute of limitations governing sex-related child abuse crimes. The new statute permits prosecution for those crimes where "the limitation period specified in [a prior statute of limitations] has expired"—provided that (1) a victim has reported an allegation of abuse to the police, (2) "there is independent evidence that clearly and convincingly corroborates the victim's allegation," and (3) the prosecution is begun within one year of the victim's report. Cal. Penal Code Ann. §803(g). A related provision, added to the statute in 1996, makes clear that a prosecution satisfying these three conditions "shall revive any cause of action barred by [prior statutes of limitations]." The statute thus authorizes prosecution for criminal acts committed many years beforehand—and where the original limitations period has expired—as long as prosecution begins within a year of a victim's first complaint to the police.

In 1998, a California grand jury indicted Marion Stogner, the petitioner, charging him with sex-related child abuse committed decades earlier—between 1955 and 1973. Without the new statute allowing revival of the State's cause of action, California could not have prosecuted Stogner. The statute of limitations governing prosecutions at the time the crimes were allegedly committed had set forth a 3-year limitations period. And that period had run 22 years or more before the present prosecution was brought.

Stogner moved for the complaint's dismissal. He argued that the Federal Constitution's *Ex Post Facto* Clause, Art. I, §10, cl. 1, forbids revival of a previously time-barred prosecution....

The Constitution's two *Ex Post Facto* Clauses prohibit the Federal Government and the States from enacting laws with certain retroactive effects. See Art. I, §9, cl. 3 (Federal Government); Art. I, §10, cl. 1 (States). The law at issue here created a new criminal limitations period that extends the time in which prosecution is allowed. It authorized criminal prosecutions that the passage of time had previously barred. Moreover, it was enacted after prior limitations periods for Stogner's alleged offenses had expired. Do these features of the law, taken together, produce the kind of retroactivity that the Constitution forbids? We conclude that they do.

First, the new statute threatens the kinds of harm that, in this Court's view, the *Ex Post Facto* Clause seeks to avoid. Long ago the Court pointed out that the Clause protects liberty by preventing governments from enacting statutes with "manifestly *unjust and oppressive*" retroactive effects. Calder v. Bull, 3 Dall. 386 (1798). Judge Learned Hand later wrote that extending a limitations period after the State has assured "a man that he has become safe from its pursuit ... seems to most of us unfair and dishonest." Falter v. United States, 23 F.2d 420, 426 (2d Cir. 1928). In such a case, the government ... has deprived the defendant of the fair warning that might have led him to preserve exculpatory evidence. And a Constitution that permits such an extension, by allowing legislatures to pick and choose when to act retroactively, risks both "arbitrary and potentially vindictive legislation," and erosion of the separation of powers. See Fletcher v. Peck, 6 Cranch 87 (1810) (viewing the *Ex Post Facto* Clause as a protection against "violent acts which might grow out of the feelings of the moment").

Second, the kind of statute at issue falls literally within the categorical descriptions of *ex post facto* laws set forth by Justice Chase more than 200 years ago in Calder v. Bull.... Drawing substantially on Richard Wooddeson's 18th-century commentary on the nature of *ex post facto* laws and past parliamentary abuses, Chase divided *ex post facto* laws into categories that he described in two alternative ways. He wrote:

> "I will state what laws I consider *ex post facto* laws, within the words and the intent of the prohibition. 1st. Every law that makes an action done before the passing of the law, and which was innocent when done, criminal; and punishes such action. *2d. Every law that aggravates a crime, or makes it greater than it was, when committed.* 3d. Every law that changes the punishment, and inflicts a greater punishment, than the law annexed to the crime, when committed. *4th. Every law that alters the legal rules of evidence, and receives less, or different, testimony, than the law required at the time of the commission of the offence, in order to convict the offender.* All these, and similar laws, are manifestly unjust and oppressive." (emphasis altered from original).

In his alternative description, Chase traced these four categories back to Parliament's earlier abusive acts, as follows:

> Category 1: "Sometimes they respected the crime, by declaring acts to be treason, which were not treason, when committed."
> Category 2: *"[A]t other times they inflicted punishments, where the party was not, by law, liable to any punishment."*
> Category 3: "[I]n other cases, they inflicted greater punishment, than the law annexed to the offence."
> Category 4: *"[A]t other times, they violated the rules of evidence (to supply a deficiency of legal proof) by admitting one witness, when the existing law required two; by receiving evidence without oath; or the oath of the wife against the husband; or other testimony, which the courts of justice would not admit."* 3 Dall., at 389 (emphasis altered from original).

The second category—including any "law that *aggravates a crime, or makes it greater* than it was, when committed"—describes California's statute as long as those words are understood as Justice Chase understood them—*i.e.,* as referring to a statute that "inflicts *punishments,* where the party was not, by *law,* liable to *any punishment.*"

After (but not before) the original statute of limitations had expired, a party such as Stogner was not "liable to any punishment." California's new statute therefore "aggravated" Stogner's alleged crime, or made it "greater than it was, when committed," in the sense that, and to the extent that, it "inflicted punishment" for past criminal conduct that (when the new law was enacted) did not trigger any such liability....

So to understand the second category (as applying where a new law inflicts a punishment upon a person not then subject to that punishment, to any degree) explains why and how that category differs from both the first category (making criminal noncriminal behavior) and the third category (aggravating the punishment). And this understanding is consistent, in relevant part, with Chase's second category examples— examples specifically provided to illustrate Chase's *alternative* description of laws inflicting *"punishments, where the party was not, by law,* liable to *any punishment."*

Following Wooddeson, Chase cited as examples of such laws Acts of Parliament that banished certain individuals accused of treason. Both Chase and Wooddeson explicitly referred to these laws as involving "banishment." This fact was significant because Parliament had enacted those laws not only after the crime's commission, but under circumstances where banishment "was simply not a form of penalty that could be imposed by the courts." Thus, these laws, like the California law at issue here, enabled punishment where it was not otherwise available "in the ordinary course of law."

[Numerous] legislators, courts, and commentators have long believed it well settled that the *Ex Post Facto* Clause forbids resurrection of a time-barred prosecution. Such sentiments appear already to have been widespread when the Reconstruction Congress of 1867—the Congress that drafted the Fourteenth Amendment—rejected a bill that would have revived time-barred prosecutions for treason that various Congressmen wanted brought against Jefferson Davis and "his coconspirators," Cong. Globe, 39th Cong., 2d Sess., 279 (1866-1867) (comments of Rep. Lawrence). Radical Republicans such as Roscoe Conkling and Thaddeus Stevens, no friends of the South, opposed the bill because, in their minds, it proposed an *ex post facto* law, and threatened an injustice tantamount to "judicial murder." In this instance, Congress ultimately passed a law extending *unexpired* limitations periods, ch. 236, 15 Stat. 183—a tailored approach to extending limitations periods that has also been taken in modern statutes....

The dissent ... emphasizes the harm that child molestation causes, a harm that "will plague the victim for a lifetime," and stresses the need to convict those who abuse children. [We] agree that the State's interest in prosecuting child abuse cases is an important one. But there is also a predominating constitutional interest in forbidding the State to revive a long- forbidden prosecution. And to hold that such a law is *ex post facto* does not prevent the State from extending time limits for the prosecution of future offenses, or for prosecutions not yet time barred....

KENNEDY, J., dissenting.

California has enacted a retroactive extension of statutes of limitations for serious sexual offenses committed against minors. The new period includes cases where the limitations period has expired before the effective date of the legislation. To invalidate the statute in the latter circumstance, the Court tries to force it into the second category of Calder v. Bull, which prohibits a retroactive law "that *aggravates a crime,* or makes it *greater* than it was, when committed." These words, in my view, do not permit the Court's holding, but indeed foreclose it. A law which does not alter the definition of the crime but only revives prosecution does not make the crime "greater than it was, when committed." Until today, a plea in bar has not been thought to form any part of the definition of the offense....

The majority seems to suggest that retroactive extension of expired limitations periods is "arbitrary and potentially vindictive legislation," but does not attempt to support this accusation. And it could not do so. The California statute can be explained as motivated by legitimate concerns about the continuing suffering endured by the victims of childhood abuse.

The California Legislature noted that "young victims often delay reporting sexual abuse because they are easily manipulated by offenders in positions of authority and trust, and because children have difficulty remembering the crime or facing the trauma it can cause." People v. Frazer, 982 P.2d 180 (Calif. 1999). The concern is amply supported by empirical studies. See, *e.g.,* Lyon, Scientific Support for Expert Testimony on Child Sexual Abuse Accommodation, in Critical Issues in Child Sexual Abuse 107 (J. Conte ed. 2002).

The problem the legislature sought to address is illustrated well by this case. Petitioner's older daughter testified she did not report the abuse because she was afraid of her father and did not believe anyone would help her. After she left petitioner's home, she tried to forget the abuse. Petitioner's younger daughter did not report the abuse because she was scared. He tried to convince her it was a normal way of life. Even after she moved out of petitioner's house, she was afraid to speak for fear she would not be believed. She tried to pretend she had a normal childhood. It was only her realization that the father continued to abuse other children in the family that led her to disclose the abuse, in order to protect them.

The Court tries to counter by saying the California statute is "unfair and dishonest" because it violated the State's initial assurance to the offender that "he has become safe from its pursuit" and deprived him of "the fair warning." The fallacy of this rationale is apparent when we recall that the Court is careful to leave in place the uniform decisions by state and federal courts to uphold retroactive extension of unexpired statutes of limitations against an *ex post facto* challenge.

There are two rationales to explain the proposed dichotomy between unexpired and expired statutes, and neither works. The first rationale must be the assumption that if an expired statute is extended, the crime becomes more serious, thereby violating category two; but if an unexpired statute is extended, the crime does not increase in seriousness. There is no basis in logic, our cases, or in the legal literature to support this distinction. Both extensions signal, with equal force, the policy to prosecute offenders.

This leaves the second rationale, which must be that an extension of the expired statute destroys a reliance interest. We should consider whether it is warranted to presume that criminals keep calendars so they can mark the day to discard their records or to place a gloating phone call to the victim. The first expectation is minor and likely imaginary; the second is not, but there is no conceivable reason the law should honor it. And either expectation assumes, of course, the very result the Court reaches; for if the law were otherwise, there would be no legitimate expectation. The reliance exists, if at all, because of the circular reason that the Court today says so; it does not exist as part of our traditions or social understanding.

In contrast to the designation of the crime, which carries a certain measure of social opprobrium and presupposes a certain punishment, the statute of limitations has little or no deterrent effect. The Court does not claim a sex offender would desist if he knew he would be liable to prosecution when his offenses were disclosed....

When a child molester commits his offense, he is well aware the harm will plague the victim for a lifetime. The victims whose interests §803(g) takes into consideration have been subjected to sexual abuse within the confines of their own homes and by people they trusted and relied upon for protection. A familial figure of authority can use a confidential relation to conceal a crime. The violation of this trust inflicts deep and lasting hurt. Its only poor remedy is that the law will show its compassion and concern when the victim at last can find the strength, and know the necessity, to come forward. When the criminal has taken distinct advantage of the tender years and perilous position of a fearful victim, it is the victim's lasting hurt, not the perpetrator's fictional reliance, that the law should count the higher. The victims whose cause is now before the Court have at last overcome shame and the desire to repress these painful memories. They have reported the crimes so that the violators are brought to justice and harm to others is prevented. The Court now tells the victims their decision to come forward is in vain.

The gravity of the crime was known, and is being measured, by its wrongfulness when committed. It is a common policy for States to suspend statutes of limitations for civil harms against minors, in order to "protec[t] minors during the period when they are unable to protect themselves." Some States toll the limitations periods for minors even where a guardian is appointed, and even when the tolling conflicts with statutes of repose. The difference between suspension and reactivation is so slight that it is fictional for the Court to say, in the given context, the new policy somehow alters the magnitude of the crime. The wrong was made clear by the law at the time of the crime's commission. The criminal actor knew it, even reveled in it. It is the commission of the then-unlawful act that the State now seeks to punish. The gravity of the crime is left unchanged by altering a statute of limitations of which the actor was likely not at all aware....

Chapter 21

Habeas Corpus

A. History and Theory of Habeas Corpus

Page 1398. Replace the text between the breaker rule and the notes on page 1404 with this material.

Yaser Esam Hamdi v. Donald Rumsfeld
124 S. Ct. 2633 (2004)

O'CONNOR, J.

At this difficult time in our Nation's history, we are called upon to consider the legality of the Government's detention of a United States citizen on United States soil as an "enemy combatant" and to address the process that is constitutionally owed to one who seeks to challenge his classification as such.... We hold that although Congress authorized the detention of combatants in the narrow circumstances alleged here, due process demands that a citizen held in the United States as an enemy combatant be given a meaningful opportunity to contest the factual basis for that detention before a neutral decisionmaker.

I.

On September 11, 2001, the al Qaeda terrorist network used hijacked commercial airliners to attack prominent targets in the United States. Approximately 3,000 people were killed in those attacks. One week later, in response to these "acts of treacherous violence," Congress passed a resolution authorizing the President to "use all necessary and appropriate force against those nations, organizations, or persons he determines planned, authorized, committed, or aided the terrorist attacks" or "harbored such organizations or persons, in order to prevent any future acts of international terrorism against the United States by such nations, organizations or persons." Authorization for Use of Military Force ("the AUMF"), 115 Stat. 224. Soon thereafter, the President ordered United States Armed Forces to Afghanistan, with a mission to subdue al Qaeda and quell the Taliban regime that was known to support it.

This case arises out of the detention of a man whom the Government alleges took up arms with the Taliban during this conflict. His name is Yaser Esam Hamdi. Born an American citizen in Louisiana in 1980, Hamdi moved with his family to Saudi Arabia as a child. By 2001, the parties agree, he resided in Afghanistan. At some point that year, he was seized by members of the Northern Alliance, a coalition of military groups opposed to the Taliban government, and eventually was turned over to the United States military. The Government asserts that it initially detained and interrogated Hamdi in Afghanistan before transferring him to the United States Naval Base in Guantanamo Bay in January 2002. In April 2002, upon learning that Hamdi is an American citizen, authorities transferred him to a naval brig in Norfolk, Virginia, where he remained until a recent transfer to a brig in Charleston, South Carolina. The Government contends that Hamdi is an "enemy combatant," and that this status justifies holding him in the United States indefinitely—without formal charges or proceedings—unless and until it makes the determination that access to counsel or further process is warranted.

In June 2002, Hamdi's father, Esam Fouad Hamdi, filed the present petition for a writ of habeas corpus under 28 U.S.C. §2241 in the Eastern District of Virginia, naming as petitioners his son and himself as next friend. The elder Hamdi alleges in the petition that he has had no contact with his son since the Government took custody of him in 2001, and that the Government has held his son "without access to legal counsel or notice of any charges pending against him." The petition contends that Hamdi's detention was not legally authorized. It argues that, "as an American citizen, ... Hamdi enjoys the full protections of the Constitution," and that Hamdi's detention in the United States without charges, access to an impartial tribunal, or assistance of counsel "violated and continues to violate the Fifth and Fourteenth Amendments to the United States Constitution." The habeas petition asks that the court, among other things, (1) appoint counsel for Hamdi; (2) order respondents to cease interrogating him; (3) declare that he is being held in violation of the Fifth and Fourteenth Amendments; (4) "to the extent Respondents contest any material factual allegations in this Petition, schedule an evidentiary hearing, at which Petitioners may adduce proof in support of their allegations"; and (5) order that Hamdi be released from his "unlawful custody." Although his habeas petition provides no details with regard to the factual circumstances surrounding his son's capture and detention, Hamdi's father has asserted in documents found elsewhere in the record that his son went to Afghanistan to do "relief work," and that he had been in that country less than two months before September 11, 2001, and could not have received military training. The 20-year-old was traveling on his own for the first time, his father says, and "because of his lack of experience, he was trapped in Afghanistan once that military campaign began."

[The] Government filed a response and a motion to dismiss the petition. It attached to its response a declaration from one Michael Mobbs (hereinafter "Mobbs Declaration"), who identified himself as Special Advisor to the Under Secretary of Defense for Policy…. The declaration states that Hamdi "traveled to Afghanistan" in July or August 2001, and that he thereafter "affiliated with a Taliban military unit and received weapons training." It asserts that Hamdi "remained with his Taliban unit following the attacks of September 11" and that, during the time when Northern Alliance forces were "engaged in battle with the Taliban," Hamdi's Taliban unit surrendered to those forces, after which he "surrendered his Kalishnikov assault rifle" to them. The Mobbs Declaration also states that, because al Qaeda and the Taliban "were and are hostile forces engaged in armed conflict with the armed forces of the United States," individuals associated with those groups "were and continue to be enemy combatants." Mobbs states that Hamdi was labeled an enemy combatant "based upon his interviews and in light of his association with the Taliban." According to the declaration, a series of "U.S. military screening teams" determined that Hamdi met the criteria for enemy combatants, and "a subsequent interview of Hamdi has confirmed that he surrendered and gave his firearm to Northern

Alliance forces, which supports his classification as an enemy combatant." ...

II.

The threshold question before us is whether the Executive has the authority to detain citizens who qualify as "enemy combatants." [For] purposes of this case, the "enemy combatant" that [the government] is seeking to detain is an individual who, it alleges, was "part of or supporting forces hostile to the United States or coalition partners" in Afghanistan and who "engaged in an armed conflict against the United States" there. We therefore answer only the narrow question before us: whether the detention of citizens falling within that definition is authorized. [On this question, we agree with the Government's position] that Congress has in fact authorized Hamdi's detention, through the AUMF....

The AUMF authorizes the President to use "all necessary and appropriate force" against "nations, organizations, or persons" associated with the September 11, 2001, terrorist attacks. 115 Stat. 224. There can be no doubt that individuals who fought against the United States in Afghanistan as part of the Taliban, an organization known to have supported the al Qaeda terrorist network responsible for those attacks, are individuals Congress sought to target in passing the AUMF. We conclude that detention of individuals falling into the limited category we are considering, for the duration of the particular conflict in which they were captured, is so fundamental and accepted an incident to war as to be an exercise of the "necessary and appropriate force" Congress has authorized the President to use....

The capture and detention of lawful combatants and the capture, detention, and trial of unlawful combatants, by universal agreement and practice, are important incidents of war. Ex parte Quirin, 317 U.S. 1 (1942). The purpose of detention is to prevent captured individuals from returning to the field of battle and taking up arms once again.... There is no bar to this Nation's holding one of its own citizens as an enemy combatant. In *Quirin*, one of the detainees, Haupt, alleged that he was a naturalized United States citizen.... Nor can we see any reason for drawing such a line here. A citizen, no less than an alien, can be part of or supporting forces hostile to the United States or coalition partners and engaged in an armed conflict against the United States; such a citizen, if released, would pose the same threat of returning to the front during the ongoing conflict.

In light of these principles, it is of no moment that the AUMF does not use specific language of detention. Because detention to prevent a combatant's return to the battlefield is a fundamental incident of waging war, in permitting the use of "necessary and appropriate force," Congress has clearly and unmistakably authorized detention in the narrow circumstances considered here.

Hamdi objects, nevertheless, that Congress has not authorized the indefinite detention to which he is now subject.... We recognize that the national security underpinnings of the "war on terror," although crucially important, are broad and malleable.... If the Government does not consider this unconventional war won for two generations, and if it maintains during that time that Hamdi might, if released, rejoin forces fighting against the United States, then the position it has taken throughout the litigation of this case suggests that Hamdi's detention could last for the rest of his life.

It is a clearly established principle of the law of war that detention may last no longer than active hostilities.... Active combat operations against Taliban fighters apparently are ongoing in Afghanistan. The United States may detain, for the duration of these hostilities, individuals legitimately determined to be Taliban combatants who engaged in an armed conflict against the United States. If the record establishes that United States troops are still involved in active combat in Afghanistan, those detentions are part of the exercise of "necessary and appropriate force," and therefore are authorized by the AUMF....

III.

Even in cases in which the detention of enemy combatants is legally authorized, there remains the question of what process is constitutionally due to a citizen who disputes his enemy-combatant status. Hamdi argues that he is owed a meaningful and timely hearing and that "extra-judicial detention [that] begins and ends with the submission of an affidavit based on third-hand hearsay" does not comport with the Fifth and Fourteenth Amendments. The Government counters that any more process than was provided below would be both unworkable and "constitutionally intolerable." Our resolution of this dispute requires a careful examination both of the writ of habeas corpus, which Hamdi now seeks to employ as a mechanism of judicial review, and of the Due Process Clause, which informs the procedural contours of that mechanism in this instance.

Though they reach radically different conclusions on the process that ought to attend the present proceeding, the parties begin on common ground. All agree that, absent suspension, the writ of habeas corpus remains available to every individual detained within the United States. U.S. Const., Art. I, §9, cl. 2 ("The Privilege of the Writ of Habeas Corpus shall not be suspended, unless when in Cases of Rebellion or Invasion the public Safety may require it"). Only in the rarest of circumstances has Congress seen fit to suspend the writ. See, e.g., Act of Mar. 3, 1863, ch. 81, §1, 12 Stat. 755; Act of April 20, 1871, ch. 22, §4, 17 Stat. 14. At all other times, it has remained a critical check on the Executive, ensuring that it does not detain individuals except in accordance with law. All agree suspension of the writ has not occurred here. Thus, it is undisputed that Hamdi was properly before an Article III court to challenge his detention under 28 U.S.C. §2241. Further, all agree that §2241 and its companion provisions provide at least a skeletal outline of the procedures to be afforded a petitioner in federal habeas review. Most notably, §2243 provides that "the person detained may, under oath, deny any of the facts set forth in the return or allege any other material facts," and §2246 allows the taking of evidence in habeas proceedings by deposition, affidavit, or interrogatories.... The Government recognizes the basic procedural protections required by the habeas statute, but asks us to hold that, given both the flexibility of the habeas mechanism and the circumstances presented in this case, ... no further process is due.

[The Government argues] that further factual exploration is unwarranted and inappropriate in light of the extraordinary constitutional interests at stake. Under the Government's most extreme rendition of this argument, "respect for separation of powers and the limited institutional capabilities of courts in matters of military decision-making in connection with an ongoing conflict" ought to eliminate entirely any individual process, restricting the courts to investigating only whether legal authorization exists for the broader detention scheme. At most, the Government argues, courts should review its determination that a citizen is an enemy combatant under a very deferential "some evidence" standard. Under this review, a court would assume the accuracy of the Government's articulated basis for Hamdi's detention, as set forth in the Mobbs Declaration, and assess only whether that articulated basis was a legitimate one. In response, Hamdi emphasizes that this Court consistently has recognized that an individual challenging his detention may not be held at the will of the Executive without recourse to some proceeding before a neutral tribunal to determine whether the Executive's asserted justifications for that detention have basis in fact and warrant in law....

Both of these positions highlight legitimate concerns. And both emphasize the tension that often exists between the autonomy that the Government asserts is necessary in order to pursue effectively a particular goal and the process that a citizen contends he is due before he is deprived of a constitutional right. The ordinary mechanism that we use for balancing such serious competing interests, and for determining the procedures that are necessary to ensure that a citizen is not "deprived of life, liberty, or property, without due process of law," U.S. Const., Amdt. 5, is the test that we articulated in Mathews v. Eldridge, 424 U.S. 319 (1976). *Mathews* dictates that the process due in any given instance is determined by weighing "the private interest that will be affected by the official action" against the Government's asserted interest, "including the function involved" and the burdens the Government would face in providing greater process. The *Mathews* calculus then contemplates a judicious balancing of these concerns, through an analysis of "the risk of an erroneous deprivation" of the private interest if the process were reduced and the "probable value, if any, of additional or substitute safeguards." We take each of these steps in turn.

It is beyond question that substantial interests lie on both sides of the scale in this case. Hamdi's "private interest ... affected by the official action," is the most elemental of liberty interests—the interest in being free from physical detention by one's own government.... Nor is the weight on this side of the *Mathews* scale offset by the circumstances of war or the accusation of treasonous behavior, for it is clear that commitment for any purpose constitutes a significant deprivation of liberty that requires due process protection, and at this stage in the *Mathews* calculus, we consider the interest of the erroneously detained individual.... Moreover, as critical as the Government's interest may be in detaining those who actually pose an immediate threat to the national security of the United States during ongoing international conflict, history and common sense teach us that an unchecked system of detention carries the potential to become a means for oppression and abuse of others who do not present that sort of threat....

On the other side of the scale are the weighty and sensitive governmental interests in ensuring that those who have in fact fought with the enemy during a war do not return to battle against the United States. [The] law of war and the realities of combat may render such detentions both necessary and appropriate, and our due process analysis need not blink at those realities. Without doubt, our Constitution recognizes that core strategic matters of warmaking belong in the hands of those who are best positioned and most politically accountable for making them.

The Government also argues at some length that its interests in reducing the process available to alleged enemy combatants are heightened by the practical difficulties that would accompany a system of trial-like process. In its view, military officers who are engaged in the serious work of waging battle would be unnecessarily and dangerously distracted by litigation half a world away, and discovery into military operations would both intrude on the sensitive secrets of national defense and result in a futile search for evidence buried under the rubble of war. To the extent that these burdens are triggered by heightened procedures, they are properly taken into account in our due process analysis.

Striking the proper constitutional balance here is of great importance to the Nation during this period of ongoing combat. But it is equally vital that our calculus not give short shrift to the values that this country holds dear or to the privilege that is American citizenship. It is during our most challenging and uncertain moments that our Nation's commitment to due process is most severely tested; and it is in those times that we must preserve our commitment at home to the principles for which we fight abroad.

With due recognition of these competing concerns, we believe that neither the process proposed by the Government nor the process apparently envisioned by the District Court below strikes the proper constitutional balance when a United States citizen is detained in the United States as an enemy combatant.... We therefore hold that a citizen-detainee seeking to challenge his classification as an enemy combatant must receive notice of the factual basis for his classification, and a fair opportunity to rebut the Government's factual assertions before a neutral decisionmaker. For more than a century the central meaning of procedural due process has been clear: Parties whose rights are to be affected are entitled to be heard; and in order that they may enjoy that right they must first be notified. It is equally fundamental that the right to notice and an opportunity to be heard must be granted at a meaningful time and in a meaningful manner. These essential constitutional promises may not be eroded.

At the same time, the exigencies of the circumstances may demand that, aside from these core elements, enemy combatant proceedings may be tailored to alleviate their uncommon potential to burden the Executive at a time of ongoing military conflict. Hearsay, for example, may need to be accepted as the most reliable available evidence from the Government in such a proceeding. Likewise, the Constitution would not be offended by a presumption in favor of the Government's evidence, so long as that presumption remained a rebuttable one and fair opportunity for rebuttal were provided. Thus, once the Government puts forth credible evidence that the habeas petitioner meets the enemy-combatant criteria, the onus could shift to the petitioner to rebut that evidence with more persuasive evidence that he falls outside the criteria. A burden-shifting scheme of this sort would meet the goal of ensuring that the errant tourist, embedded journalist, or local aid worker has a chance to prove military error while giving due regard to the Executive once it has put forth meaningful support for its conclusion that the detainee is in fact an enemy combatant. In the words of *Mathews*, process of this sort would sufficiently address the "risk of erroneous deprivation" of a detainee's liberty interest while eliminating certain procedures that have questionable additional value in light of the burden on the Government.

We think it unlikely that this basic process will have the dire impact on the central functions of warmaking that the Government forecasts. The parties agree that initial captures on the battlefield need not receive the process we have discussed here; that process is due only when the determination is made to continue to hold those who have been seized. The Government has made clear in its briefing that documentation regarding battlefield detainees already is kept in the ordinary course of military affairs. Any factfinding imposition created by requiring a knowledgeable affiant to summarize these records to an independent tribunal is a minimal one. Likewise, arguments that military officers ought not have to wage war under the threat of litigation lose much of their steam when factual disputes at enemy-combatant hearings are limited to the alleged combatant's acts…. In sum, while the full protections that accompany challenges to detentions in other settings may prove unworkable and inappropriate in the enemy-combatant setting, the threats to military operations posed by a basic system of independent review are not so weighty as to trump a citizen's core rights to challenge meaningfully the Government's case and to be heard by an impartial adjudicator.

In so holding, we necessarily reject the Government's assertion that separation of powers principles mandate a heavily circumscribed role for the courts in such circumstances. Indeed, the position that the courts must forgo any examination of the individual case and focus exclusively on the legality of the broader detention scheme cannot be mandated by any reasonable view of separation of powers, as this approach serves only to condense power into a single branch of government. We have long since made clear that a state of war is not a blank check for the President when it comes to the rights of the Nation's citizens. Whatever power the United States Constitution envisions for the Executive in its exchanges with other nations or with enemy organizations in times of conflict, it most assuredly envisions a role for all three branches when individual liberties are at stake….

Today we are faced only with such a case. Aside from unspecified "screening" processes and military interrogations in which the Government suggests Hamdi could have contested his classification, Hamdi has received no process. An interrogation by one's captor, however effective an intelligence-gathering tool, hardly constitutes a constitutionally adequate factfinding before a neutral decisionmaker. That even purportedly fair adjudicators are disqualified by their interest in the controversy to be decided is, of course, the general rule. Tumey v. Ohio, 273 U.S. 510 (1927). Plainly, the "process" Hamdi has received is not that to which he is entitled under the Due Process Clause….

SOUTER, J., concurring in the judgment.

… In these proceedings on Hamdi's petition, he seeks to challenge the facts claimed by the Government as the basis for holding him as an enemy combatant. And in this Court he presses the distinct argument that the Government's claim, even if true, would not implicate any authority for holding him that would satisfy 18 U.S.C. §4001(a) (Non-Detention Act), which bars imprisonment or detention of a citizen "except pursuant to an Act of Congress." [The plurality accepts] the Government's position that if Hamdi's designation as an enemy combatant is correct, his detention (at least as to some period) is authorized by an Act of Congress as required by §4001(a), that is, by the Authorization for Use of Military Force, 115 Stat. 224 (hereinafter Force Resolution). Here, I disagree and respectfully dissent....

Since the Force Resolution was adopted one week after the attacks of September 11, 2001, it naturally speaks with some generality, but its focus is clear, and that is on the use of military power. It is fairly read to authorize the use of armies and weapons, whether against other armies or individual terrorists. But ... it never so much as uses the word detention, and there is no reason to think Congress might have perceived any need to augment Executive power to deal with dangerous citizens within the United States, given the well-stocked statutory arsenal of defined criminal offenses covering the gamut of actions that a citizen sympathetic to terrorists might commit. See, e.g., 18 U.S.C. §2339A (material support for various terrorist acts); §2339B (material support to a foreign terrorist organization); §2332a (use of a weapon of mass destruction, including conspiracy and attempt); §2332b(a)(1) (acts of terrorism "transcending national boundaries," including threats, conspiracy, and attempt); §2339C (financing of certain terrorist acts); §3142(e) (pretrial detention)....

It is worth adding a further reason for requiring the Government to bear the burden of clearly justifying its claim to be exercising recognized war powers before declaring §4001(a) satisfied. Thirty-eight days after adopting the Force Resolution, Congress passed the statute entitled Uniting and Strengthening America by Providing Appropriate Tools Required to Intercept and Obstruct Terrorism Act of 2001 (USA PATRIOT ACT), 115 Stat. 272; that Act authorized the detention of alien terrorists for no more than seven days in the absence of criminal charges or deportation proceedings, 8 U.S.C. §1226a(a)(5). It is very difficult to believe that the same Congress that carefully circumscribed Executive power over alien terrorists on home soil would not have meant to require the Government to justify clearly its detention of an American citizen held on home soil incommunicado....

Because I find Hamdi's detention forbidden by §4001(a) and unauthorized by the Force Resolution, I would not reach any questions of what process he may be due in litigating disputed issues in a proceeding under the habeas statute or prior to the habeas enquiry itself. For me, it suffices that the Government has failed to justify holding him in the absence of a further Act of Congress, criminal charges, a showing that the detention conforms to the laws of war, or a demonstration that §4001(a) is unconstitutional.... Since this disposition does not command a majority of the Court, however, the need to give practical effect to the conclusions of eight members of the Court rejecting the Government's position calls for me to join with the plurality in ordering remand on terms closest to those I would impose....

SCALIA, J., dissenting.

... This case brings into conflict the competing demands of national security and our citizens' constitutional right to personal liberty. Although I share the Court's evident unease as it seeks to reconcile the two, I do not agree with its resolution.

Where the Government accuses a citizen of waging war against it, our constitutional tradition has been to prosecute him in federal court for treason or some other crime. Where the exigencies of war prevent that, the Constitution's Suspension Clause, Art. I, §9, cl. 2, allows Congress to relax the usual protections temporarily. Absent suspension, however, the Executive's assertion of military exigency has not been thought sufficient to permit detention without charge....

The very core of liberty secured by our Anglo-Saxon system of separated powers has been freedom from indefinite imprisonment at the will of the Executive. Blackstone stated this principle clearly:

> Of great importance to the public is the preservation of this personal liberty: for if once it were left in the power of any, the highest, magistrate to imprison arbitrarily whomever he or his officers thought proper ... there would soon be an end of all other rights and immunities.... To bereave a man of life, or by violence to confiscate his estate, without accusation or trial, would be so gross and notorious an act of despotism, as must at once convey the alarm of tyranny throughout the whole kingdom. But confinement of the person, by secretly hurrying him to gaol, where his sufferings are unknown or forgotten; is a less public, a less striking, and therefore a more dangerous engine of arbitrary government.... To make

> imprisonment lawful, it must either be, by process from the courts of judicature, or by warrant from some legal officer, having authority to commit to prison; which warrant must be in writing, under the hand and seal of the magistrate, and express the causes of the commitment, in order to be examined into (if necessary) upon a habeas corpus. If there be no cause expressed, the gaoler is not bound to detain the prisoner. For the law judges in this respect, … that it is unreasonable to send a prisoner, and not to signify withal the crimes alleged against him. 1 W. Blackstone, Commentaries on the Laws of England 132-133 (1765).

These words were well known to the Founders. Hamilton quoted from this very passage in The Federalist No. 84. The two ideas central to Blackstone's understanding—due process as the right secured, and habeas corpus as the instrument by which due process could be insisted upon by a citizen illegally imprisoned—found expression in the Constitution's Due Process and Suspension Clauses.

The gist of the Due Process Clause, as understood at the founding and since, was to force the Government to follow those common-law procedures traditionally deemed necessary before depriving a person of life, liberty, or property. When a citizen was deprived of liberty because of alleged criminal conduct, those procedures typically required committal by a magistrate followed by indictment and trial....

These due process rights have historically been vindicated by the writ of habeas corpus. In England before the founding, the writ developed into a tool for challenging executive confinement. It was not always effective. For example, in Darnel's Case, 3 How. St. Tr. 1 (K.B. 1627), King Charles I detained without charge several individuals for failing to assist England's war against France and Spain. The prisoners sought writs of habeas corpus, arguing that without specific charges, "imprisonment shall not continue on for a time, but for ever; and the subjects of this kingdom may be restrained of their liberties perpetually." The Attorney General replied that the Crown's interest in protecting the realm justified imprisonment in "a matter of state … not ripe nor timely" for the ordinary process of accusation and trial. The court denied relief, producing widespread outrage, and Parliament responded with the Petition of Right, accepted by the King in 1628, which expressly prohibited imprisonment without formal charges, see 3 Car. 1, c. 1, §§5, 10.

The struggle between subject and Crown continued, and culminated in the Habeas Corpus Act of 1679, 31 Car. 2, c. 2, described by Blackstone as a "second magna charta, and stable bulwark of our liberties." 1 Blackstone 133. The Act governed all persons "committed or detained ... for any crime." §3. In cases other than felony or treason plainly expressed in the warrant of commitment, the Act required release upon appropriate sureties (unless the commitment was for a nonbailable offense). Where the commitment was for felony or high treason, the Act did not require immediate release, but instead required the Crown to commence criminal proceedings within a specified time. §7. If the prisoner was not "indicted some Time in the next Term," the judge was "required ... to set at Liberty the Prisoner upon Bail" unless the King was unable to produce his witnesses. Able or no, if the prisoner was not brought to trial by the next succeeding term, the Act provided that "he shall be discharged from his Imprisonment." [The] practical effect of this provision was that imprisonment without indictment or trial for felony or high treason under §7 would not exceed approximately three to six months. The writ of habeas corpus was preserved in the Constitution—the only common-law writ to be explicitly mentioned. See Art. I, §9, cl. 2.

The allegations here, of course, are no ordinary accusations of criminal activity. Yaser Esam Hamdi has been imprisoned because the Government believes he participated in the waging of war against the United States. The relevant question, then, is whether there is a different, special procedure for imprisonment of a citizen accused of wrongdoing by aiding the enemy in wartime.

Justice O'Connor, writing for a plurality of this Court, asserts that captured enemy combatants (other than those suspected of war crimes) have traditionally been detained until the cessation of hostilities and then released. That is probably an accurate description of wartime practice with respect to enemy aliens. The tradition with respect to American citizens, however, has been quite different. Citizens aiding the enemy have been treated as traitors subject to the criminal process.

As early as 1350, England's Statute of Treasons made it a crime to "levy War against our Lord the King in his Realm, or be adherent to the King's Enemies in his Realm, giving to them Aid and Comfort, in the Realm, or elsewhere." 25 Edw. 3, Stat. 5, c. 2.... The Founders inherited the understanding that a citizen's levying war against the Government was to be punished criminally. The Constitution provides: "Treason against the United States, shall consist only in levying War against them, or in adhering to their Enemies, giving them Aid and Comfort"; and establishes a heightened proof requirement (two witnesses) in order to "convict" of that offense. Art. III, §3, cl. 1. In more recent times, too, citizens have been charged and tried in Article III courts for acts of war against the United States, even when their noncitizen co-conspirators were not. For example, two American citizens alleged to have participated during World War I in a spying conspiracy on behalf of Germany were tried in federal court. See United States v. Fricke, 259 F. 673 (S.D.N.Y. 1919)....

There are times when military exigency renders resort to the traditional criminal process impracticable. English law accommodated such exigencies by allowing legislative suspension of the writ of habeas corpus for brief periods....

Where the Executive has not pursued the usual course of charge, committal, and conviction, it has historically secured the Legislature's explicit approval of a suspension. In England, Parliament on numerous occasions passed temporary suspensions in times of threatened invasion or rebellion. E.g., 1 W. & M., c. 7 (1688) (threatened return of James II); 17 Geo. 2, c. 6 (1744) (threatened French invasion); 17 Geo. 3, c. 9 (1777) (the American Revolution). Not long after Massachusetts had adopted a clause in its constitution explicitly providing for habeas corpus, see Mass. Const. pt. 2, ch. 6, art. VII (1780), it suspended the writ in order to deal with Shay's Rebellion.

Our Federal Constitution contains a provision explicitly permitting suspension, but limiting the situations in which it may be invoked: "The privilege of the Writ of Habeas Corpus shall not be suspended, unless when in Cases of Rebellion or Invasion the public Safety may require it." Art. I, §9, cl. 2....

The Suspension Clause was by design a safety valve, the Constitution's only express provision for exercise of extraordinary authority because of a crisis. Very early in the Nation's history, President Jefferson unsuccessfully sought a suspension of habeas corpus to deal with Aaron Burr's conspiracy to overthrow the Government. During the Civil War, Congress passed its first Act authorizing Executive suspension of the writ of habeas corpus, to the relief of those many who thought President Lincoln's unauthorized proclamations of suspension unconstitutional…. During Reconstruction, Congress passed the Ku Klux Klan Act, which included a provision authorizing suspension of the writ, invoked by President Grant in quelling a rebellion in nine South Carolina counties….

Even if suspension of the writ on the one hand, and committal for criminal charges on the other hand, have been the only traditional means of dealing with citizens who levied war against their own country, it is theoretically possible that the Constitution does not require a choice between these alternatives. I believe, however, that substantial evidence does refute that possibility. First, the text of the 1679 Habeas Corpus Act makes clear that indefinite imprisonment on reasonable suspicion is not an available option of treatment for those accused of aiding the enemy, absent a suspension of the writ. In the United States, this Act was read as enforcing the common law, and shaped the early understanding of the scope of the writ…. Section 7 of the Act specifically addressed those committed for high treason, and provided a remedy if they were not indicted and tried by the second succeeding court term. That remedy was not a bobtailed judicial inquiry into whether there were reasonable grounds to believe the prisoner had taken up arms against the King. Rather, if the prisoner was not indicted and tried within the prescribed time, "he shall be discharged from his Imprisonment." The Act does not contain any exception for wartime….

Writings from the founding generation also suggest that, without exception, the only constitutional alternatives are to charge the crime or suspend the writ. In 1788, Thomas Jefferson wrote to James Madison questioning the need for a Suspension Clause in cases of rebellion in the proposed Constitution. His letter illustrates the constraints under which the Founders understood themselves to operate:

> Why suspend the Hab. corp. in insurrections and rebellions? The parties who may be arrested may be charged instantly with a well defined crime. Of course the judge will remand them. If the publick safety requires that the government should have a man imprisoned on less probable testimony in those than in other emergencies; let him be taken and tried, retaken and retried, while the necessity continues, only giving him redress against the government for damages….

The proposition that the Executive lacks indefinite wartime detention authority over citizens is consistent with the Founders' general mistrust of military power permanently at the Executive's disposal. In the Founders' view, the "blessings of liberty" were threatened by "those military establishments which must gradually poison its very fountain." The Federalist No. 45 (J. Madison). No fewer than 10 issues of the Federalist were devoted in whole or part to allaying fears of oppression from the proposed Constitution's authorization of standing armies in peacetime. Many safeguards in the Constitution reflect these concerns. Congress's authority "to raise and support Armies" was hedged with the proviso that "no Appropriation of Money to that Use shall be for a longer Term than two Years." U.S. Const., Art. 1, §8, cl. 12.... A view of the Constitution that gives the Executive authority to use military force rather than the force of law against citizens on American soil flies in the face of the mistrust that engendered these provisions.

It follows from what I have said that Hamdi is entitled to a habeas decree requiring his release unless (1) criminal proceedings are promptly brought, or (2) Congress has suspended the writ of habeas corpus. A suspension of the writ could, of course, lay down conditions for continued detention, similar to those that today's opinion prescribes under the Due Process Clause. But there is a world of difference between the people's representatives' determining the need for that suspension (and prescribing the conditions for it), and this Court's doing so.

The plurality finds justification for Hamdi's imprisonment in the Authorization for Use of Military Force, 115 Stat. 224.... This is not remotely a congressional suspension of the writ, and no one claims that it is. Contrary to the plurality's view, I do not think this statute even authorizes detention of a citizen with the clarity necessary to satisfy the interpretive canon that statutes should be construed so as to avoid grave constitutional concerns.... If the Suspension Clause does not guarantee the citizen that he will either be tried or released, unless the conditions for suspending the writ exist and the grave action of suspending the writ has been taken; if it merely guarantees the citizen that he will not be detained unless Congress by ordinary legislation says he can be detained; it guarantees him very little indeed....

Having distorted the Suspension Clause, the plurality finishes up by transmogrifying the Great Writ—disposing of the present habeas petition by remanding for the District Court to "engage in a factfinding process that is both prudent and incremental." This judicial remediation of executive default is unheard of. The role of habeas corpus is to determine the legality of executive detention, not to supply the omitted process necessary to make it legal. It is not the habeas court's function to make illegal detention legal by supplying a process that the Government could have provided, but chose not to. If Hamdi is being imprisoned in violation of the Constitution (because without due process of law), then his habeas petition should be granted; the Executive may then hand him over to the criminal authorities, whose detention for the purpose of prosecution will be lawful, or else must release him.

There is a certain harmony of approach in the plurality's making up for Congress's failure to invoke the Suspension Clause and its making up for the Executive's failure to apply what it says are needed procedures—an approach that reflects what might be called a Mr. Fix-it Mentality. The plurality seems to view it as its mission to Make Everything Come Out Right, rather than merely to decree the consequences, as far as individual rights are concerned, of the other two branches' actions and omissions. Has the Legislature failed to suspend the writ in the current dire emergency? Well, we will remedy that failure by prescribing the reasonable conditions that a suspension should have included. And has the Executive failed to live up to those reasonable conditions? Well, we will ourselves make that failure good, so that this dangerous fellow (if he is dangerous) need not be set free. The problem with this approach is not only that it steps out of the courts' modest and limited role in a democratic society; but that by repeatedly doing what it thinks the political branches ought to do it encourages their lassitude and saps the vitality of government by the people.

Several limitations give my views in this matter a relatively narrow compass. They apply only to citizens, accused of being enemy combatants, who are detained within the territorial jurisdiction of a federal court. This is not likely to be a numerous group; currently we know of only two, Hamdi and Jose Padilla. Where the citizen is captured outside and held outside the United States, the constitutional requirements may be different. Moreover, even within the United States, the accused citizen-enemy combatant may lawfully be detained once prosecution is in progress or in contemplation. The Government has been notably successful in securing conviction, and hence long-term custody or execution, of those who have waged war against the state....

If the situation demands it, the Executive can ask Congress to authorize suspension of the writ—which can be made subject to whatever conditions Congress deems appropriate, including even the procedural novelties invented by the plurality today.... If civil rights are to be curtailed during wartime, it must be done openly and democratically, as the Constitution requires, rather than by silent erosion through an opinion of this Court....

Many think it not only inevitable but entirely proper that liberty give way to security in times of national crisis.... Whatever the general merits of the view that war silences law or modulates its voice, that view has no place in the interpretation and application of a Constitution designed precisely to confront war and, in a manner that accords with democratic principles, to accommodate it. Because the Court has proceeded to meet the current emergency in a manner the Constitution does not envision, I respectfully dissent.

THOMAS, J., dissenting.

The Executive Branch, acting pursuant to the powers vested in the President by the Constitution and with explicit congressional approval, has determined that Yaser Hamdi is an enemy combatant and should be detained. This detention falls squarely within the Federal Government's war powers, and we lack the expertise and capacity to second-guess that decision. As such, petitioners' habeas challenge should fail....

The Founders intended that the President have primary responsibility—along with the necessary power—to protect the national security and to conduct the Nation's foreign relations. They did so principally because the structural advantages of a unitary Executive are essential in these domains. "Energy in the executive is a leading character in the definition of good government. It is essential to the protection of the community against foreign attacks." The Federalist No. 70 (A. Hamilton). The principal ingredient for "energy in the executive" is "unity." This is because "decision, activity, secrecy, and dispatch will generally characterise the proceedings of one man, in a much more eminent degree, than the proceedings of any greater number."...

Congress, to be sure, has a substantial and essential role in both foreign affairs and national security. But it is crucial to recognize that judicial interference in these domains destroys the purpose of vesting primary responsibility in a unitary Executive. [With] respect to certain decisions relating to national security and foreign affairs, the courts simply lack the relevant information and expertise to second-guess determinations made by the President based on information properly withheld. [Even] if the courts could compel the Executive to produce the necessary information, such decisions are simply not amenable to judicial determination because they are delicate, complex, and involve large elements of prophecy....

For these institutional reasons and because Congress cannot anticipate and legislate with regard to every possible action the President may find it necessary to take or every possible situation in which he might act, it should come as no surprise that [a failure to act does not] imply congressional disapproval of action taken by the Executive....

The war power of the national government is the power to wage war successfully. It follows that this power is not limited to victories in the field, but carries with it the inherent power to guard against the immediate renewal of the conflict, and quite obviously includes the ability to detain those (even United States citizens) who fight against our troops or those of our allies. Although the President very well may have inherent authority to detain those arrayed against our troops, I agree with the plurality that we need not decide that question because Congress has authorized the President to do so.

[In] United States v. Salerno, 481 U.S. 739 (1987), the Court explained that the Due Process Clause "lays down [no] categorical imperative." The Court continued: "We have repeatedly held that the Government's regulatory interest in community safety can, in appropriate circumstances, outweigh an individual's liberty interest. For example, in times of war or insurrection, when society's interest is at its peak, the Government may detain individuals whom the Government believes to be dangerous." Cf. Kansas v. Hendricks, 521 U.S. 346 (1997). The Government's asserted authority to detain an individual that the President has determined to be an enemy combatant, at least while hostilities continue, comports with the Due Process Clause. As these cases also show, the Executive's decision that a detention is necessary to protect the public need not and should not be subjected to judicial second-guessing. Indeed, at least in the context of enemy-combatant determinations, this would defeat the unity, secrecy, and dispatch that the Founders believed to be so important to the warmaking function....

Accordingly, I conclude that the Government's detention of Hamdi as an enemy combatant does not violate the Constitution. By detaining Hamdi, the President, in the prosecution of a war and authorized by Congress, has acted well within his authority. Hamdi thereby received all the process to which he was due under the circumstances....

B. *The Availability of Postconviction Review*

2. Procedural Bars

Page 1423. Insert this material at the end of note 5.

The Supreme Court has resolved several disputes over the meaning of the federal statute of limitations in favor of petitioners. In Carey v. Saffold, 536 U.S. 214 (2002), the Court interpreted the word "pending" in the tolling provision of the statute of limitations broadly, to include periods between a state court's decision on an application for collateral review and the filing of a notice of appeal to a higher state court. And in Clay v. United States, 537 U.S. 522 (2003), the Supreme Court ruled that a federal conviction becomes "final," and starts the one-year period for seeking collateral relief, when the time period for seeking certiorari runs out.

3. Collateral Review of Ineffective Assistance Claims

Page 1433. Insert this material at the end of note 1.

In Massaro v. United States, 538 U.S. 500 (2003), the defendant in a federal criminal case waited until a collateral proceeding to raise his claim of ineffective assistance of trial counsel. The Supreme Court held that the defendant did not commit procedural default, even though he could have raised the claim on direct appeal, and even though the trial record was sufficiently developed to raise the claim. The Court reasoned that it is more efficient to allow defendants to raise the claim in collateral proceedings, because ineffectiveness claims often require evidentiary hearings on whether there was some strategic reason for the lawyer's act or omission. Because appellate courts are not capable of taking testimony or other evidence, judicial economy is best served by allowing defendants to raise the claim initially in collateral proceedings. Even when the necessary facts already appear in the trial record, counsel on direct appeal must rely on trial counsel to become familiar with the case on a short deadline, making it awkward for the appellate lawyer to raise a claim of ineffective assistance.

C. Federal Habeas Corpus Review of State Convictions

1. Expansion

Page 1444. Insert this material at the end of note 3.

See Rhines v. Weber, 125 S. Ct. 1528 (2005) (district court has discretion to stay a "mixed" habeas corpus petition containing both exhausted and unexhausted claims while the petitioner returns to state court; stay in federal court tolls statute of limitations; court must find good cause for the failure to exhaust, unexhausted claims must be potentially meritorious, and there is no suggestion of intentional delay).